FAMILY, FRIENDS & FERVOURS

to Michael McDonald
William Gladstone

Family, Friends & Fervours

William Gladstone

The lines have fallen for me in pleasant places:
yea, I have a goodly heritage.
> Psalm 16

MICHAEL RUSSELL

© William Gladstone 2015

The right of Sir William Gladstone
to be identified as the author of this work
has been asserted by him in accordance with the
Copyright, Designs and Patents Act, 1988

First published in Great Britain 2015
by Michael Russell (Publishing) Ltd
Wilby Hall, Wilby, Norwich NR16 2JP

Page makeup in Sabon by Waveney Typesetters
Wymondham, Norfolk
Printed and bound in Great Britain
by Berforts Information Press

All rights reserved

ISBN 978-0-85955-327-8

Contents

Family trees   vi–viii

FAMILY & FRIENDS

1. Nanny May   1
2. My Parents Take Over   13
3. Manley and Llandulas   25
4. Fasque and Astridge   41
5. School Days   50
6. Holidays in Wartime   61
7. HMS *Wrangler*   70
8. Oxford 1946–49   79
9. Shrewsbury 1949–50   89
10. Hawarden   101
11. Our Lancing Years, 1961–69   139
12. Some Hambros and Some Beatons   166

FOUR FERVOURS

1. Birds   183
2. The Landscape Garden   201
3. Watercolour Landscape   232
4. Shooting   248

Index   277

Some Gladstones

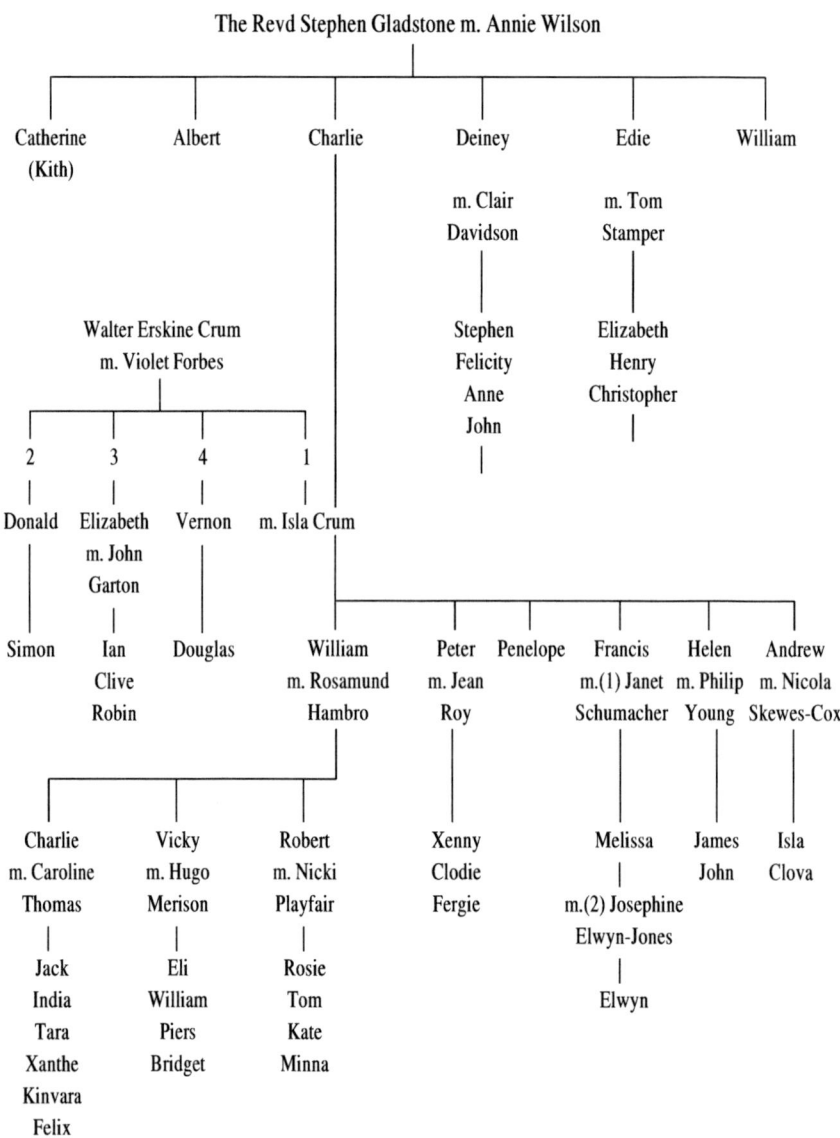

Some Hambros

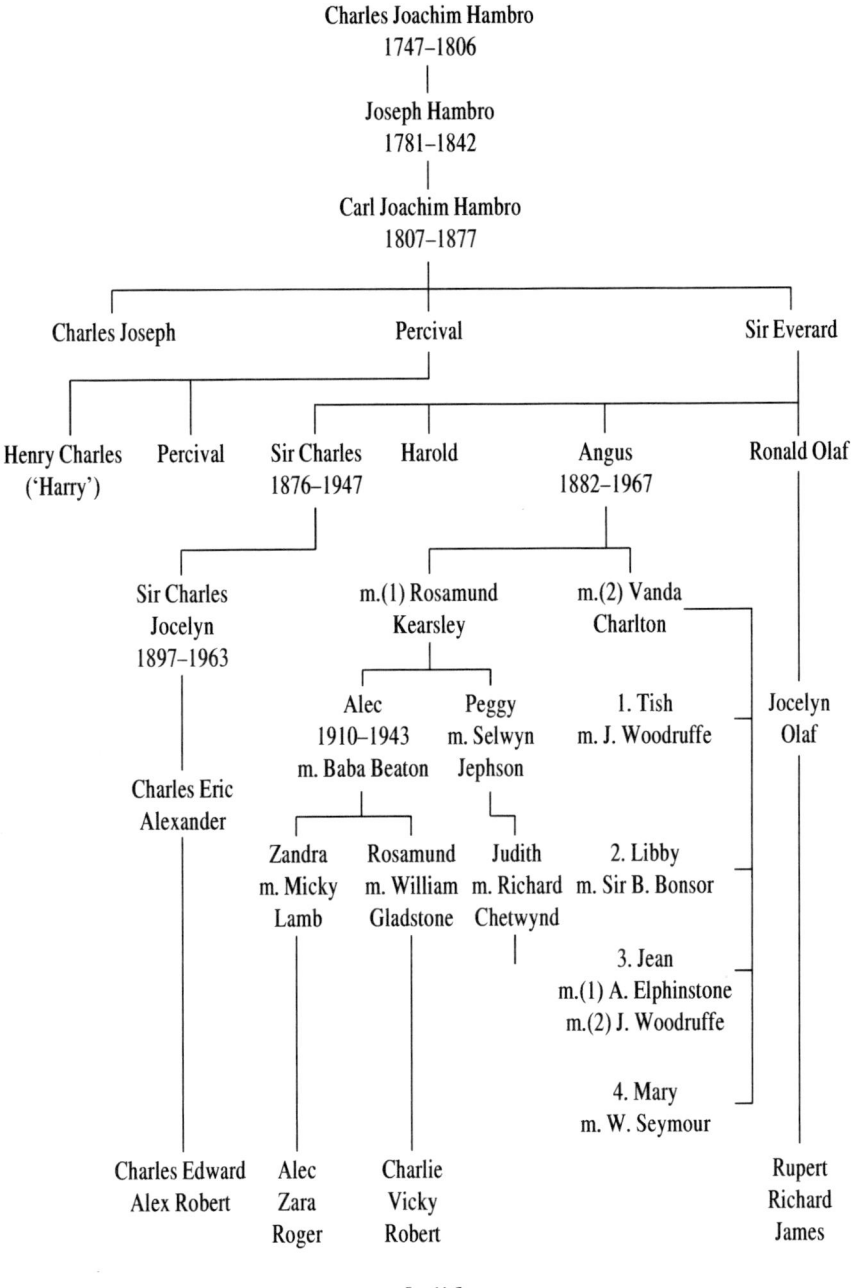

Some Beatons

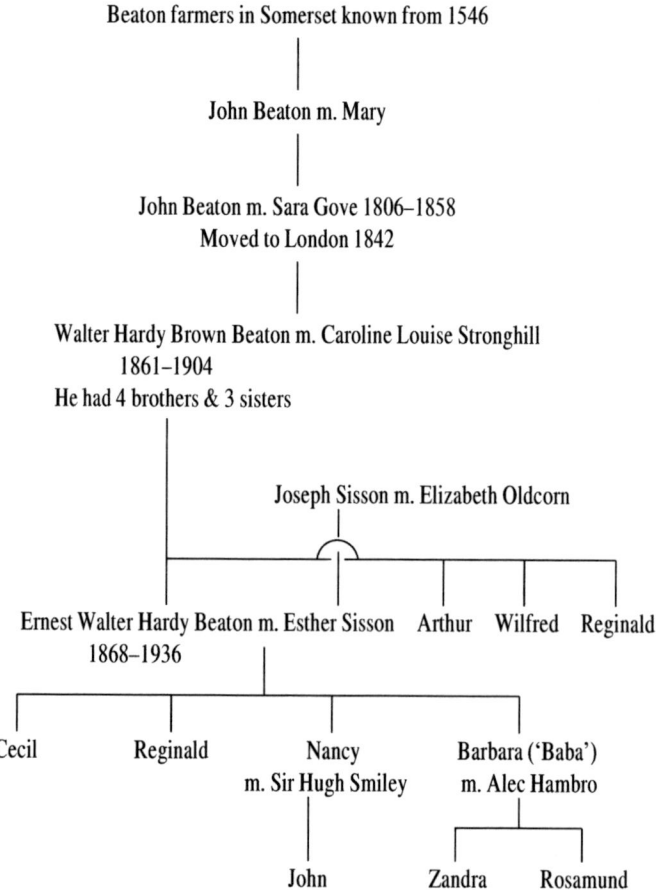

FAMILY & FRIENDS

I
Nanny May

My mother was not allowed to marry until she reached her nineteenth birthday, and she was still not quite twenty when I was born ten months later. My father was thirty-six and about to become a housemaster at Eton. During my mother's pregnancy they were housed by a bachelor master who lived on his own at Baldwin's End, Michael Bland, who was to become my godfather, before they moved to Penn House for the September term. I was born on 29 October, one day after my father's birthday. He and his elder brother Albert, sons of a parson, were both born on 28 October, St Simon and St Jude's day, two years apart. My father said it was lucky that Albert had not been christened Simon, or he would have been Jude: but reverence for the memory of the Prince Consort had been preferred to that of the Saint, and my father was named Charles after his maternal grandfather.

My mother was Isla, a rare name in those days and invariably pronounced 'is-lar' by all but the few who were in the know, mostly Scots. She was the eldest child of Walter Erskine Crum, always known as Erskine and living and working in Calcutta, and of Violet Forbes. He had recently been knighted as a member of the Viceroy's Council, but he died of a heart attack aged forty-six, leaving my maternal grandmother a widow with four children and almost no money. Expatriates in India used to take four months' leave in Britain every three years, the voyage home in a P&O liner taking thirty-one days, and for their honeymoon Erskine and Violet stayed in Angus, and walked Glen Isla: hence my mother's name.

My mother was an energetic, imaginative and artistic person, never to be defeated by a challenge, as became more and more evident to me as time passed and challenges multiplied during and after the war. She was a gifted artist, a student of architecture in west London, and my father had a magnificent oak drawing table made for her with a high stool, which lived in the drawing room discreetly isolated by an oak-framed tapestry screen; but I don't think she did much artistic work during this period; certainly none survived. She was one of a still fairly

Nanny May

small but growing number of masters' wives, most of whom were at least a decade older than she was. But she seemed to have enjoyed those years, to have fitted in as a housemaster's wife and with my father's colleagues, a group of men with remarkably diverse interests and strong personalities, and with their families. There were dinner parties for eight people twice a week, cooked and served by servants of course: she never boiled an egg before 1939. She had two more children, Peter born three years after me and Penelope five; but we were all looked after by Nanny.

Nanny May was a foundling, a baby left on a doorstep on 1 May and surnamed accordingly, baptised Phyllis and brought up by the nuns of Clewer in their convent near Windsor. Her closest childhood friend was Agnes, who stayed in the convent as a nun, while Phyllis opted for a secular life and was trained as a nanny. She was the formative influence of my early years, and when she left I felt as bereft as an orphan. She had been with my mother's siblings, Elizabeth, Donald and Vernon. Uncle Vernon was only seven years older than I, and when Nanny left him she came to me.

The housemaster's rooms, known as the private side, were separated from the boys' side by green baize doors at ground and first floor level, but there was no such door on the second floor where Nanny and I lived in splendid isolation. On the ground floor there was a stone porch and a spacious entrance hall and cloakroom, the dining room, the drawing room and my father's book-lined study. On the first floor were my parents' bedroom and bathroom and my father's dressing room, the spare bedroom with bathroom, and the Dame's sitting room, bedroom and bathroom, with her baize door to the boys' side. Dames were the house matrons who had retained the title of the ladies who used to run their own boys' boarding houses until the mid-nineteenth century. On the top floor were the day and night nurseries, Nanny's room and the bathroom and a separate loo with a fine mahogany thunder-box. As the first child, my health was fussed over. Nanny suggested a step to enable my feet to be in contact with terra firma whilst I was 'doing my business' after breakfast. As was common practice, I was given a dose of Californian syrup of figs every three weeks to keep me going. At the age of four I was considered too thin and prescribed cream, which I have disliked ever since, except with sugar. Nanny used to give me a pinch of salt to stop me from crying or making a rumpus: I have eaten too much salt ever since but, as I point out to my critics, I am still alive and kicking.

Nanny May

Breakfast, lunch and a light supper came up from the kitchen, the same food as the boys got. If it was hot, or had left the kitchen hot, the plates were under a metal cover. Later, a 'hot plate' made its appearance, a porcelain plate with hot water inserted into a metal tray underneath it through a hole with a neat little threaded metal cap. As far as I was concerned, food was food, and that was that. It occurred to me that some food was nastier than other food, notably fish on Fridays and 'frogspawn' as a variant of rice pudding; but it never occurred to me that it might be a pleasure to eat – except in the case of sweets, strawberries (a rare treat in season) and ice cream. Frigidaires were just beginning to come in, but butter and milk were still kept in the dairy, a little north-facing room with slate shelves and gauze over the window. Not until my later years at my prep school had I ever come across the idea that a meal might be a pleasure to eat, when John Corlett, the young maths master, a man of the world, used to talk to us at lunch about (among other subjects) the pleasure of a good restaurant. In the nursery there was the usual stuff about being a good boy and making a clean plate, which I often found a bit of a struggle.

Life's routine consisted of playing in the nursery, playing in the garden, going for walks with Nanny either up the High Street or in the playing fields, and playing in the drawing room under my mother's eye between tea and bedtime. I started lessons at the age of four, but before and indeed after that almost everything I remember learning came from conversations with Nanny. In the nursery I learnt to say my prayers and to try to be a good boy, but my knowledge and understanding of the world came from our walks up the High Street.

Nanny seemed to know all the shopkeepers. Just over Barnes Pool Bridge was Mr Berrow the ironmonger, neat, short and balding, with his grey moustache and fawn-coloured overall coat. Beyond him was Mr Wells the upholsterer, upright and slightly dyspeptic-looking in his bowler hat, black jacket and pin-striped trousers. His carpenters made the oak bookshelves and Norfolk fender in my father's study, my mother's drawing table, and the step to make the nursery convenience more convenient. Further on was the new Post Office, purpose-built in a style which reflected what I later recognised as the perfect taste, celebrated in his telephone booths, of Sir Giles Gilbert Scott. Then came Mr Gane the shoemaker; then New and Lingwood with the windows full of the coloured caps and scarves and shirts and stockings of the gigantic Eton boys in their top hats who strolled past the pram.

Nanny May

Opposite was the gentleman's hairdresser, Mr Jefferies, whose main shop was in Berkeley Square, creator of the fashionable upper-class hair oil Honey and Flowers, a feminine name, I thought, for such a manly requisite. His business was later taken over by G. Thomas, dark, square and severe. Once my curls had been cut off at the age of three (my babyish image immortalised by Marcus Adams, the fashionable West End photographer whose backgrounds consisted apparently entirely of clouds) Nanny and I visited Jefferies every three weeks for a haircut. I always had my hair washed that evening, because Nanny said the scissors would not have been clean. It's true that nits, so common in today's schoolchildren, were almost unknown in middle-class families, so perhaps the precaution was a wise one. No doubt Honey and Flowers was lethal to foreign bodies too, but hair oil was not *de rigueur* in our family.

Beyond Jefferies was the picture framer whom I knew as Mr Dunstan from the notice in his shop window of St Dunstan's Society for war-blinded soldiers, of whom he was one. Then came Mr Reid the chemist, his shop full of elegant shapely multi-coloured bottles with glass stoppers, jars and carboys. Like many shops in the High Street, Reid's bore above its door the decorative coat of arms of a royal appointment, Pharmacists By Appointment to His (or Her) Majesty – sometimes still King Edward VII or Queen Alexandra, sometimes to George V or Queen Mary.

On the right of the street again was Mr Garnham the electrician, who had lost an arm in the war but could still deftly handle a screwdriver; then Mills the Milliner, bigger than the other shops, fussily feminine with its dainty underwear and rows and rows of cotton reels. Anything we bought in these shops (we were often doing errands for my mother) – a light bulb from Mr Garnham or a reel of cotton from Mills – was put on account. Nothing was paid for in cash. 'What name, please?' 'Gladstone'. 'Ah! And how is Mr Disraeli today?' Thus began a lifetime not merely of being identified as somebody's great-grandson, but of the acute embarrassment caused by that unalterable distinction. Mr Gladstone, the Grand Old Man, had still been Prime Minister in 1894, and had died aged eighty-eight some thirty-two years before my first-remembered encounters with this banter: so anyone over the age of about forty remembered Mr Gladstone in his lifetime, a living rather than a historical image.

Mr Gladstone had done much for the emancipation of women,

Nanny May

especially in education and in their admission to the professions; the first steps are the most difficult. The 'flapper' vote for women under thirty did not come until 1930. (How typical of the British upper-class male to insult the notion of the young female having a vote by comparing her to a 'flapper', a young duck which no gentleman would consider shooting in September, although the legal season had opened.) One of my early memories is of Nanny voting at the polling station in the Porny School in the High Street and explaining to me that she thought it a good idea to give 'the other people' a go this time. Thus I learnt about the swing of the pendulum.

Windsor Bridge was of course open to traffic, and since there were no parking restrictions and still some horse-drawn vehicles there was a good old traffic jam in Eton High Street every day, accompanied by much tooting of horns. Often there was a policeman (policemen looked like policemen in those days) signalling priority first in one direction and then in the other. He could alleviate the problem, but had no power to solve it: the shops had to receive their deliveries.

Just before Windsor Bridge, on the left, owned by a lady who was a good friend of Nanny but whose name I have forgotten, was a tiny sweetshop with quaint bow windows, and a good chance of a gratuitous sweetie. Over the bridge and on the right before Windsor Hill was Mr and Mrs Messenger's toyshop where Nanny bought me my fire engine and, some years later, Peter his double-decker, as birthday presents. The metal fire engine was a dark reddish purple, with its hose reel and a retracting ladder on top. The staircase and upper deck of the double-decker bus, like the ones in the High Street, were open to the weather. These were phenomenally generous presents from Nanny's tiny remuneration, each costing 25/- or 30/-, say about £100 to £150 in today's figures. I collected lead (called tin) soldiers: guardsmen just as they look today, but with longer and more formidable rifles and bayonets; Highlanders in kilts and white helmets, with plenty of white piping on their red coats, firing their rifles in three ranks, standing, kneeling and lying down. It evidently hadn't occurred to toy soldier makers that there had been a Boer War, let alone a World War. Only a few mounted Life Guards or Blues could be afforded. Unlike me, Peter was not meticulous, nor a hoarder, and his bus was an unpredictable weapon of mass destruction for my parades on the nursery floor.

Peter arrived three years after me: his howling in his cot in my father's dressing room on 16 October 1928 is my earliest conscious memory of any event. He must have accompanied us in the pram on most of our walks.

Later we had clockwork Hornby trains, Peter a goods train and me a GWR passenger train with two coaches in its yellow and brown livery. There were two stations in Windsor, but the Southern Railway was being electrified, so only the Great Western had proper engines.

Beyond Messenger's, halfway up the hill, were Mr Fuller's and Mr Tull's next door to one another, famous for their chocolate cakes and truffles respectively, both of them also proper tea shops with doylies and maids in lace caps and aprons and cuffs, with tablecloths to match, and dainty flowery china. A visit to one of these was 'a treat of rare order'. Higher up was W. H. Smith with a varied stock of books. It is still there, the only survivor of all those shops. On the corner of Peascod (pronounced 'pescot') Street was Pratt's, a big store full of decorative household goods, ornaments galore, and many other things. It had one of those wonderful aerial ropeways from each counter to the one central till. They whizzed a little cup containing your invoice and the cash tendered to the till on a system of taut wires suspended from the ceiling and fired like a catapult; it would then come back with the receipt and the correct change. These systems were eventually replaced by National Cash Register tills of extraordinary mechanical ingenuity, the successors of the eighteenth-century Jacquard loom and the nineteenth-century typesetting machine. Each cash register cost about the same as a small car. It was not until the 1990s that they disappeared in favour of digital systems.

We did not often go beyond Pratt's, which was where the band appeared for the changing of the guard at Windsor Castle, the culmination of our expedition. To this day I cannot witness a marching band of the Foot Guards without a surge of nervous excitement.

When we did go further and then turned down Sheet Street, it was to see, and later to climb on, the tank opposite the Barracks. This was a First World War lozenge-shaped tank with its gun barbettes either side and its hefty iron tracks. Sadly its metal was to be sacrificed to the war effort in 1940. One day when we were down there we saw the R100. I was playing on the tank when one of the two great airships newly built to carry passengers (with disastrous consequences) came flying low overhead.

Occasionally we turned down Peascod Street. About a third of the way down were Woolworth's ('3d and 6d Stores') and Marks and

Nanny May

Spencer (maximum price 5/-), opposite one another. M & S was not yet a national institution with high quality food and comparatively cheap but up-market clothing. The concept was more along the lines of good value resulting from the economies of scale. Woolworth's, although American, was already an institution, again as a result of the economy of scale, simply on the basis that everything there was cheap. I did all my Christmas shopping there.

The usual alternative walk, rustic rather than urban, was the playing fields via Weston's Yard with its ancient brick buildings along the main road, and on the other side the still comparatively vulgar and new-looking patterned brick of the New Buildings of College. As we turned into College Field, a high wall on the right more or less screened the disused stables, soon to be demolished and replaced by the open King of Siam's garden with its striking statue of Perseus holding the snake-haired Gorgon's head. In spite of periodic explanations I never grasped what Perseus had to do with the King of Siam. On the left was College Wall, sometimes with the Wall Game to gaze upon. Then came the Leg o' Mutton pond with frogs and moorhens, clad in its shield of magnificent elm trees planted in the reign of Charles the something, or perhaps James the something, a long time ago. Then over Sheep Bridge with its striking cascade on the right, and Sixth Form Bench, a name meaningless to me, overlooking the river bank with its view of Romney Weir and, beyond it, Windsor Castle.

Beyond Sheep Bridge was Upper Club, with its spreading chestnut trees and the benches intended for watching cricket but used by two or three nannies for a rest and a chat. Peeling the leaves until they looked like fishbones kept us quietly occupied. We told the time by blowing the down off dandelions and we made daisy chains. We used to meet Bluebottle, Mr Butler the park keeper in his brightly coloured livery, who had lost an arm in the war and wore a black glove on his immobile cosmetic hand, making him look even more like a waxwork. Occasionally we walked past the 'Triangle' (official name The Upper Shooting Fields, where presumably the bowmen had practised in days of old), now a small football field where Charles Mayes, the most spherical of the housemasters, ran a weekly football match for the sons of masters. The soles of our football boots had bars rather than studs, which were beginning to come in but were considered rather dangerous The path took us to the little iron bridge over the Jordan where we could play Poohsticks, a time-honoured game recently given its name in the books of A. A. Milne, children's favourites. We crossed the Datchet Road and set out on the continuation of the long straight path. It led to the village of Langley, now in the outskirts of the jumped-up town of Slough, a long walk we only took occasionally.

The other variant of a country walk was along the Eton Wick road. Where Eton town ended and the old common began stood the brick-walled sheep pound, now disused, and then a slight dip in the road where in times of flood the Thames had expanded its course for centuries, turning Eton again and again into the island which its name represents. There were steel posts on the right of the road with projecting arms to take a raised board-walk, and with holes for the handrail, when the footpath was under water. Then came the Great Western Railway on its arches of yellow brick. It had been excluded from Eton by the College, and runs on a wide curve between Slough and Windsor. Beyond it there were some new houses along Broken Furlong on the right, and on the left South Field, full of skylarks and lapwings, stretching as far as the river. The footpath ran along the right of the road, the big hedgerow trees with their climbable Arthur Rackham roots bulging on to it. Eton Wick was no more than a hamlet: there were no council houses in those days, but there was a magnificent clump of elm trees dividing the narrow road like a sort of village green, massacred some years later in the name of the local council in case one happened to fall on a villager or, perhaps, a motor car. (The Dutch elm disease would have wiped them out in the 1970s anyway, as it did all the elms in the playing fields.) In Eton Wick was Mr Woolridge with his bicycle shop and his marvellous dexterity in mending a puncture, tightening the brakes or adjusting the saddle.

Nanny taught me the difference between right and wrong, not to waste things, to do my best, and to be kind to others. Her generosity and her conviction that money was not the main source of happiness could not but have rubbed off on those around her, unless they were very stony ground. A loving and forgiving God was a presence and indeed an assumption in her life but she never preached nor proselytised.

My pocket money was three pence a week. Pennies were much bigger in those days, which gave them status, although there were 240 of them to the pound. A penny went in to the Dr Barnardo's Homes collecting box, and a penny into my money box as savings, leaving a penny to spend. A careful poor person could live on five shillings (sixty pennies) a week, the old age pension. Nanny said we were not rich but

Nanny May

not poor: 'happy medium'. When I consider the size of my grandmother's house which we visited for our holidays, and of her team of servants indoors and out, I do wonder whether we were perhaps high medium rather than low medium. But that is not the point. Britain was still copiously littered with the idle rich, as it had been since the eventual economic recovery from the Napoleonic wars in the days of Jane Austen. By modern standards most of them were idle rather than rich, living on a few hundred pounds a year, the interest on their holding of Consols. Their pleasant houses were cheap to build and their two or three or more servants cheap to pay. My grandmother had a big house and a whole team of servants. One must reach the age of the dining room rather than the nursery to become aware of such things, which I shall therefore return to later.

Nanny, like everyone else, was convinced that Britain was top nation, deserved to be so, and was likely to go on being so for ever. This belief was not shaken by hard times, which affected foreigners just as much as they affected us. There were beggars selling matches or trinkets on street corners, and after our picnic lunches on our car journeys we gave the left-overs to the first tramp we saw, always within a few miles. They were gratefully received.

Our top-nationhood was undoubtedly deserved. We were a virtuous nation – hard-working, enterprising and clever. We had invented almost everything, and we made it better than anyone else, except wine and cheese, dominated by the French. If we didn't make it, or grow it, we bought it and sold it. Foreign stuff was labelled 'Foreign'. It was preferable to Buy British for quality. We built, and owned, far more ships than anyone else, including ocean liners. The Red Ensign dominated world trade. Pax Britannica depended on the Royal Navy, still the largest in the world; and although the United States was catching us up it did not have squadrons of cruisers, and the coal or oil and dockyards to run and maintain them, on the China Station or in the South Atlantic or India, nor a nascent independent Navy in Australia and Canada. We had dug the mines and built the railways in India and South America. Now we were doing the same in most of Africa, and it was British investors who provided vast loans of money for the development of emergent nations, even if the results often tended to disappoint. We had brought peace and civilisation to India and now we were doing the same for Africa. On the map of the world there was more pink than any other colour, and not only so if you used Mercator's projection. These were matters of fact, not opinion. They were everybody's, or almost everybody's, assumptions. This was the Empire on which the sun never set, the white man's burden. Nanny taught me to be proud of it. I was. I still am, with some reservations of course.

One very seldom saw a coloured person in Britain, even in London. Cargo ships were manned largely by lascars, but not many people went on board a merchant ship and most of them were in quarantine anyway. Negroes were known as niggers, but without malice as far as the population of Britain was concerned. They were thought of as mostly primitive people or 'savages'. *Little Black Sambo* was one of my earliest books. But slavery was regarded with disgust: the Navy had spent vast resources over many decades suppressing it in the Mediterranean and the Atlantic.

Nanny did not hold outdated ideas. She was up-to-date in all respects. She had a wireless in the nursery. It lived on the top of a high cupboard in order to improve the rather crackly reception from London, about twenty-five miles away. The announcers were male, and had correct accents: they spoke the King's English.

The holy Mrs Crace, a housemaster's wife with a son called Christopher who also exuded an impression of holiness (he looked to me like a wingless angel), ran a Sunday school for infants, which I attended from a very young age, learning the stories of Jesus's life, illustrated by little stick-in pictures which we took home and stuck in. Another housemaster's wife, equally holy, Mrs Sladden, had a severe governess, Miss Scott, for her two pious sons, both of whom became clergymen. Duncan, the younger, was my contemporary. He became vicar of Lower Peover (happily pronounced 'Peever') in Cheshire. He and I and one or two others (I am uncertain about who precisely was at this school, my first, and who was at my second) were the sole pupils at Miss Scott's School. The only experience I remember there was drawing and then painting a picture of a flower in a flower pot. The sole objective in the painting was Not To Go Over. 'Art' at Miss Scott's School was strictly representational. Notions like freedom of expression or using one's imagination were unheard of, and would indeed have been frowned upon. I took care, using thin horizontal brush strokes for the flower pot, and did not 'go over' (I kept the picture for many years) in spite of the temptation – soon to produce in me me a heady mixture of excitement and fear of the consequences – to 'go over' in my general behaviour, if not in art lessons.

Nanny May

After a year under Miss Scott I joined a very different school, run by Miss Keay and Miss Drake, first in Eton High Street and then in a cavernous Victorian semi-detached house in Windsor, in which both Miss Keay and Miss Drake lived. Miss Keay's junior part of it consisted of six or seven children, all or almost all the children of Eton masters (but including Jeremy White, son of the Adjutant of the Eton Corps, an officer in the Greenjackets). Miss Keay was comfortable and feminine in shape and personality, like a kindly but efficient aunt or governess, and she taught us more than we needed to know to make a good start at our preparatory schools. Miss Drake was absolutely different, and out of our orbit. She took only the older pupils who stayed on, rather than going away to preparatory schools: she had dark cropped hair with a fringe. Her horn-rimmed spectacles seemed to us to suit her academic credentials, and emphasised in our minds the contrast between these two ladies.

The main business of our school life was a grounding in the three Rs. We learnt to read and write and our arithmetic not only taught us our times tables but got us as far as fractions, HCFs and LCMs, which did not come into our preparatory school syllabus until our second or even third year. I think we did understand what a highest common factor and a lowest common multiple were, but that was not the point. The point was to know how to do them. But we had a broader education too, of which I remember botany. We collected and pressed wild flowers and counted and recorded the number of their petals, sepals and stamens. Miss Durnford gave dancing classes in the Castle Hotel, which I hated. There was no joy about them: the ethos was too theatrical for me.

When Penelope arrived Vera Moody was recruited as nurserymaid, Nanny's assistant, learning and accumulating experience on the job. A delightful person, she stayed with us until I was about twelve years old. By then Peter had joined me at Scaitcliffe, our preparatory school, and Penelope was old enough to benefit from a governess.

Just before I left for Scaitcliffe, it was announced that Nanny was leaving. I was dumbstruck. It had never occurred to me that she would 'leave'. Apparently she was to retire. She lived in London and worked without remuneration in a hospital until her eighties, acting I think as what might be called a 'greeter' now, directing visitors to patients and giving information; but for all I know she may before that have been involved in a children's ward. Perhaps her vocation had been with

Nanny May

babies and young children, whereas Vera was more interested in older ones. I never heard any suggestion that she had not gone by mutual consent. As I consider that early phase of my life, I can see now that my parents were gradually taking over. We kept in touch, and Nanny gave me a watercolour of the warship I had served in for my twenty-first birthday, and a set of tablemats with birds by Vernon Ward, gliding seagulls, serene swans and springing teal, for our wedding present. Peter and I attended her funeral at the convent at Clewer. In the cold, bare red-brick Victorian Gothic chapel there remained three aged nuns, the service sung in the wavering reedy tone of their ancient voice-strings. The graves, without permanent tombstones, had taken up less than a single row in the large cemetery. Nanny's mortal remains were laid close to those of her dear friend Agnes with its little wooden label. This was a last object lesson for us from Nanny – in humility.

2
My Parents Take Over

I realise now that as I started to grow up my parents played an increasing part in my life, especially in encouraging my interests and my curiosity. My morals were the morals of the nursery. They still are. But my parents also contributed to keeping me on the straight and narrow path while at the same time broadening my interests, which perhaps is the best way of encouraging a child to think. I cannot claim that I thought outside the box, whatever that is supposed to represent. The box for me was the set of assumptions for which Nanny laid firm foundations. She was not dogmatic and the knowledge she imparted was based not on prejudice but on facts as she saw them, so the box had an organic nature and was capable of expanding as I did; but it was a box all the same, and my mind has lived within it comfortably ever since (in the sense of the 'comfortable words' for those few who are still conversant with the Book of Common Prayer). On the other hand, my problem – according to my father, conveyed with gentleness and sympathy but invariably opening the tap of childish tears of contrition – was that I was over-excitable: I could not resist the temptation to get up to mischief. I joined a boarding preparatory school just before my ninth birthday. What my school education taught me was not to get caught, facilitating my ability to live within the box apart from occasional forays outside it, most of them followed by a quick and painless retreat. These childish capers seem to have come under better control when I was in my upper twenties, which is when most young men develop a sense of social maturity.

Looking back at this gradual transition from the nursery, I suppose that the milestone came when I was allowed to sit up for dinner with my parents, except on dinner party nights. Then in the school holidays I had breakfast and lunch with them too, and I remember being appalled by my father throwing most of his letters straight into the waste paper basket, some of them unopened. 'They're advertisements,' he said. Some things haven't changed since my childhood.

One of the most valuable lessons I learnt from my mother was that it was possible to discern what was 'in good taste' and what was not, although she had the imagination not to use such an abstract and explosive term, and indeed not to seem to be dogmatic. What I learnt from her was proportionality, a word with a wider sense than a mere 'sense of proportion' which we use as an abstract concept. This was much more, too, than a sense of moderation, which would not appeal to children, although they might appreciate it later as undergraduates of the University of Oxford, if they were amongst the fortunate few who were privileged to attend it, as a virtue – at least if applied to others than oneself. Proportionality could only be taught by learning to observe things, and to realise that some things were nicer than others. It was also sowing the seed in a young mind of the notion that beauty lies in the eye of the beholder, which is not simply a cynical statement that beauty is what any individual thinks it is, but that the wise beholder sees better than the fool. Many children who are brought up to understand these ideas are over-stimulated, and tend to grow into precocious prigs. My faults no doubt are legion, but I have never been accused of that, because my mother had the instinct to understand how children's minds worked. She did not treat us like tiny adults.

Part of this lesson came from my mother's efforts to teach me to create a picture. She was a gifted and original artist and she tried to explain to me the concept of composition. I drew a train in a station. It did not take up much of the paper, just a narrow strip. She said 'Put some people in', which I thought was rather boring. However, I did meticulously draw one person, on the platform, in the bottom left-hand corner. The shortcomings of this picture were the first lesson in composition that I remember, although they didn't impress me at the time. When I drew matchstick men she encouraged me to look at a person and draw what I saw. She taught me that water was not always blue. 'Look at it,' she said. But I was not capable of doing so: convention had already gained a front place in my mind, blocking out more elementary observation. Yet her words did sink in: later on, I began to look at things, to ask myself what they looked like, even if I couldn't get a clear answer.

'Look and learn' is a phrase from nursery or at best primary education; very good in its way, yet it is often more concerned with the result of looking than the art of looking or what to look for, or in other words how to observe, which means how to interpret and understand. It must be considered elementary by teachers, since it is not pursued in secondary education. Baden-Powell did not use such an attractive phrase when he taught 'powers of observation', yet his objective was to train young soldiers to look for and interpret things they might not otherwise be aware of, and his method was sounder than 'look and learn'. Later he emphasised its value in *Scouting for Boys*. Unfortunately, many young people leave school at sixteen without having a clue how to observe their surroundings.

How to use one's eyes specifically as a source of knowledge and understanding was a lesson my mother taught me. I wish I had learnt it more thoroughly. I can walk through a wood and see every tree and every flower; but when I walk through an airport I find it hard to see, let alone interpret, the signposts.

My mother taught me to use my eyes, and my father taught me to use my ears. He was a sophisticated ornithologist, and he showed me that the way to identify birds on our walks was to listen. For as long as I can remember I have found it difficult to sort out what people are saying, although I have no problem with the volume. But birdsong (like music) comes to me easily, and I can often hear and interpret sounds which other people can't.

My father also introduced me to gardening and to carpentry, although he himself was gifted at the former but not the latter. These interests have given me lifelong pleasure. I used to go with him to Waterer's nursery at Taplow to choose alpines. As with my mother's lessons in seeing, I did not fully appreciate them at the time, but the special blue of the gentian and the name of the saxifrage somehow sunk in. Marigolds were easier to appreciate: they invaded his rock garden and I was horrified at the way he tore them out. Mr Quarterman the gardener (yes, we had a full-time gardener) got hold of a mould for making concrete blocks. We laid a foundation for a greenhouse where my father could propagate his own cuttings. Crocks were collected for the bottoms of the terracotta flowerpots to ensure good drainage, and loam, sand and granite grit were required for the compost; we collected grit from far afield. I still have that greenhouse, eighty years on. The soil at Eton was alkaline, but my father wanted to grow azaleas, so we used to take the trailer and a wheelbarrow to collect leafmould at Hedgerley, a Buckinghamshire beech wood granted to Eton by Henry VI but subsequently sold by the Governing Body because it didn't produce enough income. The lesson I learnt there was that a small child towing a heavy wheelbarrow makes all the difference. I also learnt the song and

My Parents Take Over

the flight of the wood warbler, a scarce species, which occupied the same site on the edge of the wood year after year.

My parents' car for my first few years was a Studebaker. It was draughty even with the hood up and it didn't have a self-starter, so the engine had to be wound into life with the starting handle or 'crank' before the driver could (in the words of a prewar book – First War, of course – still in my possession, called *Motor Car Maintenance and Management*) 'mount the seat, advance the ignition, depress the clutch and engage the change-speed lever'. When Peter arrived the Studebaker was disposed of in favour of a Chrysler, RX 4846, which had a more modern seating arrangement although the windows were still cellophane panels with metal lugs, which had to be inserted in the doorframes and stored somewhere when removed in fine weather. My father made a wooden tray which he slung with ropes from the roof-bars to carry Peter in his cot.

At the end of 1934, during my first term at my prep school, came the 1935 model 27 horsepower Vauxhall BUU47, one of the first batch of cars with three registration letters, very modern: light grey with blue leather upholstery, with wide mudguards integrated into the bodywork and glass windows fitted within the door frames, which could be wound up and down. Its hood was secured with just one clip either side of the front windscreen and could be put up or down by one person in a few seconds. The canvas was stretched on a solid wooden frame which hinged at the centre, and the whole thing lay happily behind the top of the back seat. This design seems to have been forgotten about during the war, and was not recovered, let alone improved on, at least until the 1980s.

The Vauxhall at 27 horsepower rather than the standard 24 could effortlessly pull the trailer which accompanied us on our holidays. Its acceleration was astonishing and it could cruise (well, more or less) at 70 mph, which one could reach on a long stretch of straight road. It cost £375, £25 more than the saloon model, and the same price as one of the numerous three-bedroom houses which were springing up on new estates and along the main roads on the outskirts of towns – ribbon development which was shortly to be stopped by the Town and Country Planning Acts. People said these houses were 'jerry-built' but nearly all of them are still in good order and sought after now. They are now at least twenty times as expensive as an average new car.

Quite early in the Vauxhall's life the 30 mph limit was introduced in

My Parents Take Over

towns, as were 'Major Road' signs at crossroads, and then in the late 1930s Belsiha beacons named after the minister of transport Mr Hore-Belisha (now called 'pelicans' or 'penguins' or something equally unmemorable).

'Major Road' signs were rather scoffed at by my father whose stock joke was 'watch out for the Major', but they served society better than the tactics of one of my father's colleagues who drove the Yellow Peril, another Vauxhall, more sporty and breezy than ours with a cruiser stern like a boat. He figured that the quicker you crossed a crossroads the less likely you were to collide with another car. Roundabouts had not been invented.

Every school holidays we travelled to my paternal grandmother's house, Manley Hall in Cheshire, and I soon became familiar with the route: Maidenhead, Henley with its Fair Mile; Oxford; over Magdalen Bridge and turn right down Longwall Street, noting Mr Morris's bicycle shop; Banbury and its cross and circular church; Warwick with the view of the castle from the bridge; Kenilworth with its castle and two fords over the road; Stoneleigh; Castle Bromwich with the now iconic Dunlop factory; Erdington with a couple of miles of very early dual carriageway; Brownhills in the Black Country, and thence on to Watling Street to Weston-under-Lizard; then Newport, Whitchurch and Chester. Our favourite picnic places were Kenilworth Castle, a wooded spot by the river near Stoneleigh, and a field off Watling Street after Ivetsey Bank. The journey was boring but most of the town centres had interesting features.

Cars were not used as runabouts for short errands, which presumably is why my expeditions alone with my father or my mother in the Chrysler and then the Vauxhall were more memorable than they would be nowadays, when piped music or mobile phones preempt conversation. I accompanied my mother on shopping trips to London. It seemed that most of them (but probably in fact only two or at most three) were for the purpose of buying her an expensive hat – ridiculously so, it seemed to me at the time, when you considered the number of lead soldiers or ice creams that could have been bought for the price, two or even three pounds. Like all our clothes they were made in England, and every hat was different. I recollect my mother sitting in front of a mirror in a posh shop, rejecting one after another ('it simply isn't me') and dithering over this mighty investment for The Fourth of June, Lord's and Henley, until eventually she made up her mind, the rejects were

My Parents Take Over

tidied away and a hatbox provided and a small fortune changed hands. She had a natural gift for fashion and design, and very little money. She could cut and sew anything from a dress to a dressing gown and run it up in a couple of days at most. She was a miraculous knitter: socks or stockings or a cable-stitched sweater grew in front of one rather like those ghastly gimmicks of speeded-up pictures on the television of flowers growing and opening before your very eyes, while at the same time she read a book, and probably carried on a conversation as well. As she had very little money I conclude that hats were the exception: the only thing she couldn't make to her full satisfaction.

Those trips to London were treats to me: just my mother and I on our own in the breezy open car, along the Great West Road past all the new factories which I now realise were the pioneers of mass-produced modern light industry, each with its name in shining letters and its distinctive logo: Coty perfumes, Janzen Swimwear, Gillette razor blades; most of the way, it seemed, from Slough to Chiswick. As we got into the West End we would leave the main road to find a car park in a square. There always seemed to be a space: often my mother said she 'knew the man', who was liable to find somewhere for an attractive lady with a sixpence. As one moved towards the West End the crossing sweepers became more frequent, with their stylish broad-brimmed hats, one side pinned to the crown like an Australian soldier's, their brooms and shovels and low-slung metal carts to take the horse-dung.

Occasionally the objective was to buy my school clothes from the designated supplier, or to fit a new pair of shoes by looking through X-ray machines, or perhaps to go to Harrods for a special purpose – for her to buy a wedding present, or for me to spend a birthday present in the toy department. It was my father who took me to St Paul's, where we climbed to the top of the dome, and to the Science Museum where the latest sensation was the blue Supermarine seaplane which had won the Schneider Trophy, hung from the roof: the forerunner in design of the Spitfire. There were some grand old working steam engines with both beam and piston movements and some splendid models of sailing and steamships. We also visited the Natural History Museum where the biggest exhibit was the life-sized whale and where even in those days there were skeletons of gigantic dinosaurs.

My longer journeys with my father were satisfied by the *Times* crossword puzzle and a pound of grapes. Grapes in those days actually had a

My Parents Take Over

taste. A pound was generous measure, and could be made to last for a journey. My father patiently taught me the conventions of the *Times* crossword, which was unmatched in style and quality by any other, and was composed by two or three people with crossword puzzle minds. The particular conventions they used had to be understood. Very clever individuals could solve the puzzle every day in a given number of minutes, or while shaving, or even in outstanding cases like the vicar of Peppard, without actually deigning to write in the answers. Many of these feats were, in truth, 'almosts', but with no admission that the final answer didn't come to them until later in the day, or that their wife had filled it in at breakfast time. My father and I took most of the journey to get as far as we did. A multiple clue like 'The first swallow?' (5,7,3,2.3) was easy, and the answer helped with several shorter ones; whereas the longer one-worders like 'By abstention spoil a mouthful?' (9) might need confirmation later from a dictionary.

As the family grew in size, my father and I sometimes went by car while my mother and the younger children went by train; but my most exciting trips with him were to visit my godfather Michael Bland, who had retired from teaching modern languages at Eton to Falkenham near Woodbridge in Suffolk. Uncle Michael was a real old bachelor, generous and considerate but also pernickety to a whim, and he treated me as a grown-up, or rather in a way which made me feel grown-up, as he and my father and I sat at dinner, cooked by his cook and served by his maid. A primary purpose of these holidays was to teach me to sail, which he and my father had used to do at Freshwater on the Isle of Wight. At first he had a 17-foot open clinker-built varnished boat, but this was succeeded by the larger *Odile*, which might I suppose just qualify nowadays as a small 'cabin cruiser', Bermuda rigged (meaning it had two triangular sails, a jib and a mainsail) and built by Nunn Brothers at Waldringfield with no expense spared, including teak decking curved to match its lines. Odile was the Girl in the Alice Blue Gown, which on the face of it seemed an odd choice for Uncle Michael. In the next berth was the *Hermione*, referred to by Ernie Nunn as the 'ermy one'.

Michael carried the pram dinghy on his back, to the surprise of onlookers, to the point of launch where he could scull us to *Odile*'s moorings. Later on I was allowed to scull the little tub-shaped pram ashore on my own: I remember a hair-raising experience with a strong tide running, but it was a good way to learn.

Michael was an ideal instructor, kindly but insistent that there was one right way and any number of wrong ways to do anything, and able to reduce complicated matters to their basic elements. We rigged the sails and hoisted away as we cast off. He taught me to coil the ropes clockwise and not to snag them, to belay round a cleat or pay out over a fairlead and, most importantly, always to keep the sails full. I learnt what it meant to be close-hauled, and to watch over the bows for a fair puff or a foul puff, a catspaw approaching. He taught me how to go about, and to watch out for the boom and not to broach-to with the wind astern. The principles are easy to grasp and once learnt they are not forgotten.

The timing of our daily sail depended on the tides. Michael knew the river well and never deigned to use a chart or take the smallest risk of going aground even with a rising tide. Often we saw a boat stuck on the mud, silently mocking the crew for their ignorance or stupidity. And then one day the dreadful happened: Michael ran us aground. He took the kedge anchor to the bows, belayed its rope and threw it out so as to be able to pull us off before anyone could witness our plight. Unfortunately the fluke caught in the pocket of his shorts, and the kedge took him with it – a sickening splash! After a seemingly endless pause Michael's upper half surfaced. Carefully he removed his rimless spectacles – 'Please take my spectacles, Charles' – but not his cap; and waded out with the anchor until only his head and shoulders were visible. Then he returned on board. At that moment a friendly boat came past: 'Want any help?' 'No thank you,' said Michael, 'I've waded out with the kedge.' I have never forgotten that answer. It told the truth, and nothing but the truth. Whether it told, or ought to have told, the whole truth, was an interesting question, but fools rush in where angels fear to tread.

My father admired Michael's answer as much as I did. If my old friend Robert Armstrong, now Lord Armstrong of Ilminster, had been there on that occasion he might not have admitted, as he did many years later as Cabinet Secretary, that he had on a famous occasion been 'economical with the truth', for which he was unjustly much criticised. We have no duty to be officiously and irrelevantly detailed in our responses, and when we swear by Almighty God in a court of law to tell the whole truth we are entitled to bear that in mind.

Our visits must have been at the beginning of the summer holidays (in late July) because I remember the partridges on the dusty Suffolk lanes with their huge broods, almost always more than twenty chicks and often more than twenty-five. You never see anything like that

My Parents Take Over

nowadays, even in East Anglia. Nor do you see hosts of sparrows round every house, a nuisance in those days but a treasured sight now. The partridges have been the victims of sustained chemical warfare supported by the tactics of scorched earth, the sparrows of millions of acres of tarmac. The sparrows on the dusty August lawn outside Freshfields annoyed Michael by taking the food he had put out for non-proletarian species. He caught them by the dozen in a trap and despatched them by a deft pressing of the thumb into their tiny brains. He preferred the swallows which nested under his verandah – the same families came back year after year.

My interest in sailing inspired by these visits to Michael Bland made our annual visit to Cowes regatta by my parents and myself the most exciting expedition of the summer. My father's friend 'Scottie' owned a motor yacht berthed at Hamble on Southampton Water. It had quite a stout hull and high freeboard, somewhat similar in shape to what was generically known as a 'motor fishing vessel' but rather more luxurious in its fittings; but anyway I spent every moment on the upper deck, with my father's binoculars and my own Box Brownie camera. Mr Scott was severely lame, whether congenitally or from a war wound I never knew. I have forgotten his Christian name; perhaps it was never used, for in those days friends commonly addressed one another by surnames or nicknames. Nor did I ever know how the friendship had come about, although the war was the most likely context. Anyway, Scottie was a splendid host, took us on the best routes to see the big yachts, and explained their classes and races to me: they were the 'J&K' class, the twelve-metres and the eight-metres.

The 'J&K' class were the sensational boats one came to watch. They were all about the same size but their rigs varied slightly, hence the 'J&K'. Most of them had the simplest and most modern rig, the Bermuda rig. Although the size of the jib was increased by a bowsprit, the mainsail was far the larger of the two sails, with two of its three sides attached to the mast and the boom, and thus kept almost flat when close-hauled to sail into the wind. The masts of most of the yachts in this class were now made of hollow metal, both stronger and lighter than a solid mast. A few of the older boats still had a separate topsail above the mainsail, but the sensational variant was the *Westward*, a two-masted schooner and a wonderful sight in a stiff breeze: indeed so sensational that now seventy years later a replica of her with the same name has been built.

My Parents Take Over

All these yachts also had a spinnaker, a massive bulging sail to catch a following wind, rigged in place of the jib. The size of these sails had gradually increased and the latest science was to cut a spinnaker with a small hole in it so that some of the wind could pass through it and preserve the most desirable shape while preventing wind from eddying out at the edges.

Most of the 'J&K' yachts were owned by foreigners, except for the *Shamrock* which belonged to The King, who was often at the helm, and the *Endeavour*, actually first the *Endeavour* and then *Endeavour II*, owned by Mr T. O. M. Sopwith, the millionaire well known for his company's First World War aircraft including the Sopwith Camel and the Sopwith Scout. These were our British challengers for the America's Cup. Since the cup was held by the U.S.A. the races were held on the American coast, and it was a rule that the challenger could not be shipped across the Atlantic but had to sail to its destination. It thus required qualities of seaworthiness far beyond those normal for a racing yacht, automatically putting any challenging nation at a disadvantage. There was a shortage of millionaires in the 1930s, and Mr Sopwith's willingness to lay out huge sums in spite of this inevitable handicap was much admired. There was speculation about the secret design details whilst the yacht was building. The most important rule regarding the permitted specification for the America's Cup was the length of the waterline, measured when the mast was vertical (and this applied to the smaller classes too: hence the twelve- and eight-metres were described by their length); because the longer the waterline the faster the potential speed of a yacht sailing close-hauled into the wind. The art of the designer was therefore to achieve a maximum increase in the length of waterline for the minimum angle of heel, so that even in a light breeze, when a boat was only heeling a few degrees out of vertical, her waterline would be as long as possible. The *Illustrated London News* was the best of the weekly magazines for the quality and variety of its articles as well as its illustrations, whether drawings, diagrams or photographs, and I used to follow the yachting news in my parents' copy for the many weeks when the new challenger was on the stocks. Unfortunately neither *Endeavour* nor *Endeavour II* succeeded. The next British challenger was *Rainbow*: its most original feature was a snub-nose (rather than a 'cutting edge') to increase its Atlantic seaworthiness without sacrificing speed. I am not sure how many decades passed before it was generally realised in ship design that a bull-nose could provide a more efficient streamline than a cutting edge, as is now almost universal. Perhaps the design of nuclear submarines was the decisive factor.

Apart from *Shamrock*, *Westward* and *Endeavour*, the yacht I most admired was *Velsheda*, perhaps for no other reason than her striking pea-green hull and mellifluous name. These three were captured on my Box Brownie in images so handsome that my parents allowed me to get enlargements printed and framed. The twelve-metres were also superb yachts to see in the course of a race, not least because they were separated by much shorter distances than their larger sisters. A twelve-metre was a yacht for a millionaire: the eight-metres, also exciting to watch, were a new class requiring a smaller crew for owners who lived at a slightly less rarefied level of affluence.

My other godfather was my mother's first cousin and closest childhood friend Arthur Forbes. His father, like hers, had been in India, and Isla and Arthur grew up with their grandmother, 'Granny Crum', at the exquisite medieval Fyfield Manor near Abingdon, leased from St John's College, Oxford. Arthur went to Sandhurst and joined the Cameronians. His battalion were much in India until the war and after that he lived in the Sudan as a, and then the, senior game warden. His postal address was Major Arthur Forbes, Game Warden, Sudan. Sudan was about the size of France, Spain and Britain combined (a point missed by Mr Gladstone's critics after the Gordon affair, who said that the British army could and should keep the peace by 'occupying the forts in the Sudan'). The postman in Arthur's day never seemed to have a problem in delivering my letters to my godfather, who was exceedingly generous and once sent me , to my great embarrassment, the handsome sum of £7 (add two noughts for today's value) for riding lessons, the mere thought of which filled me with dread. The money was put in my Post Office Savings Bank, an admirable but now long defunct institution. We quite frequently visited Fyfield to see my great-grandmother and Arthur's mother Agnes, and we watched the village blacksmith at work under the spreading chestnut tree.

My mother's other grandmother, 'Grannyma', lived in Porlock in an ancient thatched cottage and looked like a ripe, smiling Cox's orange pippin. She was a good sport and throughout her life had hunted with the Devon and Somerset Staghounds. Her family seemed to have been of the same bent: three Forbes brothers in India had each lost an eye pigsticking. At Porlock as at Fyfield the main village amusement was watching the blacksmith, again under a chestnut tree. This acquaintance with Exmoor later stood me in good stead, because Rosamund had been brought up there. She and her sister had hunted with the foxhounds and knew every inch of the moor, so my memories of Porlock (including my father driving the car up the hill) helped me to fit in when we visited her mother's cottage near Exford.

I have mentioned that my mother's father had died young, leaving a widow who lived in Thornham Cottage in Henley, and four children, the oldest eighteen; and that her grandmothers, both widowed, lived at Fyfield and Porlock. But my father's mother lived at Manley Hall, a large house in Cheshire, with a bevy of my first cousins and periodic uncles and aunts, and we always went there for the school holidays.

3
Manley and Llandulas

My grandfather Stephen Gladstone, the second son of the Prime Minister, was rector of Hawarden for thirty years before moving in 1904 to a less demanding country parish at Barrowby near Grantham. In his upper thirties he married Annie Wilson, daughter of a Liverpool surgeon. All their six children were born in Hawarden rectory, from which by dint of conscientious hard work their father had developed a model large Victorian country parish in which he employed three curates, two of whom, serving at the same period, were the Reverend Mr Cain and the Reverend Mr Abel. Stephen's marriage brought a new breadth and a new fulfilment to his work, and his children's memories of Hawarden were happy ones; but their time at Barrowby was the golden era of their later youth and early adulthood. When Stephen retired from Barrowby he bought Manley Hall in Cheshire, on the red sandstone ridge above Helsby with a fine view over Chester towards Hawarden and the Welsh hills to the west. This was a kind of homecoming, but at a discreet distance from Hawarden Castle where Stephen's nephew William was now the 'young squire'.

My grandfather died before I was a year old, but my grandmother, known as 'Muzzie', not only continued to live in Manley but soon enlarged it to accommodate a growing tribe of grandchildren. It seemed big enough to me. It was a delightful two-storey, late Georgian house with a few gothic windows on the ground floor of the sunny side: the long, low, chintzy sitting room, the billiards room and a little study beyond it. The drawing room with its big Georgian window was not much used – certainly not by us. The dining room was on the right of the entrance hall and on the left was a chapel (later removed) where Granny conducted prayers every day after breakfast, the grown-ups in the front row, the children and nannies behind them and the servants at the back. Even before joining my prep school I became familiar with some of the words of the Prayer Book because Granny, presumably following her late husband's choice, recited the Benedictus every day: 'the dayspring from on high hath visited us' seemed vaguely reassuring, although I don't suppose anyone except the front row knew quite how to interpret it.

My grandmother died suddenly in 1930 aged sixty. Uncle Albert, with his sister Catherine, Aunty Kith, took over Manley. He worked in London during the week and came up by train for the weekends; as was customary in the family firm, partners who had been in Calcutta were able to come home to the London office in their forties.

When we children were seven or eight we were promoted from the nursery to the dining room. There was a slide – and a slab – by which the dishes could be delivered from the kitchen to the dining room. Breakfast of course was a proper breakfast with porridge followed by a choice of eggs, bacon and sometimes kippers. When Aunty Kith dished out the bacon for the children the treat was to have a- spoonful of 'dibbery', the grease now supposed to be so bad for one, on top of it. Lunch was also a proper full meal, namely a first course of meat and two vegetables – with fish on Fridays – followed by pudding. Mutton was as much valued as beef, and was not held to be worth eating until it was four years old: a good leg of mutton would appear on Sundays as often as a joint of beef. As the week wore on, the Sunday joint was eaten cold on Tuesdays and then became perhaps shepherd's pie or cottage pie or toad-in-the-hole, and finally Irish stew. The puddings were traditional – apple dumplings or fritters or plum pudding, castle puddings, spotted dog or roly-poly pudding with occasionally the less welcome bread-and-butter pudding; but there was always rice pudding placed on the table in front of Uncle Albert as an alternative, subject to the ritual of removing the skin, which must come off in one piece, browned but not burnt, and thus demonstrate that the cook had hit the happy mean and that it was neither stodgy nor navigable. There was always a proper Cheshire cheese on the sideboard, orange, cylindrical, about five inches diameter and seven or eight inches high. All the children wanted the elastic band which kept the little wrinkled paper cap in place on Uncle Albert's screw-topped beer bottle: 'Please, Uncle Albert, may I have the elastic band?' 'Please, Uncle Albert, I asked first.' Uncle Albert soon decreed that the person who asked last should have it.

The knives were silver-handled but steel-bladed, and were cleaned and sharpened simultaneously in those wonderful circular grinding machines which held several knives at a time round their circumferences. We enjoyed turning the handles and indeed a good deal of our time was spent in the back passage with its flagstones – chatting and no doubt asking endless tiresome questions in the kitchen, pantry and scullery, leading to the back door and the little yard which was our normal exit and where our bikes were kept. The steel knives had a 'G' engraved on the handles: the fish knives and those used for dessert and cheese had silver or silver-plated blades and horn handles, and woe betide anyone who cut their fruit or cheese with a G knife. On one occasion it was discovered that an ignorant maid had provided a G knife for the cheese. 'A G knife in the cheese!' said Henry, aged about seven, in a loud voice. 'What next?'

It can be understood, therefore, that some manners and conventions were strictly enforced in this household, but they had to be picked up as one went along. One lunch-time when I was already at my prep school I spilt something and said in a loud voice 'Damn!' A horrified silence followed and I was escorted from the room by my mother like a prisoner en route to the cells; I can remember to this day her telling me that saying 'Damn!' was simply Not Done.

Kith and Albert were both unmarried; but the next three of the family – Charlie, Deiney and Edie – had all married in 1924 and 1925. Charlie, my father, was a schoolmaster and we came to Manley for the school holidays. Deiney and Edie with their respective spouses were in India, so they homed in on Manley when they were on leave. Moreover, in those days children were sent home from India at the age of four, because the Indian climate was not considered suitable for European children to grow up in; so my first cousins were parked with their grandmother and, after her early death in 1930, with her elder and unmarried daughter, Aunty Kith. It seems extraordinary that parents should be confined to seeing their young families during a few months' leave at three-yearly intervals, but that is how it was. Later on, they spoke to their parents on the telephone once a month, for three minutes at £1 a minute. The telephone was of the old upright type: one lifted the receiver off its hook. So an additional earpiece was fitted at Manley to enable two children to listen, though only one at a time could speak.

Catherine, Aunty Kith, was the eldest of the family. Perhaps the strict morals of a Victorian clerical family, even one which was full of fun and laughter, coupled with a growing number of younger brothers and sisters whose mother needed help and support in looking after them, were circumstances which tended to inhibit marriage. Whether or not that was the case, the mission and fulfilment of Aunty Kith's life was her devotion to her nephews and nieces.

Manley and Llandulas

Next in age came Uncle Albert, who began his career as a partner in the family firm of merchants in Calcutta, but by the time I first knew him was a partner in London. He had been an exceptionally distinguished oarsman at Eton and at Oxford. He was the only man in his year at Christ Church to enter trade. During the war he joined the Gurkhas and survived service at Gallipoli, and later in Mesopotamia, where his younger brother Uncle Deiney was also an officer with the Gurkhas. The only way of thwarting the midges was by smearing themselves with the axle grease provided for the motor lorries. The Turkish army was an even more formidable enemy than the midge. Uncle Albert was awarded the military MBE and Uncle Deiney the MC for his leadership during a river crossing under heavy fire. He was recommended for the VC. Mesopotamia became a British Protectorate and was turned into the nation state of Iraq, its boundaries drawn by a Whitehall Arabist doing his best.

When he had been promoted to the London office, Uncle Albert had at least one serious stab at getting married, but it came to nothing and maybe he thought, as bachelors sometimes did – and probably still do – that he was getting too old. He was a most generous man, with a dry sense of humour and a terse turn of phrase, but modest to the point of being self-effacing: photographs of him are hard to come by.

My father, exactly two years younger than Albert, was also an oarsman of great distinction at Eton and Oxford. After university he spent the best part of two years perfecting his French and German, mainly in Paris and Heidelberg, before becoming a master at Eton. He had been a member of the Oxford University Officers' Training Corps. The Oxford Corps were field gunners, borrowing the municipal tram horses, which were accustomed to following the tramlines into Carfax and could only be cajoled with difficulty into turning down St Aldate's en route to artillery exercises. The whole enterprise was carried out in quite a relaxed atmosphere and there were various anecdotes of cadets mounting their steeds facing the tail or falling between two horses after consuming too many pints of 'tupenny' (the very best beer, at 2d a quart) at lunch. My father joined the staff at Eton in 1912 to teach French and German. Here he became an officer in the Corps as did his closest friend Eric Powell, and it is clear from his diary that he was really keen on this, and not merely a young master who had been 'volunteered.' His time spent in Germany must have enhanced the sense of foreboding common to many British people that the militarism of the

Manley and Llandulas

Kaiser and the German army and navy had to be stood up to – or, at the worst, prepared for. When in the late days of July the War Office telephoned the head master* to say that the Expeditionary Corps were about to embark for France and they needed three officers with fluent French and German as interpreters, he immediately volunteered. Thus he became one of the only four identified volunteers in the 'Army of Mercenaries' known as the Old Contemptibles, three of them being Eton masters. As a despatch rider he conveyed messages to Allied headquarters. He was issued with a motor bike (having a few hours of training) and seconded to the Royal Flying Corps, but in spite of suffering endless punctures caused by countless nails on the cobbled roads shed by the boots of the marching infantry, he claimed to have retreated further from Mons than anyone else: a formidably difficult and challenging feat, fraught with every kind of difficulty and danger – including Uhlans on the lookout for potential prisoners. After nights spent in pouring rain under trees, he became ill (field hospitals were mostly in trains before tactics got bogged down in trenches) and after recovering was thrust into his role as an observer. He found his first flights frightening experiences; his life was always dependent on the skill and judgement of his pilot. He recorded his experiences in his diary and in a long letter to his siblings, which I have published separately.

He and his pilot were shot down behind enemy lines in April 1915 and became prisoners of war. Evidently my father as a fluent German and French speaker was either a potential or an actual nuisance in a normal prisoner-of-war camp or 'Offlag', and he was shipped to the island of Stralsund in the Baltic, from which it was virtually impossible to escape. Most of the prisoners were Russian officers and he learnt Russian from them, later becoming the first schoolmaster in Britain to teach it as a modern language. He became ill and lost so much weight that he was selected for exchange and repatriation just before the war ended, and had reached Holland at the time of the armistice. It took him a long time to make a physical recovery but he was fit enough to return to Eton in September 1919. He and Uncle Albert had lost most of their male contemporary friends. Looking at their group photographs from school or university, one could ask 'Who is that?' only to receive the answer 'He's dead, poor fellow'.

*Headmaster/head master. I have followed the usage that the respective schools themselves adopted.

Manley and Llandulas

I have a photograph of my father as one of nine boys in his house at Eton as 'members of the boats' dressed in their Fourth of June uniforms, their beribboned straw boaters naming their boats: *Monarch, Victory, Prince of Wales, Britannia*... Only three of the nine, including my father, survived. One of them was posthumously awarded the VC and several earned DSOs and MCs.

The consequence was that the survivors had few surviving friends from school and university. In the case of Uncle Albert, Neville Rolfe had been a regular Gurkha officer who had been his mentor at Gallipoli; Harold Barker was a rowing friend who lived near Nettlebed; 'Barmy Gilbert', a sportsman who had played cricket for England against the West Indies, and Douglas Smyth-Osbourne, a Darjeeling tea planter: but that was about it. In my father's case, his colleague Eric Powell's death in an Alpine accident in 1930 was a sore blow. Two or three other friends sent their sons to his house at Eton. For the girls, of course, the consequences were even worse.

My mother was, as I have said, much younger than my father. Her mother Violet Crum, Lady Crum since Erskine had been knighted, took the name of Erskine into her surname; a young widow living in Thornham Cottage at Henley, whom I got to know quite well; but my young maternal aunt and uncles did not play much of a part in my life until later. Consequently we spent our holidays with my father's family: I have described our journeys to Manley.

Next in age came Uncle Deiney, the tallest of the brothers, a finelooking man and a gentle giant. He too rowed for Eton – in the recordbreaking crew which won the Ladies' Plate in 1911. When his son Stephen and I were in the Eton Eight in 1941, the prow of the 1911 boat with the names of the crew painted on it was still a trophy in the 'Eight Room' at the boat house: in that crew were one current Eton housemaster, A. C. Beasley-Robinson, and no less than four fathers of sons at his house, including Stephen. More people of his generation had survived than was the case with his elder brothers. Deiney was not considered academic enough to go to Oxford and chose to try his hand at farming in Canada, but it did not suit him and he became a partner alongside Uncle Albert, in the family firm in Calcutta. He married Clair Davidson whose family lived at Aboyne.

Aunty Clair came from a good old Scottish imperial family. Her father 'Poppa' had been a colonel in the Indian Army, as had his father before him in the days of the East India Company, which in most respects governed India until the Mutiny in 1857. Poppa's numerous sisters, all over ninety, were orphan pensioners of the Company. Poppa had an economical bent, a traditional Aberdonian characteristic, splitting his matches with a sharp knife in order to get two for one, but lacerating his waistcoat in the process, casting doubt on the actual economy achieved, especially as he seemed to use half a match about once a minute as he puffed away at his pipe. His wife, for some undiscovered reason, was known as 'Bowlie'. They lived appropriately at Aboyne, in a house called Allt Dinnie, so we used to visit Aunty Clair's family once or twice when we were on holiday at Fasque or later at Glen Dye. Her sister Jean lived in a smaller house which she and her husband Brigadier Jackson, with his fearsome scrubbing-brush moustache, had built next door to them, Burnside. He was one of those clever army officers who appear just a little bit too clever to their superiors and hence do not rise to the rank of general. The brigadier built exquisite models of ships of the line with every rope and every block and tackle rigged exactly as had been the Navy's practice, and he could (and did) demonstrate, correctly, the instances in which the design of the rope work with all its tackles was inefficient, and would have worked better if arranged differently. He would not have hesitated to explain this to Nelson, had he been his contemporary.

It did not take the brigadier long to realise that the Aboyne Highland Games might be better organised. He arranged for the flags of all the local Highland chiefs and chieftains to fly round the perimeter of the ring, and insisted on inventing and adding a flag using the Gladstone coat of arms for Uncle Albert, as a local laird, although we were a Lowland family. Unfortunately Highland games are extremely boring for spectators, but the funfair turned the expedition into a treat and after a rather less than a decent time had elapsed watching the tossing of the caber, we would escape from the arena to the fun fair in the hope of seeing the freaks, perhaps a two-headed sheep and a bearded woman, and riding the dodgems and shooting at little balls suspended by a jet of water.

Aunty Clair inherited her family's inclination to economise. Once when my father met her at King's Cross on the train from Aberdeen she complained that it had been absolutely packed full. He said that there seemed to have been plenty of room in the front coaches. 'Yes', she said, 'but I'd paid for my seat.' During our holidays at Glen Dye she would go round the breakfast table putting precisely one spoonful of sugar into each person's cup, whether they wanted it or not, one day doling out salt by mistake, with entertaining results. Then she went round, through force of habit, collecting from each plate the bacon rind and the skeletons of the kippers for the hens, forgetting that they were in Kent. There was an element of absent-mindedness about her: once in Calcutta she had forgotten how to switch off the engine of the car (a de Dion Bouton, by the way) and had driven it round and round the circular entrance drive until it ran out of petrol. She was, however, both shrewd and intelligent, and good at the *Times* crossword, which the grown-ups used to do every day (yesterday's edition in Scotland, of course). Sometimes in the evening – perhaps at dinner – she would suddenly hold up her hand – she had thought of the answer to the clue which had baffled everybody. Uncle Deiney and Aunty Clair had four children: Stephen, Felicity, Anne and John. My age fell between the elder two.

After Uncle Deiney in my grandparents' family came Aunty Edie, who like her elder sister was educated at home and was put in charge of the Girls' Friendly Society and the Girl Guides. It would be hard to imagine anyone with a kinder and more affectionate and tolerant disposition. She was proud of the athletic achievements of her three elder brothers. Once my father, putting down the newspaper, said 'I see we have won the Test Match.' 'Oh, have you?' she replied. 'Well done!' She married Uncle Tom and they had three children, Elizabeth, Henry and Christopher. Again, I fell between the first two in age.

Uncle Tom was the son of a railwayman and himself became a railway surveyor. He joined the Territorial Army (it had been inaugurated in 1908 to replace the Militia and the Volunteers, and included the Yeomanry) and by the time of the outbreak of war in 1914 he was a sergeant. He ended the war as a major who had been awarded the MC and two bars: this triple award was very rare indeed, as also it was in the Second World War. He joined the Indian Civil Service and, based in Bombay (Mumbai), living in Poona in the monsoon season, he became a senior surveyor, receiving the CIE, equivalent of the CBE, on his retirement at the age of forty-five. He was the kindest of men. He was a good shot with a rifle, less so with a shotgun, and in old age could be coaxed to retell well-worn anecdotes of sporting incidents in India: not of the trophy-hunting pursuit of big game, but more in the character of removing a threatening but elusive boar.

Thus the company at Manley, both the grown-ups and my contemporaries, could not have been more delightful: my parents, three uncles and three aunts, and the eight children of the first two batches; for Penelope, born at the end of 1930, and Clair's youngest, John, who was still crawling after the move to Hawarden, were not ready to join in during the vintage years from about 1929 until 1935.

As we grew older, Aunty Kith secured the services of a series of French governesses, Mam'selles, but we treated them ruthlessly, as children (and others) will treat innocent strangers whose function is to challenge their liberty, giving none of them the slightest chance of obtaining order, let along speaking French. But we got on very well with the domestic staff, notably with Big Elizabeth (tall but thus named to distinguish her from little Elizabeth), the head parlourmaid, and Eva Pate, head housemaid, who returned after the war to look after Uncle Albert and Aunty Kith. We liked and respected Mr Carter, the chauffeur, who mended all our punctures without complaint unless we had aggravated the problem by riding with a flat tyre. He wore the leather gaiters of the groom and looked after and washed all the cars during the holidays, but his special care was the 'Ark', the generic name for the big car, of which there were two or perhaps three over the course of years; a name first used under Mr Carter's predecessor, Mr Twinning, whose Christian name was later discovered to be Noah, causing some embarrassment. There was an odd job man in a green baize apron who did the coal and polished the shoes and cleaned the back passage. The head gardener, mainly responsible for the kitchen garden, was Mr Keeling, and I remember him repeating time and again at the end of this era 'Well, I never did expect to live to fall the hew edge.' Mrs Keeling had a kindly wrinkled face and their son was the under-gardener: sadly he died with the army in North Africa during the war – of 'malicious ammonia', as his parents told us. Mrs Mussons, Martha, was another good friend. She ran the tiny post office from the front room of her cottage round the corner, where we could cash postal orders, perhaps for 9d or a shilling, and buy our postage stamps for thank-you letters for a penny-halfpenny.

Occasionally we went to Chester for shopping, notably at Mr Dutton's in Eastgate Street, one of those delightful grocers with tiles on the floor and walls and dark, solid, wooden counters of which only a few successors survive nowadays in the richest areas of large towns. Aunty Kith would seek his advice whilst dictating her lengthy order, which he delivered to Manley. We bought bits and pieces, bells and saddle bags, for our bicycles at Halford's in Northgate Street. We had

Manley and Llandulas

our hair cut at Proud's in St Werburgh Street and then, if we had been on our best behaviour, we might visit Bollands for a cream bun. Bollands had an 'orchestra' – two refined ladies with a grand piano and a violin.

Liverpool still counted in our family affairs and traditions, although the old family firm there, incapable of responding to changing conditions, was moribund. Raising money for Liverpool Cathedral was the object of garden fêtes at Manley; one of them was to be opened by (the other) Aunt Maud, just after Uncle Harry had got his peerage. She had already been awarded the CBE for her work for the Red Cross. To be cynical, if you knew the right people and asked often enough, you usually got something in those days, and I remember Aunty Kith checking the proof of the programme stating that the fête in aid of the building of Liverpool Cathedral was to be opened by THE Lady Gladstone of Hawarden, C.B.E. The Lady Chapel, almost big enough to be a cathedral in its own right, was already open and the family of Lord Vestey, 'Provision Merchant' as the plaque says, was paying for the tower from the profits of South American beef.

The annual treat in Liverpool was to go to the pantomime: afterwards we remembered, retold and varied the jokes according to context time and again, even for years. My father said that all the best jokes originated in Liverpool and that they were tried out there before arriving at Drury Lane for the pantomime in London; and indeed the only time we ever went to Drury Lane we heard the jokes we had heard in Liverpool two years before.

Each holiday we used to visit Aunt Maud in Princes Road. Not the Aunt Maud of Hawarden but Aunt Maud Wilson, Granny's unmarried sister, who lived in her spacious, almost cavernous, late Victorian house with its large garden in Princes Road, in the smartest residential area in the city. She spoke of 'going down town' to the shops. She was a kindly and delightful aunt, always good for half-a-crown for a well-behaved nephew. We also used to visit her unmarried brother, Uncle Bertie, at Hooton on the Wirral. He seemed to me to be typical of the contented and mildly eccentric bachelors of those days, who lived on a modest income in a nice house with a couple of servants and had never done a day's work in his life. Each time he took a sip of tea, his left hand held flat below the cup to prevent a drip from soiling his shirt, he would raise his head and move his lips to relish the flavour before returning the cup to its saucer. He did so, he said, because he had watched hens

Manley and Llandulas

drinking like that, and they seemed to enjoy it so much. After tea we would go in to the garden for a game of quoits. Then we would play a game of catch, which simply meant that the three of us stood in a triangle and threw the ball to each other.

My most memorable visit to Liverpool was my birthday treat for which I had chosen to see a liner. My father duly arranged this and we travelled northwards along the docks from Pierhead, where the ferry from Birkenhead landed us, on the overhead railway. The view from the train astonished me: motor lorries, horse-drawn carts and handcarts, wheelbarrows and sack trolleys and men rolling barrels or walking purposefully in their hundreds to and fro in every direction or standing around in groups, a scene of milling activity, continuing for mile after mile – there was a train stop at every dock, of course. The size of the liner we saw impressed me, although what I remember most vividly about the docks themselves was the anti-rat metal discs on all the hawsers. I could never quite get it clear in my mind whether they were intended to stop rats from getting on to ships or getting off them. But the unforgettable part of the day was the view from the overhead railway. The Gladstone Dock was being built at the time. I was not there for the official opening, nor did I see the launch of the *Ark Royal* at Cammell Laird in Birkenhead like other members of the Manley party; I think because of my prep school terms.

As we were returning to Manley from Birkenhead in the evening, we passed a massive fire at the oil refinery near Ellesmere Port. When I thanked my father for the treat I told him that it had really been two treats, because I had intended to choose a house on fire for my treat the following year. Actually, the next really big blaze I saw – on the horizon one evening from the dormitory of my prep school – was the burning of the Crystal Palace; and the next after that was the blitz on the London docks from the upper floor of Uncle Tom's house in Hertfordshire in the early autumn of 1940.

Our recreations at Manley fall into fairly clear categories; the earliest included walks with Nanny May. Either we turned right out of the gate and went down the long hill past the quarry to see the kingcups in the roadside ditches below, or we turned left towards Mouldsworth to see the ducks on the duck pond and occasionally, when Nanny had found out the day and time, to see Tommy Carter, the blacksmith (who had some sheds in a yard rather than a chestnut tree as at Fyfield or Porlock), fitting the red-hot steel rim to a cartwheel and plunging it into

[35]

a bath of water to shrink it on, with an impressive hiss and a cloud of steam.

Then came the sandpit, which was not a mere ordinary sandpit with defined boundaries but the whole area between the garages and the Dutch barn, where a load of sand for our enjoyment had been dumped by a horse and cart from the Aston quarry. Four or five of us had ample space to make roads and bridges and tunnels and cuttings and embankments and hairpin bends and garages for our Dinky toys, together with houses and castles which were more to the taste of the girls. Dinky toys were not cheap. They cost around 1s/6d and we would have perhaps one or two or three each, but by no means a whole collection. The sand got dispersed over the course of time and I remember when it was agreed that we should have a new load; a 'yard' of sand – which meant a cubic yard, a cartload! I was amazed to discover that a whole yard of sand cost precisely the same as one Dinky toy.

We were a hands-on family. All the grown-ups had a good knowledge of gardening. The rhododendrons had to be kept under control, and trees which had outgrown their sites were felled with axes and long crosscut saws. Large bonfires were enjoyed by all. Expeditions were arranged with walks and games and picnics, mostly in the summer when we were at Llandulas. I remember one in 1930 to the Denbigh moors, when our cars had to be parked close to the road because Great-Uncle Harry and Aunt Maud were coming from Hawarden to join our picnic tea.

A remark made by Aunty Kith that afternoon in a context I have forgotten stuck in my mind. She simply said 'Nobody has any money this year.' This struck me as distinctly odd, because I hadn't noticed much difference, although with hindsight I suppose there were some minor grumbles about the need to economise – as Nancy Mitford put it, the writing paper got thinner and the lavatory paper got thicker. I was vaguely aware of mention of remote acquaintances who had lost their whole fortunes overnight in the Stock Exchange crash. But the news that 'nobody had any money this year' struck me not simply with disbelief (Uncle Harry and Aunt Maud turned up in their Rolls with two chauffeurs, looking rich enough to me), but I suppose also with that faint kind of foreboding which can fairly easily be transferred to a back drawer in one's mind. But I have never forgotten that remark. Later I realised that many people like Aunty Kith depended for their whole incomes on interest from government stock and

Manley and Llandulas

dividends from companies, and that when a company did not make a profit it did not pay a dividend. It was as simple as that.

Uncle Harry and Aunt Maud duly turned up but she did not deign to dismount – she was always delicate – so one by one we had to climb in to the spacious back of the car with its deep-pile grey carpet to pay court to her.

Manley had a few fields and a wood and as we grew up the 'Runaway' became a chief diversion. Occasionally the girls would run away but much more often it was the boys, signalling the advantage of their masculinity. The girls were usually sporting enough to chase us, so this turned in to our private version of hare and hounds. There were not many hiding places – the hayloft in the Dutch barn was best – but no credit was lost to the girls by having the sense simply to ignore us. There were rabbits in the fields and the best remembered feat at Manley was when Henry chased one and killed it with a cricket stump. Later we all got bicycles which were the source of much enjoyment.

Uncle Deiney, home on leave, bought Stephen a magnificent hut with a verandah in kit form, and it was granted a prime site near the front gate. Elizabeth and Henry (Stamper) decided that this was simply not good enough. A smart and spacious hut professionally made had no place in the culture of Manley as they perceived it, a culture of improvisation. Stephen's hut required some site preparation in the form of clearing undergrowth and levelling, and even laying a foundation, giving time for a rival project to pre-empt it.

A large pile of sawn and creosoted fencing timber happened to be delivered for the orchard. Elizabeth and Henry decided to appropriate it together with a big box of nails and they used it to erect a rival hut, literally overnight. This was such a remarkable *fait accompli* that the grown-ups felt unable to insist on its being dismantled. The orchard fence was put on hold and the hut gave us endless enjoyment, a headquarters in which we could devise all sorts of projects and gossip privately to our hearts' content. The hut was square in all dimensions except for a slight lean on the roof, so very little sawing was required except for making the door, which was hung with the gate hinges intended for the fence. It was equipped with a bench, and the fact that it had no windows enhanced its privacy.

Manley Hall, like its surroundings, was ideal for hide-and-seek or sardines, and in the evenings we could play charades and dumb crambo. It became habitual for us to write and perform a play every holidays, but these dramatic efforts had no merit except in absorbing our time.

We graduated to grown-up breakfast and lunch, but not to grown-up dinner. We had 'tea' on a low table at the end of the sitting room and it became a matter of honour to empty a large packet of corn flakes or Force every evening, followed by bread, butter and jam. Then Aunty Kith used to read a chapter of one of Captain Marryat's novels. The mournful end of *Masterman Ready* made a deep impression.

LLANDULAS

Each summer the Manley house party, following family tradition, set off for a seaside holiday on the North Wales coast. W. E. Gladstone and Catherine with their large family had stayed year after year at Penmaenmawr. He recorded those holidays in his diary, numbering every bathe in the sea. Swimming in salt water he found 'a most powerful agent'. We stayed at Llandulas, just east of Colwyn Bay. During the early years Granny hired a large house named Bryndulas, but when the tribe of grandchildren outgrew it, we took a preparatory school, Arnold House. Evelyn Waugh taught there for a brief while; but what went on during the term time did not concern us. The village was built on a steep hill overlooking the sea, but there was ample space for us to play and a tennis court on which we raced our tortoises won as prizes at the Rhyl funfair, which with its hair-raising rides was the best treat of the whole holiday.

Most days we went down to play on Llandulas beach. The dickey of Aunty Kith's bullnosed Morris Cowley, with room for two children in the area nowadays occupied by the boot but with ingress by a hinged lid, was the most sought after conveyance, closely followed by Uncle Albert's Wolseley ('The Cardinal', of course) which had room in the front seat for one child on the right of the driver (and several on the left). The tide had to be right: pebbles at high tide were of no use to us, but once the sand appeared we could build dams and castles or paddle or bathe. Granny still had a bathing machine, a substantial hut on steel-rimmed wheels from which she could launch herself knee-deep down steps at the right state of the tide, in a costume which discreetly covered most of her. Our picnic designed to suit our taste consisted mostly of jam sandwiches, as attractive to wasps as they were to us, producing some traumatic moments. 'That child's swallowed a wasp' I

Manley and Llandulas

remember my father saying on one occasion. I think the victim was Peter.

Depending on the tide, we sometimes played at Arnold House in the morning and visited the beach in the afternoon. The only unwelcome item in the day's programme was the compulsory rest on our beds after lunch, as it was also at Manley: an hour's inactivity was essential to enable us to digest this substantial meal. As it happens, these were the days when Henry won his laurels as a trencherman: a poached egg and toast in one mouthful, the main course at lunch in twelve – or was it nine? Henry was to achieve a height of six feet nine inches in his prime. He joined the Navy but was too big to occupy a fighter aircraft. He slept in two hammocks sewn together. He had chronic scars on his shins because all the doors in warships had a coaming, a barrier about two feet high to prevent water caused by damage from sloshing from one compartment to another, and Henry had to bend at both ends to get through them. Eventually his breathing was affected by the confined spaces and a promising career in which he had looked set to become an admiral came to an end. He joined Stephen in the family firm in Calcutta. Tallness was hereditary in the Gladstone family. It was said that you could always recognise the first Sir John in a crowd: he would be the tallest man. Our cousin John of Capenoch was six foot eight: my father said his boots had to be laid down at Cammell Laird. Christopher Parish was almost as tall as Henry. My father and some of his children had John Gladstone's nose, which perhaps was preferable to his height.

We found the rests after lunch unbearably tedious, and simply used to advance the clock we were provided with, get up long before the appointed time and generally make a fuss about returning to our beds. There was, incidentally, also a rule that nobody should bathe until an hour after a meal. That was sensible, even if a little over-cautious.

Once on a foul stormy day, when the best we could manage was a walk along the coastal cliffs, a rocket went up from a ship at sea to summon the lifeboat. Nanny hastened us back to witness the launch of the Llandulas lifeboat, hauled down the beach by ropes on its huge wheels by a team of villagers until the water was deep enough to launch it. For us, although we were disappointed that there was no shipwreck, the splash as the boat entered the water and began to plough through the breakers was memorable.

Often we went on expeditions, either to the beach at Penmaenmawr

Manley and Llandulas

or to Snowdonia. At Penmaenmawr the beach was reached through a long, low passage under the railway, known as Granny's Tunnel, perhaps after my father's Granny Catherine. Here the Irish Mail, still the most important train in Britain even though most of Ireland was now independent, running from Euston to Holyhead drawn by two mighty steam locomotives, thundered past us even more impressively than at Llandulas on the low embankment with the mountain as its backdrop: an unforgettable sight and sound.

We walked up Snowdon as quite young children, usually either taking the easy route more or less as followed by the railway, but once from the south, which involved my father giving me a piggy-back, as Uncle Deiney did for Stephen, wading more than waist-deep over the submerged causeway across Llyn Llydaw. There is a path now, so you can walk round. The reward at the summit was a bottle of ginger beer, with a glass ball as a stopper. We also climbed the Glydyrs.

The vintage years at Manley ended when Uncle Deiney came home to the London office and bought a substantial house, Lewins, at Crockham Hill in Kent, and soon afterwards Uncle Tom retired and bought the Old Rectory at Munden in Hertfordshire. Uncle Harry died aged over eighty in 1935, Aunt Maud moved to Plas Warren nearby, and Uncle Albert with Aunty Kith were at last able to occupy his inheritance and move from Manley to Hawarden Castle. During the following years I enjoyed delightful stays at Lewins, Munden and Hawarden. Manley, left to my father as the second son, lay empty for lack of buyers or tenants.

4
Fasque and Astridge

In 1936 Uncle Albert was able for the first time to reside, at least for some weeks in the summer, at the palatial house in Kincardineshire in Scotland which he had inherited from his bachelor cousin John Gladstone ten years earlier. John's unmarried sister and lifelong companion Mary had occupied the house in solitary splendour until her death in 1932, the last few years bedridden and demented in her room on the top floor. It would have been absurd for Albert to retain a full team of servants at Fasque whilst he was still the senior partner in London of the family business of East India merchants; but when he came into his other inheritance, at Hawarden, in 1935, he realised that he could transport the core servants from there to Fasque for a summer stay. The Ark was available for the purpose: an Armstrong Siddeley (they were advertised as 'built like a battleship') with a timber-framed back end (or stern) like a 'shooting brake'. The team at Fasque during Uncle Albert's six-week stay was stiffened by local people, notably by Miss Towns as cook, daughter of the former estate joiner, who had worked as a junior in the kitchen before the First World War; and Mrs Menzies, daughter of one of the gamekeepers John had imported from Suffolk.

The Fasque Estate was a fine inheritance, which I will describe in another context. As far as we were concerned – I mean we ten first cousins, Uncle Albert's nephews and nieces – it was a huge holiday house with ample room inside and out for every kind of enjoyment we cared to devise. We were aware that the electrical installation and the central heating had been worn out by the time of, if not before, John's death, but the use of candles and tilly lamps made our stay all the more romantic. The house had been built for show rather than for usefulness. In relation to its size it did not have many rooms, but they were large. The entrance hall with the cantilevered double staircase in the distance beyond it was impressive, but we children had to use the back door and the servants' stairs. Our quarters were on the top floor, the 'boys' dorm' at the south-east and the 'girls' dorm' at the south-west corner of the

Fasque and Astridge

house. Each 'dorm' consisted of a bedroom, which would accommodate three or even four children, a dressing room larger than a normal double bedroom, and a turret; and, on the north side of the house, a bathroom. Thus the batch of three older boys, and similarly of girls, could sleep in the bedroom and the younger batch in the dressing room. The nannies and governesses lived in the more than ample servants' quarters in the north wing.

The turrets were small but romantic, havens for chatter and for treasures: the boys' turret contained the old collection of birds' eggs, stored in purpose-built trays with cotton wool in each little square space. Birds'-nesting in its old form was beginning to be frowned on, but it was still acceptable to remove carefully, and then blow, one egg from a clutch, except with rare species. The boys' bathroom was a *tour de force*, the bath of a kind seen nowadays only in those very few stately homes open to the public still in their pre-First-War state. It would easily accommodate three children at a time and above the massive brass taps was a semi-circular shelter accommodating the wave, the spray and the shower. The wave came through a slit about waist height. The spray consisted of several rows of small holes around the semi-circle, which did literally spray one with water: a much more efficient system than the now universal shower. The shower itself was about a foot in diameter, unlike the puny lift-off showers of nowadays which are anyway used mainly as sprays. The girls' end only had a normal bath, although it was much larger than anything obtainable nowadays.

Between the boys' bathroom and the servants' stairs was the lift, the size of a modern hotel lift and worked by ropes and pulleys, for bringing up the coals. I learnt later that a condition of each farm tenant's lease was that he should cart four tons of coal annually to the big house from Laurenckirk station, about four miles away.

Between the two 'dorms', at the centre of the house, was the nursery, an attractive room with its huge bay window and its cupboards full of Victorian toys. Opposite, on the north side of the house, was Cousin Mary's bedroom, unoccupied not as a gesture of piety but because there was no particular use for it and it was full of unwanted furniture and pictures anyway; and between these two rooms was the oval stairwell, with its high wrought-iron railing to prevent us, or anyone else, falling down it. One can only describe it as a stairwell, although in fact the staircase from first to second floor discreetly occupied an adjacent space and was never used anyway because we had to use the back stairs. In

Fasque and Astridge

our pyjamas we used to gaze through the railings to watch the grown-ups in their finery moving from the drawing room on the first floor towards the great double staircase to descend for dinner. Our avowed sport was to spit on them and then withdraw from sight before the target grown-up could look up to see where this unwelcome dropping came from.

During the summer when we had passed the entrance exam to our public schools we were allowed down to dinner once with the grown-ups, one at a time. For this single special occasion the boys had to be bought a dinner jacket and the girls an evening dress. Why we were not invited in pairs, or even all together for one evening, was never adumbrated; presumably because one child was generally agreed to be quite enough. The dinners were as grand as you could wish, elaborate and formal. There was one standard joke. On the north wall of the dining room were two sideboards with mirrors below them, a by-product of which was that those sitting on the south side of the table could observe the feet of those sitting opposite. The trick was for the gentlemen on the south side to fish up the shoes, temporarily kicked off because of their tight discomfort by the ladies on the north side, and to put them on their laps with the toes showing above the level of the table.

The children's meals were taken in the servants' hall. The 'pug's parlour' which was originally the dining room for the senior servants only – the housekeeper, butler and cook, served by their juniors – was now large enough to accommodate the whole indoor staff. There was one large beech table in the servants' hall, with room for all of us and our nannies and nurserymaids.

Evening clothes were not the only new outfit required. Aunty Kith decided that the children should form the choir in church, and that they should wear kilts. Each of us was thus fitted out at her expense in a smart London store with full Highland outfit. Humiliatingly, the smaller boys' hips were inadequate to support the kilt, so we had to wear a built-on bodice under our shirts and our silver-buttoned short jackets. We put our collection money, probably a threepenny bit, in our fur-lined sporrans and tucked our skianddhus with their cairngorm jewelled tops into our stockings.

The church had been built, about a hundred yards from the house, by the first Sir John, in 1847, and was one of the earliest in the Episcopal revival. His grandson the second Sir John had had it lined with Caen stone at hideous expense, so the interior was quite light and cheerful. Most of the Scottish people who attended the Episcopal church were those with English connections or education: the established church in Scotland is the Kirk, the Presbyterian Church, with no bishops. It played an integral part in Scottish life, guardian of a strict moral code with a puritanical flavour. The Episcopal church was thus the innocent agent of the class divisions in society. Thanks to the good manners of our aristocratic neighbours, there was no such division between the two families who made up most of the Episcopal congregation, one of them ancient and the other nouveau.

On the left sat the Gladstones, members of an ancient Lanarkshire family but merchants until 1830; on the right the Hepburn-Stuart-Forbes-Trefusis family from Fettercairn House: Lord and Lady Clinton, their daughter and Bowes-Lyon son-in-law, their two granddaughters and their guests.

In the late Sir John's time it was, of course, compulsory for the servants to attend. Now it was voluntary. A few of them might be there, but on the whole the seats behind the two families were used by the few Episcopalians who lived in the area. The only rivalry between the two families was in the singing. We had the advantage both of numbers and of the unilateral occupation of the choir stalls, but Lady Clinton was a determined cheerleader for her family. Stephen, Henry and I were on the right (cantoris to be correct); Elizabeth, Felicity and Anne on the left (decani, pronounced dec-cane-eye in those good old days). The younger members sat in the front rows, mere probationers. To give us our due, I'm sure we all sang rather well.

Except on Sundays, when as at Manley and later at Hawarden having fun was rigorously forbidden, much of our lives was lived outdoors and bicycles were our essential equipment. Each morning we would cycle to Fettercairn, ostensibly to buy sweets or perhaps a small item such as a pencil from the village shop but actually in the hope of receiving a free apple, pear or orange from Willie Neal, the proprietor, a qualified pharmacist, scholar and by general consent a kind of village elder. In his lilting Scottish accent and impeccable Inglis of the south and east, white-haired and gazing prophetically skywards, his circular horn-rimmed spectacles parked on his forehead, he would remind us that our grandfather had been the greatest statesman since Pericles, and would recognise the fact by presenting us with the best pieces of fruit from his stall.

Our favourite outdoor pursuit was damming the burn in the little glen below Ivy Bridge, which seemed to be an inexhaustible occupation, either to improve our previous efforts and create a bigger pool, or after a spate had washed our dam away. This burn was too small to hold trout worth catching except in a couple of its lower pools, where we learnt to tickle them, taught by Ernle Gilbert who was a few years older than us. We biked over occasionally to the slightly larger Phesdo burn, which held a few fish weighing five or six ounces; respectable 'breakfast fish' which could be fried for lunch on a log fire on the pebbles almost while still wriggling, together with plenty of three or four ounces which were just about worth catching. But the best pools were rather deep for us to stand up in or crouch to get our fingers tickling the belly of a fish lying complacently under a big boulder or a rocky ledge.

Every year there was an expedition to Montrose to go to sea with Mr Pert in his motor boat to catch mackerel. Each line held several hooks, baited with a section of seagull feather. Once a shoal had been located from a raucous crowd of diving seagulls sweeping up whatever morsels they came across, we could pull them out two or three or even four mackerel at a time. Once or twice we caught more than a hundred: they were not overfished because they were considered 'dirty feeders', liking to lie around sewer outlets, and they would not sell for more than a penny each. It was only after modern technology had destroyed the stock of herrings, the 'silver darlings', and of cod and even haddock, that the market realised that, after all, mackerel were fine. Certainly the ones we caught were nowhere near sewers and cooked fresh they were delectable. We soon learnt to overcome our foibles and gut our trout or mackerel in little more than a few seconds.

From the age of ten or eleven it would be a treat to go out with our fathers and stalk and shoot a rabbit with a .22 rifle on the Garrol Hill. There were so many rabbits that, within a few minutes of a shot sending them scurrying for their burrows, a few heads would begin reappear to check that all seemed to be clear. There were so many rabbits at Fasque that Uncle Albert was able to pay the wages of the three gamekeepers from the proceeds of selling them. They were an acceptable and commonly used meat in those days before myxomatosis; tasting like chicken but, unlike chicken, cheap enough for ordinary people to afford. When we were twelve we were allowed to start with a sixteen-bore shotgun, going out with one of these keepers who could easily drive a succession of rabbits through one of the holes in the fences created to hold a snare. These forays might also with luck give us our first shot at a hare or a partridge. A sixteen-bore was too hefty for a twelve-year-old, but twenty-bore guns were excluded because there had been too many accidents arising from people putting a twenty-bore cartridge in a twelve-bore gun by mistake, where it would stick unseen half way up the barrel. School holidays in those days began in late July and ended at Michaelmas in late September, so the partridges were quite well-grown and, as God had evidently decreed, feeding on the stubbles and sheltering in the corn-stooks.

Fasque had a small grouse moor. My father and the uncles, often with one of Uncle Albert's friends who was staying – perhaps Ernle Gilbert's father or Douglas Smyth-Osborne – would walk up the grouse twice a week, usually getting a bag of about twenty brace and perhaps a few blue hares, walking home at teatime sweating and contented. There were four or five lines of butts and if the grouse had done well there would be two or three days' driving towards the end of the holidays. The ladies and older children would walk up on to the hill for lunch with the pony and cart which carried the hampers and brought back the bag of game at the end of the day. The treat at lunch was jam puffs, like a sort of croissant filled with strawberry jam; and ginger beer in a stone bottle. We stood in our fathers' butts for the afternoon drives, were told to keep our heads down and mark the fallen birds, and were surprised that it was possible for anyone to miss birds which flew past us so close to the butts.

There were regular expeditions for a picnic at Loch Lee or to climb Ben McDui or Lochnagar or to the beach at St Cyrus. There was a long steep path down, and back up, the cliffs at St Cyrus, and the sea was on the cold side for bathing, but we enjoyed those trips and learnt to watch the eider duck and the diving terns.

ASTRIDGE

My mother had suffered from over-Gladstonisation during our holidays, and in 1936 it was agreed that we should spend the greater part of our summer holiday as a family on our own, and then go to Fasque for just a couple of weeks in September.

There were plenty of empty farmhouses in the 1930s. A suitable one, but without mains water or electricity, was identified by my mother in Pembrokeshire, to let unfurnished at £3 a week. My father discovered that we could take our own furniture by selecting fairly compact and

Fasque and Astridge

lightweight items from his boys' house at Eton to be conveyed door to door in a railway container, to Astridge near Tenby, at a cost of £14 there and back. This was feasible because the Great Western Railway had developed small articulated lorries which could load and unload one-ton containers from a goods yard provided that a crane was available, and deliver them anywhere within a few days. The equivalent of £23 for the rent of a furnished holiday house for three weeks was affordable, and led to three memorable seaside summer holidays. We selected everything we needed from folding beds to pots and pans, from armchairs to sheets, pillowcases and candlesticks, and then set off in the Vauxhall with our luggage and bicycles in the trailer at the right moment to be available to unload the container on arrival. This added to the fun and adventure of the holiday. There were six of us: our parents and their three children and a girl enlisted as a holiday help. I think the only guest who came to stay was Harry Babington Smith, who had become my father's closest male friend after the death of Eric Powell. Harry was a good companion. He ingeniously concocted windmills and other working toys from flotsam and jetsam on the beaches, including seagulls' feathers and pieces of cork from fishing nets. He was good at pushing the four-foot- wide shrimping net along the sand when wading almost shoulder-deep, with which we provided ourselves with a luxury for many of our suppers.

The only logistic problem at Astridge was that the domestic water was pumped by a windmill, and in calm weather we could and did run dry, watching anxiously from an upstairs window for every turn of the pump. We shopped in Tenby, a delightful small town then as it still is now, but without parking problems. I have two memories: the first was my horrified discovery that our Sunday joint of beef cost 25/-, the equivalent nowadays of about £125. It continued to make its appearance throughout the week, of course, first cold, then as mince, then stew and finally soup. This is a reminder, if anyone wants to be reminded, of how cheap our food is nowadays. The second was of hearing Len Huttton's latest score in his record test match innings, extending over three days, on the wireless in (and outside) most of the shops as one wandered round the town: 320 not out in the butcher's might be followed by 330 not out in the baker's.

We lived in Astridge in delightful simplicity: without, for instance, curtains or carpets. The holiday had something of the flavour of camping, without the discomfort. The farmyard was full of wandering, scratching ducks and chickens and there was a robust old pony which Peter and Penelope could mount in tandem. For myself, I experienced for the first time the pleasure of strolling on my own in exquisite countryside, along old grass paths with high rambling hedges and through ancient oak woods with, somehow, just the right amount of undergrowth. I learnt to listen to and watch the birds without anyone's help and something entered my soul which has lodged there ever since, as it has done in countless of our countrymen in times past and present, although it is more elusive now than it was then: the sense of peace and gentle growth and creation in the slowly fading light of a summer evening.

Our holiday was conventional. As families still do, we visited the round of south Pembrokeshire's wonderful and varied beaches in the open car with our picnic, voting our choice of destination each day; and the ruined castles too – Kidwelly, Carew, Manorbier, much as they still are now, though rather less organised. What has gone however – vanished without trace – was the most characteristic vernacular feature of that Little England Beyond Wales, the countless ancient limewashed cottages, some of them thatched, painted in white, pink, light blue and yellow, giving the whole county an understated colourful, cheerful, workmanlike appearance unique in Britain. Unlike the modern bungalows with their vile artificial utilitarian character and dreadful proportions, dark slates and grey pebbledash, which have universally replaced them, they looked as if they ought to be there, and probably had been there as long as anyone could record or remember. They sat well with the ancient village churches.

Each Sunday morning we went to church at St Florence, the stone arches of its whitewashed interior – perhaps Saxon work – clumsily related to geometry. In walked the squire with his wife and three children, each of the five bearing a striking resemblance to Humpty Dumpty: the Egg Family, we called them. The vicar had a huge lump near the top of his head which tended to divert our attention from his admirable sermons.

Our third Astridge summer holiday in 1939 came to an abrupt end and I did not visit the house again for seventy years. It had not lost its remoteness, tucked away in quiet lanes. Rosamund and I had a job to find it. When we did, we saw that it had been tidied up, perhaps rebuilt, and the old farm buildings converted. The uneven cobbles of the farmyard had become the tarmac access so convenient for modern

Fasque and Astridge

dwellings. As far as I was concerned, it had lost its soul; but we had our lunch picnic on the fringes of the ancient oak wood which still retained its magic.

In 1939 war was imminent and my father returned to Eton by train. A few days later we saw the furniture in to its container, packed our bags, loaded the trailer, and set off in the Vauxhall late in the afternoon. We were stopped by policemen: the blackout was in force, only sidelights were allowed. We found one room vacant in a hotel: a bed for my mother and Penelope to share; another for Peter and me, end to end; and a small one for our Austrian helper, Maria. We reached Eton the following afternoon. We three children were soon packed off by train to Fasque for the tail end of the summer holiday. Most of the guests there were leaving or had left. Uncle Albert and Aunty Kith had retreated to the smaller rooms at the east end of the house, where we heard the news of the invasion of Poland on the radio. The Polish cavalry was no match for the German tanks: 'C'est magnifique,' we thought, or words to that effect, 'mais ce n'est pas la guerre'. And we felt a bit like Pitt when he said 'Roll up the map of Europe'. Thus, just before my fourteenth birthday, our memorable series of holidays at Fasque and Astridge came to an end.

5
School Days

In 1934, just before my ninth birthday, I joined my boarding preparatory school, Scaitcliffe, which I have described in detail elsewhere, only about five or six miles from home. It never occurred to me to consider whether or not I was happy there. On the whole I wasn't, although I had plenty of good friends. School was just something which happened, and one took it as it came. Looking back, I can make two judgements, which did not strike me as my business at the time: first, that the education was excellent, and has stood me in good stead; secondly, that Ronald Vickers, the proprietor and headmaster, was responsible for this excellence, and that in spite of the difficulties of recruiting pupils in the 1930s he managed to attract the kind of parents who appreciated his genius and were willing to put up with his uncompromising methods, sometimes bullying and menacing, of achieving what he and they required of the school. There was a right way, and only one right way, of doing everything, whether in work or games, down to the smallest details. But although Vickers was a master of simplification without trivialisation, he also conveyed to us the unforgettable and unforgotten beauty of the English language, especially by the Old Testament of the King James Bible; and indeed I am aware now that seeds of the same quality in French and Latin were sown in our minds, too.

There were never more than about forty-five pupils, but I now realise that many if not most of them came from either academic or aristocratic families. My father who was a schoolmaster chose the school because it was educating the sons of his friend the headmaster of Oundle so well; the headmaster of Bedford School sent his son there; and one of H.M. Inspectors of Schools, a very select band in those days, sent his three boys, two of whom got scholarships to Eton. Four Scottish earls sent a total of eight boys to Scaitcliffe, one of whom later suffered the unusual and unwelcome experience of having Queen Mary in his grouse butt when he was a teenager. Photographs of queens and princesses in crinolines watching Edwardian pheasant shoots are not uncommon; but Queen Mary giving advice in a grouse butt is a different matter

School Days

altogether. Also among my contemporaries at Scaitcliffe were the heir to a certain marquess who had been Viceroy of India, a peer of the realm whose father had died young, the elder son of another peer, the youner son of an English duke, and the son of a famous Norfolk banking family, heir to a mere baronetcy, but an old one.

Nothing, or almost nothing, struck me as odd about Scaitcliffe, except perhaps one or two of the masters who arrived for one term and had departed before the next; not for the reasons one might nowadays suspect, but simply because they were bogus. As far as I was concerned, it was just school as I found it, and I was aware that we were smaller than the other schools we played at cricket and football. I'm not conscious of having enjoyed the work – rather the opposite if anything. It was just what had to be done. My attitude to games was much the same. They had to be done correctly, as far as possible. Yet I remember a great deal of what I was taught about both. With one or two notable exceptions, I liked my contemporaries and we were always on the lookout for opportunities for trivial pranks. I made several abiding friendships – with Christopher and Roger Pemberton, Andrew Gibson-Watt and Geordie Leslie-Melville, and there were several others I was glad to come across from time to time. Sixty years after leaving Scaitcliffe I went to a reunion for the school's centenary in 1998 and we found the same dark green linoleum in the bathrooms, a little more worn.

Richard Vickers, one of Ronald's twin sons, succeeded him as proprietor and headmaster, but unsurprisingly the son, although he was competent and conscientious, did not have exactly the same touch of genius for the job as the father. He brought in his father's number two, Dennis Owen, as his partner, and people would say that it was really Dennis who ran the school. Dennis was, indeed, the very model of the ideal prep school master, and had already been a vital element in the school's life when Ronald was headmaster.

Ronald saw out my brother Peter, but the education meted out by orthodox preparatory and public schools did not suit him. He had no gift or liking for languages or for ball games, nor was he a compliant character who fitted comfortably into the strict framework of school life. Only when he had passed his school certificate at Eton and entered what is now called the lower sixth form did he blossom. He was a gifted zoologist – a born zoologist – who kept a menagerie of one variety or another from early childhood, and he was a brilliant oarsman who rowed number six in an Eton eight which won the

School Days

Ladies' Plate, occupying the thwart behind Christopher Davidge and David Callender who were to become the best known amateur oarsmen of their day, as he did a few years later in the Oxford crew. He became a master and housemaster at Shrewsbury, threw out all the stuffed animals and replaced them with live ones, and coached crews which won the Princess Elizabeth cup three times. He had a tame badger which he trained to live in the wild and bring up a family, and when it had done so it used to visit his house for titbits for its young. At other times he had a tame goose which followed him everywhere; he had found it abandoned at Henley and brought it back to Shrewsbury in his pocket; and a tame fox. Peter was a brilliant shot after every kind of quarry, and if ever I caught a trout in the lake Peter had caught it before me, coded its dorsal fin with beads and put it back.

My two much younger brothers, Francis and Andrew, whose arrival I have not yet chronicled, also went to Scaitcliffe, and it served their needs well. They regarded Dennis Owen rather than Richard Vickers as the headmaster. Eventually it merged with and became absorbed by another school whose name it later adopted.

In September 1938 I went to Eton, just in time for the disruption caused by the Munich crisis when Hitler marched into Austria. Most of the boys went home. Those who remained were occupied filling sandbags to shelter the windows of one room in each boys' house against German bombs. But Neville Chamberlain returned from Munich, his message of peace broadcast on the radio from Heston Airport (now Heathrow); there were pictures in the newspapers of the little flimsy piece of paper which promised peace in our time, illegibly signed 'A. Hitler' in a scrawl running downhill to the right – the kind of signature, I had been taught, which you should never trust. But it gave me one pre-war summer at Eton, and an ambivalent attitude to luxury which has lasted me for the rest of my life. The extravagance displayed on the Fourth of June and at the Eton v. Harrow match at Lord's stunned me, and left me with a lifelong distrust of ostentatious vulgarity. Henley regatta was much more to my taste, with the first cherries at our a picnic lunch on the cricket field, and the Stewards' Enclosure with its temporary flower beds filled with geraniums and the Guards band resplendent in the bandstand; the mahogany umpires' launches, *Amaryllis* and *Magician*, gliding up the Thames. During the long drab years of the war I wondered whether those halcyon days would ever return.

School Days

I have described the inward workings of Eton as an institution, and the impact of the war on life there, elsewhere. The metamorphosis from a prep school boy in shorts to an Etonian in top hat and tails, or in my case, since (like many others) I was less than 5 foot 4 inches tall, a short Eton jacket or bumfreezer, had to be accomplished between the beginning and the end of one long summer holidays. Now I had a room to myself, a tiny kingdom open to invasion by contemporaries at any time yet at specific times sovereign in its privacy, and I had to get to a schoolroom perhaps five minutes' walk away several times a day at the right time with the right books and preferably with the right work prepared and ready for a test. Yet a small room of one's own could bring isolation as well as privacy to a boy who was not gregarious, or who had either a negative or an aggressive personality.

In this very big boarding school with comparatively small houses, mostly of 40 to 45 boys, where eccentrics were tolerated and, indeed, admired, there was perhaps less protection than in a smaller school against psychological bullying, or simply being mildly teased and otherwise ignored. Much depended on the year's intake in one's house, which was largely a matter of luck. Names were entered at birth and some of the better known Old Etonian housemasters tended to get first pick, but how these children, often entered whilst still in their mothers' wombs, would turn out twelve or thirteen years later was surprisingly unpredictable. My housemaster, always referred to at Eton as 'M'Tutor', Charles Rowlatt, was such a one. He was a scholar and an athlete and a strict disciplinarian who realised that teenagers need to know exactly where they stand in terms which are simply and unambiguously applied and understood. Actually he had become a master during the First World War, to help out after being so severely wounded in the head and the stomach that he would never be fit to return to the front; and, because it became apparent to him and to his colleagues that he had the relevant gifts, he had stayed on and made teaching his career. By luck, my year was a good one; but the year above was not. They were led astray by a couple of rogues, sons of famous families who perhaps had been ignored by their parents and ill-served by their nannies in their early years. There were two or three quite pleasant people of that year, but as a group they did not serve the house well. As we grew up we reacted against them, and tried to exercise a fairer and less vicious regime.

The houses were, indeed, largely run by the boys, subject to the housemaster's veto if he had the wit to apply it; and subject, too, of course, more subtly and intangibly, to his guiding hand. He chose the Captain of the House and probably saw him daily to discuss problems, but he was expected to apply his veto very sparingly, and on the whole the house prefects, known as The Library, were genuinely self-elected. The Captain of Games was the senior person to have received his house colours for the Field Game, the school's own version of football. That was the system, and as far as we were concerned it was the Law of the Medes and Persians, which changeth not. Schoolboys (and perhaps schoolgirls, for all I know, which is not much) are conservative: they take like ducks to water to the rules of the institutions of which they are members, and their security depends on everybody knowing and understanding these rules, which therefore must not be altered. Whether they choose to conform to these rules is a different matter altogether. This kind of framework seems to encourage individual responsibility, and the sense of self-confidence which arises from the obligation (and hence the right) to make decisions.

My contemporaries were Francis Dashwood, Michael Merriam, Nicholas Horton-Fawkes and Martin Hudson, closely followed by Nicholas Headlam and Colin Macpherson. Martin messed with his elder brother and was one of those self-sufficient Etonians who passed through the system satisfactorily without causing a ripple. A little younger was Jeremy Benson, who had two older brothers in the house. All the rest of us were gregarious, and all were quite strong characters whose strengths and weaknesses made life more colourful.

Francis was socially ambitious and attached himself to the year ahead of us for a time, but he and I were always in the same form and since he was cleverer than I, I relied on him to see me through my construe. The word order of Horace's Odes and the snippets of Ovid served up to us did not baffle him as they baffled me. For continuous literature, notably Greek plays and Latin authors from Tacitus to Virgil, we could purchase cribs in Windsor or from our predecessors, but it still helped to go through the daily grind with his guidance. He was hooked on jazz, which never appealed to me, and became quite a virtuoso on the trumpet. He was devoted to money and spent much of his energy throughout his life trying to acquire it. The reason may have been that he inherited West Wycombe Park in rather a dire state. His father very cleverly had contrived to present the house to the National Trust before the Second World War with their undertaking to maintain it, provided that it was appropriately opened to the public, without

School Days

insisting on an endowment, while still allowing the family to live there; but this seemed to have been about the only clever thing Francis's father ever did; so he had to struggle to recover his family's position and to create an income from what remained of the estate, including the premises of the Hell Fire Club. He invited me once or twice to his commercial shoot. He had to be rowed about in a dinghy flapping a large umbrella to put up the reared (and almost tame) duck, compelling them to take timidly to the wing as targets for the clients. Actually, I think the duck were kept in reserve in case all else failed, and that I was invited to a partridge shoot. A line of guns about five yards apart walked through a root field. Only one partridge got up and eleven shots were fired at it. Since it then appeared as a rather modest bag for an expensive day's shooting for ten guns, we had to resort to the unfortunate duck. Francis made a good deal of money at Lloyd's and by dint of hard work he did get the estate back on its feet, although his biggest project, to create a new village, was an expensive failure financially because the people he hoped to attract did not buy the houses he built. Francis and I were contemporaries at Christ Church and I kept up my friendship with him throughout his life. We were not kindred spirits but in spite of his social ambitions and his passion for money he was a man of fine character, a good judge of people, and generous to his friends.

Michael Merriam was my closest friend at school, and although we often disagreed and were 'not on speaking terms' on numerous occasions, we were actually kindred spirits who were able to talk about anything and everything and to enjoy all those numerous and often trivial occasions which are the salt of school life. We had clear ideas about how a house at Eton ought to be run. Michael was bigger and stronger (and some months older) than I was but we both enjoyed football and rowing and were ambitious for personal success and for the success of our house. We both felt ourselves to be countrymen, and particularly enjoyed shooting, especially 'rough' shooting of one kind and another which was the only kind available in wartime and for many years thereafter. He left school and joined the Navy two terms before me and we both acquired a lifelong respect for that extraordinary institution. Unlike me he married very young but Anne accepted me as part of the furniture and our respective families were close in many respects. Michael's father, a huge man and a rugby blue, had been at Oxford with M'Tutor and was a plastics guru, his family having invented the first commercial product, Bakelite. He was knighted as

School Days

Controller of Plastics during the war. Michael's mother was a delightful, hospitable and mildly absent-minded daughter of the Kennedy family, Marquesses of Ailsa (a rock). Michael followed his father in to the rapidly developing plastics industry, hoping for the day when people would throw away their plastic bags as they did their paper bags.

The last of my exact contemporaries was Nicholas Horton-Fawkes, whose father, a regular army officer in the Greenjackets, had been Adjutant of the Eton Corps, the Officers' Training Corps as it still then was, and who, like more than one of his successors, had decided that the life of an Eton master was so much more interesting than that of an Army officer that he would like to become one. He must have been well thought of, for he was accepted subject to his learning French, for which he had no gift and which he never mastered, although he was better at writing it than speaking it. Presumably French was selected because his wife, a much more scholarly and even donnish person, was herself well qualified to teach it and was always said to correct the essays written by her husband's pupils. Nicholas inherited this gift from his mother and he also had an artistic flair which later enabled him to make a career designing carpets in order to keep the family estate at Farnley Hall in Yorkshire going. His father was plain Major Horton until he inherited this estate subject to adding the surname Fawkes. The famous Fawkes was Guy Fawkes but the Fawkes of Turner's time had been one of his most assiduous patrons: the house had been full of Turners, but most of them had been sold and some of those which remained were being put on the market from time to time.

Nicholas was a delightful friend who made plenty of contributions to our jokes and our pranks, but he had a problem which might have been described as being accident prone, except that in his case the accidents all seemed to have been carefully planned. There are people (like myself) who have a penchant for falling into a deep pond or a stream by mistake, but whereas, I have said, one of the most important lessons I learnt at school was to keep out of trouble, it was as if Nicholas had learnt how to get in to it. Using a crib to help us with our construe was essential to survival, but if we were caught the sentence was a dire one. As to cheating in Trials, the termly exams, the penalties were even more severe, and the rules of common sense dictated that it should only be resorted to in a serious crisis. Moreover, there was an unwritten rule that you never cheated in order to gain an advantage over your fellows, but only to escape the penalty of failure. There was honour among thieves.

I remember to this day how Nicholas was caught translating a randy joke by Aristophanes which was included in the text of the crib but bowdlerised in our edition. He had not surprisingly found the text of the crib extremely difficult to reconcile with the version in our textbooks, but instead of smelling a rat he had gone to the trouble of learning the version in the crib by heart. And I remember him cheating in Trials, in the most unguarded way, in order to improve his marks in a French paper which he must have found easy anyway, thus not only breaking the school rules and our own moral code but also neglecting to take elementary precautions to prevent detection, all in one fell swoop. If we had all been involved in some collective form of mischief, he was always the one who was caught. He joined the Navy as Michael and I did, and was a member of The Hard Core, the little group of public schoolboys amongst the six thousand trainees at HMS Collingwood, which used to meet from time to time for reunions for many years, but he never got a commission and ended his service as an able seaman.

Nicholas Headlam belonged to an academic and scholarly Etonian clan. His Uncle Tuppy had been the second Eton master appointed to teach modern history; his father was a civil servant of the old stamp who had spent his best years trying to reduce the National Debt, servicing which had been the main consumer of the Inland Revenue since the days of Pitt the Younger, but achieving after many years' labour a reduction of only one million pounds, peanuts. Like Michael's father he had married into a grand family: his mother was a daughter of the Earl of Verulam who had been a nurse during the First World War and had developed a passion for cleanliness: the floors of their house were always covered in newspapers, as if the cleaner had left in a hurry. Nicholas's two elder brothers were King's Scholars and I think he was a late entry on Charles Rowlatt's house list when he became the first Headlam not to get a scholarship himself. But it was a near miss. He, too, was a kindred spirit and a lifelong friend, and as it happened, like Michael and me, he was a countryman and keen on shooting; but he was much more academic than Michael and to that degree he satisfied another facet of my interests. When Freshfields, who had been our family solicitors since 1830, lost interest in their private clients, I asked him to succeed them. His willingness to accept original and ingenious solutions to difficult and complicated legal problems, coupled with prudence and meticulous care over detail made him an ideal choice. Rosamund and I still keep up with Nicholas and Jane and as with Michael Merriam I am godfather to his son.

I knew Colin Macpherson, the last member of this little vintage, less well. He was a formidable athlete who gave up cricket because it bored him and became Captain of the Boats, and who was also a Keeper of the Field, a virtuoso dribbler of the ball who had the rare skill of changing his pace as he avoided one attempted tackle after another. His father was an esteemed financier who made pots of money for Trinity College, Cambridge amongst others, but whether he was a mere stockbroker or something grander I never discovered. Colin was the eldest of several gifted brothers. In those days quite a few boys came and went at Christmas and Easter, partly because the exams were not subject to such rigid syllabuses as nowadays. Moreover, during the war one tended to be called up within a month or two of one's eighteenth birthday and it would have been pointless to kick one's heels for months in order to conform to an academic year. I had one or two good friends in the year above me, and several in the year below, including Hugh Percy, Hugh Stanley, John Swire and John Cator.

When we had passed School Certificate and were in what would now be called the Lower Sixth we began to make close friends in other houses. We now had only two main subjects of study, and although there were school periods designed to prevent of education becoming narrow we tended to meet many of the same people for at least one period every day. We now had specialist tutors rather than the 'classical' tutors of our first three years, and we met people from other houses in the seminars which were known as 'private business', often the same people as we met in school periods. About 750 or almost three-quarters of the boys were 'wetbobs' who had preferred rowing to cricket, with the result that in our early years most of our rowing was either individual or in house crews such as the 'Baby Four' and the 'Bumping Four'; but as we got older we might be competing for places in the school crews: four Novice Eights and four Lower Eights, two Trial Eights and finally three School Eights.

Francis Dashwood, ever the ambitious social success in Eton and London, was kind enough to put me up for Pop, the members of which were elected on a system of blackballing. This was an unhealthy system because it led to bargaining: 'if you don't blackball my candidate I won't blackball yours', but as with some other indefensible electoral systems it worked fairly well in practice – perhaps because a small group of electors know more about the qualities of the candidates than a large group could – at least to the extent that most of the people elected were good candidates. The weakness of the system was that many of members came from just a few houses, so some equally good candidates from other houses had little or no chance of being proposed; and just as they tended to 'bunch' in certain houses, there were hardly any wetbobs – the Captain of the Boats (*ex officio*) and myself, to be precise. This makes the point irrefutably that if I had not been a friend of one particular individual I would not have got in. It was a matter of luck – pure luck. And what difference did it make? Well, it let me in to a charmed circle (my reader can make what he or she likes of that) and it made a huge difference to my self-confidence, just what I needed as I was about to join the Navy. I had learnt in my early schooldays to keep out of the light when trouble was brewing. Now I was beginning to learn also how to sidle my way into the light when opportunity suggested that it might pay a dividend.

Early in my Eton career, in the spring of 1940, my brother and sister and I were summoned by our parents into the drawing room. Clearly there was some big news afoot, and a faint sense of foreboding, as when we had listened as a family to Neville Chamberlain announcing on the wireless that 'we are now at war with Germany'. It was announced that we were to expect the arrival of a little baby brother or sister. I do not know what reaction was expected of us. As far as I was concerned we were all right as we were. The idea of a baby arriving was mildly disconcerting. Peter was three years younger than I, and Penelope two years younger than he. The regime of nannies and boarding prep schools had meant that we were much less mixed up like plums in a pudding than families are nowadays: so our differences in age limited our intimacy as brothers and sister (the word sibling was never used until the 1980s or 1990s). Peter and I had got over our nursery combat, were happy to live and let live but also to take some interest in each other's activities. Pene and I got on very happily, notably in being able to share jokes. Our holidays at Astridge had been a powerful agent in drawing our family of five together as an entity. It would not have been appropriate to be displeased that there was going to be a new arrival, but I cannot pretend that I was enthusiastic.

When Francis duly arrived on the scene on 20 June I took to him

School Days

immediately – partly no doubt as a result of our mother's perception that I should be given some apparent responsibility for looking after him, or perhaps I should say handling him – holding him over my shoulder to encourage him to belch, turning him on his front on my knee and administering a tentative tap in the back for similar reasons, fastening his nappy with one of those fearsome pins, and pulling out his elbow to prevent him from burying his nose when asleep. More than twenty years later when Rosamund presented me with Charlie I was more conversant with baby-handling than she was. Helen arrived a couple of years after Francis just before I joined the Navy and Andrew on VJ Day when I was in south-east Asia. The difference in age between me and my youngest brother was longer than that between me and my mother. This delightful trio changed our lives: my parents continued to take an extraordinarily close and devoted interest in the older trio, but we never experienced that period when a family of teenagers put away childish things in close companionship with their parents.

6
Holidays in Wartime

My father could not get away from Eton much during the school holidays in wartime. For one thing, the Luftwaffe's attention was not programmed to fit in with school terms. Incendiary bombs in the loft or the back yard and a landmine in our neighbours' garden, which blew out our dining room windows, were holiday excitements. Petrol rationing prevented long journeys, but we managed well by railway, although discouraged by posters on every station asking 'Is your journey really necessary?' I had learnt in the 1930s that investment in the railways had been minimal for many years and that the fastest journeys had peaked in 1912. The rolling stock was ancient. You could read the age of every goods truck by the dates on the axle hubs, almost all pre-1900. Passenger coaches had a forlorn appearance. In wartime, trains were usually crowded and often late, but they got you there, on the whole in only moderate discomfort. There were large trolleys on the platforms and plenty of room for luggage, bicycles and dogs.

In 1941 Uncle Albert offered my mother the opportunity to stay at Glen Dye, the shooting lodge over the hill (the Cairn O'Mount) from Fasque, which had been let to well-heeled clients for the grouse shooting during the peacetime years. Grouse populations have been cyclical for as long as they have been recorded. The 1930s had been a vintage decade, but as it happened disease and heather beetle took their toll in 1939 and there were then very few birds until the early Fifties. But organised shooting would have been impossible during the war anyway. We enjoyed three memorable summer holidays there. My father joined us for a time in 1942 and 1943, as did my first cousin Stephen, his father Uncle Deiney and his sisters Felicity and Anne. Francis remained with Nanny Thatcher at Eton.

No house could enjoy a more idyllic Highland setting than Glen Dye, high above a bend in the tumbling Dye, sheltered by giant trees of the American north-west, douglas, nobilis and grandis, silver firs and wellingtonias, mixed in with oak and ash and birch, but with its view to the north of Cloch-na-ben, a big lump of rock on the top of a hill, one of the best known landmarks in eastern Scotland. The estate had been owned by the Farquharsons and then the Carnegies before the Gladstones came along, but nobody knows who built the lodge or when. The main part of it was there by the 1830s, pink granite late Georgian but with more of an early Victorian look, with three large bedrooms, each with a dressing room big enough to serve as a double bedroom, and a bathroom. Since then it had grown into a sort of U-shape with one wing providing more space for servants and services, and another for three gentlemen guests without spouses, with a battery of three elephantine baths for them and a room for each of their valets: Victorian accommodation. It was a light and airy house, sumptuously furnished, for six guns, who would ride out on ponies in pairs, to shoot grouse over dogs, pointers or setters, in the years before grouse driving was invented. Their gamebooks survive.

John Gladstone had got tired of drinking port, or maybe it had started to disagree with him as he grew older, and he changed to champagne, leaving a handsome quantity of 1908 vintage port in the cellar. Uncle Albert, always generous, lent my mother the cellar key, which she rashly entrusted to me. I found a bottle of the 1908, opened and decanted it – I knew how to do that – and Stephen and I consumed it in one evening. My mother was horrified: 'one glass is quite enough,' she said, 'or at the very most two if you are very tired.' But we were not impressed, although we may have modified or disguised our consumption after that. Unspoilt palates are sensitive, and we knew that the 1908 was something special. This splendid vintage had aged well in a Highland cellar, perhaps marginally cooler than the orthodox 50 to 52 degrees. And thus for years it became a feature of our Glen Dye holidays, more sparingly as the cellar shelves were emptied, until the very last bottles in the 1960s had become distinctly thin.

We walked what seemed to be enormous distances after grouse in company with Mackay, the middle-aged under-keeper, one of the thinnest men I have met, who lived solely on potatoes. All the younger men, of course, were in the Army. I waded through long heather with a heavy gun – my cousins and other contemporaries were all larger than I was – and we tramped home with perhaps four or five birds in the bag. I cannot claim that I enjoyed my first experience of walking-up grouse, although throughout the 1950s it became one of those fervours which have punctuated my life.

Holidays in Wartime

In 1942 and 1943 my father and Uncle Deiney joined us for a time, and we had one or two contemporary friends to stay. The head keeper Duncan Fraser had an old Morris which he ran throughout the war on high octane aviation spirit siphoned from no less than eight Fleet Air Arm aircraft from Arbroath which crashed on the moor, mostly on training flights. Duncan rescued the crew first and the petrol afterwards. The Morris made a buzzing sound in response to this rich repast, and was known as 'the Spitfire'. Aircraft not irreparably damaged were taken back to base on the earliest long articulated lorries, built for the purpose. One of them got stuck for several days *ventre à terre* on the Bridge of Dye, a steeply arched bridge on the military road leading from Deeside over the Cairn, built by General Wade, by then guarded against German invasion by two beautifully built granite pillboxes (which are now listed buildings) manned by a Home Guard of gamekeepers.

Duncan Fraser was diabetic (one of the earliest age group to be saved by insulin injections) and now getting on in years. He took me out to stalk my first red deer. There was a double-barrelled side-by-side .303 rifle with a very shallow v-shaped backsight which enabled one to see the target in a poor light, and fortunately I had been well taught with an air-rifle at my prep school. The trouble about stalking is that it depends on the skill of the keeper, or 'stalker', rather than on the person who is there to shoot the deer. So you do not have to plan the stalk, but are presented with a target, often with an incomprehensible whispered instruction which deer to aim at; and you then take aim with the knowledge that if you miss the whole operation is rather pointless. 'Aim low on the beast,' Duncan would say, if it was on the skyline; and then, with luck, 'It's a hit', for he could hear the impact of the bullet, which is more than I could. A stag hit in the heart will move some little way before it falls dead, so there was a period of suspense. I observed the gralloching and bleeding as nearly as I could with the casual air of a habitual spectator, and enjoyed the sense of success when the beast was lumped on to a sledge and attached to the pony for its journey to the road and transfer to the cart. To me, however, the interest of a day's stalking with Duncan, who had been at Glen Dye since 1912, was that, mercifully pausing on a steep slope as old men do, he would tell me that this was where His Grace the Duke of Wellington had killed a stag at 400 yards, or the late Sir John had told him to put stones round yon lone tree to prevent the deer from rubbing it to death, or where he

Duncan had stood, flanking from behind the line and sending the grouse round three times during a drive in the vintage year, 1930; or that this was one of the paths which had been built in 1935 at a cost of £400 for the American syndicate with their twenty-four ponies, eight for the guns, eight for the ammunition and eight to carry the game. He pointed out the path by which the crofters at the Charr had taken their eggs over to Fettercairn on their donkey to sell them; he showed me the pool where he had spotted a big fish from the wave it made moving upstream and caught a twelve-pound salmon with his first cast in this little fierce river where grilse and sea trout ran. He would tell me where Sir John had killed a hundred wild pheasants to his own gun in one little drive along an esker on the low ground; and how the dour head forester McGregor had driven his fiancée in the sidecar of his motor bike to Lynn of Dee; and when he dismounted his sole conversation was 'Are ye cold?' – snippets of information which stuck in my mind and perhaps formed a kind of foundation for my lifelong love of the place.

The Spitfire was used to convey my father and Uncle Deiney to the end of the road along the Glen where there were more grouse, but Stephen and I had to bicycle the six miles including the ascent of Netty Haugh, before we began to walk to the higher ground where more birds might be found. The sole consolation for the consequent exhaustion was that I have been able to recite these details ever since, for the benefit of those who can nowadays be taken all the way by Land Rover – an audience likely to be already familiar with them as year succeeds year.

Duncan also took me down to the Feugh and taught me the rudiments of fishing for salmon, grilse or sea trout on a small river with a wet fly. The Dye joins the Feugh below Bogendreip and the Feugh joins the Dee at Banchory. The fish begin to run up the Feugh and the Dye around the end of June, when the wild rose blooms. In the Dee, fishing begins in February, with what is known as a spring run, when the salmon returning home after years in the Atlantic move up river towards their spawning grounds in the little gravel pools of its uppermost tributaries; but the Feugh and the Dye only have an 'autumn' run. When the height of the water is just right – falling after a spate – the fish can swim upstream, and that is the time when even a novice has a good chance to catch them. You can cast right across the river and allow the fly to float down and across it temptingly. Concede a bit of line as a fish takes the fly: unlike a trout, he will try to take the fly down and will catch himself in the process. Keep the rod point up to retain tension, reel in quickly and stay opposite your fish if you can get up or down the length of the pool, whether wading or on the bank, and hope for the best: it's a very exciting sport. If he goes off with a determined dash, let him go, or he'll break your line, and then bring him back, firmly but without hurry, until he's opposite you again. As the fish tires it helps to have somebody handy with the landing net or the gaff, but if you can inch him up gingerly on to a shingle beach he can't go into reverse and will wriggle and flip himself further up every time he attempts to move. At last, a big sigh of relief.

Eleven o'clock in the morning, with sunshine and cloud, and you're just as likely to be successful within a matter of minutes as you are after having worked conscientiously down two or three pools several times, had a rest, eaten your piece and tried again. Given the right conditions, it's an easier form of fishing than a dry fly on a chalk stream, or a big salmon river where you have to wade up to your armpits and know every lie, deep behind an unseen boulder perhaps, and understand how every eddy varies with the height of the water. If you're an opportunist, rather than a connoisseur or an addict, fishing a small river offers an ideal day's sport, varied, eventful and exciting; or if you're still full of energy after a long day's rough shooting you can go down to the river at dusk on a summer evening and try your luck with sea trout as the light gently fades. I'm grateful to Duncan Fraser for introducing me to the Feugh. And I can see Penelope, aged about ten or eleven, fishing patiently for little breakfast trout in the Dye on a huge rock right below the lodge. Peter was probably occupied getting them out some other way, or stalking rabbits, or discovering some rare form of wildlife.

Our northward journeys on the sleeper produced a sense of adventure and anticipation – flick, flick, flick as the girders of the Forth Bridge passed the window. We plod over the Tay Bridge: the sea is in sight north of Dundee and we curl into Montrose with water on both sides of the line; then come the sea-cliffs, with soaring gulls and fulmars, as far as Stonehaven. On the southward journeys we loaded our luggage, our bikes and our gun cases onto the hefty four-wheeler trolleys on the platform, together with a massive haunch of venison, a couple of brown hares and a brace or two of grouse to supplement our meat ration at home, and heaved them all into the luggage van with sense of accomplishment and gratitude for the holiday.

Holidays in Wartime

A couple of times I stayed on at Fasque for a fortnight in September to help with the harvest in company with Michael Merriam, Nicholas Horton-Fawkes, Nicholas Headlam and Charles Pickthorn. Four Scotsmen too old for the Army were left on the farm, four Irishmen appeared for the harvest, there were four Italian prisoners-of-war and four English public schoolboys. None of these groups could understand what any of the others were saying, but our tasks were fairly straightforward, notably collecting the sheaves as they fell off the reaper-and-binders and making stooks from three or four pairs of sheaves, which would stay on the stubble field until they were dry enough to stack. The main crop was oats. There would be only a few fields of wheat and barley.

If the weather was unsuitable for harvesting, we had to perform humdrum jobs, including cutting the thistles in the permanent grass fields with two-handled Scotch scythes before they went to seed and, as Mr Tough the grieve (the foreman) put it, 'setting up the doon stooks' in the harvested fields when they had fallen down in rain and wind. These jobs were our first experience of the grinding boringness of a long day of unskilled manual work. They made us realise that this life on the farm might actually be even worse than Latin or Greek construe. The 'farm servants', as labourers are known in Scotland, did not have much to amuse them in the evenings: the one of them living nearest to us in a butt and ben cottage had twelve children, a baby every year, several children to a bed. We lived in a vacant part of the stable yard with minimal furniture and equipment and the delightful Mrs Hendry, the estate mason's wife, who lived next door, cheerfully cooked for us and kept our quarters from descending into total chaos.

Whether we earned our keep or not is a moot point: the grieve reported to Uncle Albert that we were good workers, which was not true. When the reapers got near the last patch of standing corn in the middle of a field we would stop work, take up our guns, and shoot the rabbits as they bolted. Uncle Albert had said we could do any rough shooting we liked in the evenings: there were no other sportsmen available to enjoy the shooting, rough or smooth. We collected our guns after work and spent some wonderful evenings after partridges on the stubbles. They could take cover in the stooks, from which they could be flushed a few at a time. There were plenty of brown hares on the grass fields in those days, and we managed to bag a few ducks and pigeons, all of which we plucked and gutted and popped into the pot for Mrs Hendry's culinary attention. A few days later we had reconverted ourselves into Etonians ready 'in all respects', to use a naval phrase, for the Michaelmas Half.

Our parents were pinned to Eton by the need to look after the house and the second brood of our family, but they were imaginative in suggesting short holidays for me with my grandmother, uncles and aunts. I could bicycle to Henley, about fifteen miles, to stay with Gran, who by now was usually on her own. Her elder son Donald like his father had been a rowing star, Captain of the Boats at Eton and President of the Oxford University Boat Club. He had gone out to Malaya to plant rubber, supposed at that time to be a likely money-spinner, where he met and married a divorced lady, sending shock waves (by means of rude or pained letters) through the family. But the marriage lasted and produced my first cousin Simon. Donald learnt to fly and joined the Air Force on the outbreak of war, where he was rated such a skilled pilot that he was put on training duties. He was always a good organiser was enlisted in 1944 to represent the R.A.F on his staff by Mountbatten as Commander-in-Chief South-East Asia, based at Kandy in Ceylon, now Sri Lanka. Gran's younger daughter Elizabeth married John Garton, who had also been the Captain of the Boats at Eton and the President of the Oxford University Boat Club, and had admirably joined the Oxfordshire and Buckinghamshire Light Infantry as a Territorial officer before the war. The wedding was one of those hurried affairs while he was on leave in the early days of the war. They had three sons, Ian, who was a contemporary of my brother Francis, Clive and Robin. Vernon, the youngest of Gran's family, was at New College, Oxford when the war broke out. He joined the Scots Guards, winning the MC as a captain in the Guards Armoured Division in northern Europe in 1944. At the end of the war with Germany he was recruited by Mountbatten as his aide-de-camp: so when I was a junior officer in a destroyer at Trincomalee, I had two uncles serving in the more elevated climate (in both senses of the word) of Kandy, an hour or two's journey away from us, yet as remote as if they had been on the moon. Mountbatten did visit the fleet, including HMS *Relentless*, before the invasion of Malaya in order to encourage us. He arranged through his staff that a wooden box should be available near the fo'c'sle, where he addressed the ship's company of two destroyers moored alongside one another; and when he arrived there he asked whether perhaps a wooden box could be found and brought along for him to stand on: bogus, I thought, a playboy; and the style of his pep talk confirmed my opinion, although I admit that it was well performed. Vernon, who knew Mountbatten well, had a high opinion of him, and remained his aide-de-camp after V.J. Day when he became the last, short-lived, Viceroy of India. Still in his early twenties, Vernon was rewarded with the CIE, the last recipient of that honour.

So Gran was on her own when on several occasions I biked over to spend a few days with her. The main activity was golf, of which she taught me the rudiments. I enjoyed it but I did not keep it up. I found my evening conversations with her interesting and instructive. She had written a long series of articles for the *Illustrated London News*, which produced some much-needed income. She had a knack of bringing characters she had known alive with a vivid phrase.

Uncle Albert and Aunty Kith had sensibly retreated from Hawarden Castle at the beginning of the war, and lived in Broadlane nearby, a house with a symmetrical Georgian brick façade concealing a haphazard but charming assembly of timbered rooms which had performed various functions – Catherine Gladstone's orphanage and then also her old folks' home, and then servants' quarters, plus the domestic laundry and dairy. Shrewdly, Uncle Albert had offered the Castle for the duration of the war to the Royal Air Force as the officers' mess for R.A.F. Hawarden, established during the early months of the war to train Spitfire pilots, sharing the airfield with the Vickers bomber factory. This ensured that the Castle would not be commandeered and vandalised by the licentious soldiery.

I travelled to Hawarden station from Slough to Paddington and thence to Wrexham General, crossed the bridge to Wrexham Exchange and took the (oddly enough) London and North Eastern Railway line which led via Hawarden and Broughton and Bretton to Chester Northgate (now buried under the leisure centre). These visits enabled me to explore the park and lake at Hawarden, which were becoming delightfully wild as the war wore on. Grey squirrels were newly invading vermin, working their way northwards – I last saw reds in Booberry Wood in 1938 – and I discovered that if you chased a grey on the ground it would panic, climb once round the nearest tree and, having thus given its pursuer a chance to catch up, take to the ground again, where I could despatch it with a stick. I bagged quite a number on each of my Hawarden holidays, to the surprise of the grown-ups.

Holidays in Wartime

Ever enterprising in devising ways and means by which I could get away on holiday, my father instructed me how to bicycle from Paddington to King's Cross: the route was simple and there were hardly any private cars in London, just buses, some taxis and a few lorries. So I biked from Eton to Slough, put my bike in the train to Paddington, biked to King's Cross where I got on the train to Ware and then biked the eight miles to Munden to visit Uncle Tom and Aunty Edie. Elizabeth and Henry were old friends of course, and my stays (for I did this more than once) were most enjoyable. One day we three bicycled the thirty miles to Cambridge and back to inspect some of the colleges. I also paid some visits to Uncle Deiney and Aunty Clair at Lewins in Kent, keeping up with Stephen, Felicity, Anne, and John who was just about coming on stream.

There was no 'long leave', or half-term holiday, at Eton during the war, just a short weekend: once we went to Brighton, where our lunch in a hotel began with Windsor soup and ended with college pudding, rather spoiling the idea of getting right away from home for a day trip. The beach was heavily barricaded with steel stakes and barbed wire, but I remember the dry invigorating sea air for which Brighton was (and is) justly famed. It was in stark contrast to the fog-prone Thames Valley with its pea-soupers often limiting visibility in winter to a few yards.

7
HMS Wrangler

I have done my best elsewhere to describe the Navy as I found it, not merely a small fish in a big pool but a minnow in an ocean, during the later years of the war. My ship returned from the Eastern Fleet to its home port, Chatham, to pay off in November 1945, but servicemen were released from the armed forces only gradually during the next couple of years. At the end of the First World War they had been demobilised *en masse* immediately, flooding the labour market and leaving heroes of the battlefields unemployed, many of them standing as beggars on the street corners. After August 1945 everyone was allotted a release class depending on their age and length of service, and I anticipated at least one year more in the Navy.

    The Admiralty were willing to take trouble to place even junior officers in the kind of job they preferred, provided that they arranged to visit the offices at Queen Anne's Gate for an interview with a retired commander. Regarding myself as fortunate to have served in one fleet destroyer, I said I would like to repeat the experience. Asked what I proposed to do on leaving the Navy, I said that I hoped for a career in teaching. Those two considerations led him to send me to HMS *Wrangler* which was just about to recommission as a training ship to give young entrants to the Navy their first taste of life in a more or less normal warship. They were the pick of the boy seamen who had been trained at HMS *Ganges* at Felixstowe and who had been selected as likely to make the Navy's next generation of petty officers. For the six years of the war the Navy had had to rely on men who had been trained before the war, an elite which had to be very thinly spread, their numbers declining by the wastage of age and battle, but bolstered by many who had joined during the war and who had undergone shortened training courses, but who mostly had simply depended on learning and acquiring experience on the job. There were many who had been promoted out of their depth, nearly all of whom were doing their best and coping well: but clearly the future of the Navy was going to depend on a new generation of professionals. It was an interesting experience to witness the formation of this elite of the future. So HMS *Wrangler* and her sister ship *Wakeful* were to do all the things a normal ship would do in peacetime, but in home waters, and with many of its ratings trainees.

Wrangler was similar to *Relentless*, but being a couple of years younger her weapons and equipment were more modern — updated rather than transformed. Both ships were of the type known as 'emergency programme' fleet destroyers, built during the war as rapidly as possible without the refinements of peacetime ships, in flotillas of eight, the initial letters of their names following alphabetical sequence. All the ships of the Navy were manned from one of three port divisions, Chatham (where the command was still known as The Nore), Portsmouth and Devonport, which was originally Plymouth but had spread out westwards to a new site where there was room for a modern dockyard. Each of the three ports had a very large (and unpleasant) barracks where sailors could be temporarily housed as they moved from one ship to another.

Traditionally a new ship would be commissioned, which meant being equipped, armed and manned, except for its officers, from one of the three port divisions. At the end of its commission it would be paid off at its home port and eventually recommissioned if required. Peacetime commissions tended to last about three years, but in wartime they were inevitably very irregular and replacements for the crew during the course of a commission came from wherever they were available. The growing variety of special skills required also made it more difficult to provide an entire crew at the right moment from one port division. However, *Wrangler* was a Devonport ship and during my year in her I became more and more aware of the special qualities of west countrymen as sailors. I could not define these qualities then or now. They just seemed to fit in more naturally and do the jobs required more effectively than crews from other parts. I can only put this quality down to an unspoken pride in an ancient tradition, together with the continuing importance of maritime life in Devon and Cornwall. It seemed to me to give *Wrangler* something special, and as it happened her captain was a west countryman, too: Edgar Warren, for whom I developed a deep respect and from whom, therefore, I learnt a lot.

Edgar Warren came from St Austell and had joined the Navy as a boy seaman. He had worked his way through the ratings as an able seaman, a leading seaman, petty officer, chief petty officer, warrant officer, and commissioned warrant officer, specialising throughout this career as a torpedoman; and then eventually, having passed the necessary exams, he was promoted to lieutenant (equivalent in rank to a captain in the Army). After the required eight years in that rank he had become a lieutenant-commander and had been given command of a destroyer. Like the gunnery branch, the torpedo branch were first and foremost seamen, and secondly specialists in one type of weapon. Edgar had been through the mill, he had done it all again and again, and he knew everything there was to know about a warship and the duties of her crew. His career was in complete contrast to that of my much-respected captain in *Relentless*, George Barstow, Dartmouth-trained and the very model of the pukka naval officer, who had lived the life of the Navy from the age of thirteen and who had acquired a rock-like reliability in knowledge, skill and judgement, but had never served on the lower deck. This contrast between my two captains made it the more interesting to serve Edgar Warren. Anything done sloppily or incorrectly would simply not be tolerated. Nobody would dream of saying 'I'm sorry, sir', let alone 'I'm sorry, sir, but...', or of questioning any detail of the particular way the captain did things or required that they should be done, but he was much liked as well as respected.

Most of the officers except the engineer officer were 'seamen' because a destroyer, with a crew of about 220, was not big enough to have, for instance, a supply and secretariat or an electrical branch officer, or a specialist gunnery or navigation or signals officer; so each of the 'seaman' officers had to do one or two jobs in specific areas. I was made fo'c'sle officer and also captain's secretary which involved running the ship's office with the help of a trained clerk known as a writer. In these two functions I saw both sides of Edgar Warren.

The main function of the fo'c'sle officer was to supervise the use of the anchors and hawsers. It was preferable if possible to tie the ship to a quay by hawsers rather than to lie at anchor, because this made storing ship and getting the crew ashore so much simpler. As we came alongside, with luck a rating ashore had been sent to catch the hawser and put the loop at the end of it over the selected bollard – otherwise one of our fo'c'sle party had to jump at the appropriate moment. The fenders were put out, pads to prevent a dunch, with one or two held until the last moment so that they could be placed at the critical point of contact. On board, the hawser was taken through a fairlead and then round a bollard or capstan. With two or three turns it could either be held or slowly paid out by three or four men as the ship came to a halt. During our training we had been warned of the dire consequences if a taut hawser, made up of many a strands of 'flexible steel wire rope' (FSWR for short), snapped – principally that the whiplash might take a man's leg off, not something one wished to risk. Actually, for a number of complicated reasons, the circumstances in which this could happen were not as common as we had been led to suppose, but it would have required a good deal of experience to understand them and gain the confidence of an old hand. So in most ships both the captain and the fo'c'sle officer tended to err on the side of caution. But not Edgar: he would have his ship neatly tied up and the hands dismissed in half the time required by others. On the other hand, if the fo'c'sle officer allowed the bows to get a dunch there would be the devil to pay: a public balls-up was not easily forgotten. The fact was that actually you had no choice: he might approach the quay at twice the speed of other captains, but the ship had to be brought to a standstill in the same amount of space. For me, this was what one might optimistically describe as a shortcut to gaining experience. Having started out thinking that the snapping of a hawser was a rare event, I actually snapped three or four of them in *Wrangler*, mercifully without serious injury to anyone.

The alternative, anchoring a ship, is a much more complicated procedure than you might imagine, but nearly all the responsibility falls on the captain and on the navigating officer on the bridge who has to work out a neat triangle on the chart, to take account of the effect of the current on the ship's course as it approaches the spot where the anchor is to be let go. All the officer on the fo'c'sle has to do on the command 'Let go port anchor' is to order a rating with a sledgehammer 'Let go'. He knocks off the Blake slip with one blow and away goes the anchor. The petty officer at the capstan will have the brakes off, and the chain known as the cable rattles away. The ship is usually going astern, and when there is enough cable on the sea bed the order will come from the bridge, the brakes and the slips will be secured and that is that.

In a confined anchorage there may be a buoy, which entails the anchor being separated from its cable and a short length of cable being eased out, which a rating who has jumped or climbed down from the fo'c'sle (there are usually a few who enjoy this kind of job) secures to the buoy. If there is no buoy, two anchors have to be laid out roughly at right angles so that shorter lengths of cable will hold the ship and she will not need so much space in which to swing with the wind and the tide. The problem is that the two cables may become twisted round one another. So the 'pusser' (meaning strictly orthodox) way of avoiding this is to 'moor ship', which involves breaking both cables just outside the hawse pipes at the bows of the ship and inserting a mooring swivel to the four ends. During this complicated operation you have to be one hundred per cent sure that you do not lose one of the anchors with cable attached. This involves an absolutely rigid adherence to the various procedures and the order in which they are performed by the officer and the petty officer on the fo'c'sle, and the absolute certainty that a dozy rating with a sledgehammer won't knock off his slip when an order is given to another rating to do so.

It takes a long time for an inexperienced crew to moor ship, and numerous practice drills to speed up the process. The necessary skill and experience used to be acquired in peacetime before the war when it was often difficult to fill the ship's company's time and the Navy resorted to 'evolutions' in order to do so. Evolutions were preferably competitive: each ship would be given some complicated task like mooring ship, or rigging sheerlegs and hoisting a gun barrel aboard, and the credit went to the ship which first hoisted the appropriate flag to signal completion. But apart from the fact that nobody had time during the war to learn these skills, mooring ship would not have allowed a ship to hoist her anchor and get under way quickly in response to an emergency.

The captain of *Wakeful* was senior to the captain of *Wrangler*, a commander with a distinguished record and a member of a well-known naval family with rather a grand idea of his own standing. The objective of the two ships was to train the Navy's future petty officers without the shortcuts that had been inevitable in wartime, and one day when we arrived at Stornaway, quite a small anchorage and subject to swift tidal currents of the Hebrides, he decreed that we should moor ship. I took a lot of trouble to get the right procedures in the right order in my head, going over them again and again and understanding precisely why they had to be performed in the given order, and how to check that one had been completed before going on to the next. The petty officer and leading hands had a good idea of the order of play, although no experience, and I could probably rely on them for reassurance if I panicked. The only man on board who had ever performed the procedure, and knew it backwards, was – needless to say – the captain. And needless to say, too, he was keen that *Wrangler* should complete the evolution before *Wakeful* did.

We were in the middle of fitting the mooring swivel when there came a shout to me from the bridge 'Come on, Sub, knock the bloody slip off.' That was the one thing I knew I must not do. I looked up querulously and I suppose I said, 'But, sir...'. 'Knock that bloody slip off' came the repeat. 'What, the port cable, sir?' 'Yes,' he said, 'knock the bloody slip off.' So we did, and everything fell with a mighty clatter miraculously into place. The flag which signalled completion was hoisted. *Wakeful* seemed to take ages – perhaps a mere long quarter of an hour – whilst we absorbed the pleasure of cutting our rival down to size. Edgar knew what shortcuts were possible: when I went through the procedures in my mind I realised that, provided (but only provided) that you had got the earlier stages right, this shortcut was obvious.

Working the hawsers and anchors was a nerve-wracking business. Edgar expected to take his ship-handling to the limits of what was possible. On the other hand, if he wasn't sure of the protocol for writing letters to senior officers or other high authority, he had no problem in tacitly admitting the fact and asking me to do it for him. Actually, we had all been taught how to do it during our training – it was one of the few appendages of OLQ, 'officer-like qualities', which could easily be taught. Letters would begin 'I have the honour to submit..' and would end 'I am, sir, your obedient servant' – or, to the Admiralty, 'Your Lordships' obedient servant' and since we all had School Certificate English we could be expected to express the subject matter correctly. There were not many letters to write. The office was tiny and I think the individual pay packets were made up ashore for us to collect, which had not been feasible in wartime. But we had to keep crew records up to date, including punishments meted out by the captain, and there were always envelopes or signals coming in which had to be dealt with, such as amendments to K.R.& A.I. (King's Regulations and Admiralty Instructions) or to charts, all addressed to the commanding officer, which had to be distributed. The captain didn't in the least mind whether or not people were aware that he wasn't confident of his mastery of formal or bureaucratic English.

One of the closest friends I had amongst the officers was Anthony Morton, the first lieutenant, that is to say the second-in-command. Grey hair gave him the appearance of experience in his upper twenties.

HMS Wrangler

He was one of those officers whose whole life was the Navy. He had few if any outside or family contacts although he was sociable enough in his ways and had an excellent and balanced relationship with the crew. He was thorough and conscientious over every detail. We were based at Rosyth where there was not much available by way of recreation except the officers' club where we could play billiards. He was interested in birds and we explored the southern shore of the Firth of Forth where there was a good variety of waders, we saw phalaropes near Lerwick in the Shetlands and fulmars, still quite rare in Britain, or rather localised to a few areas, near Stornaway. I never met him in later life but after a time his name started to appear in the promotion lists of senior officers in the newspapers, and he became Admiral Sir Anthony Morton.

Ken Lorimer was the only Reserve sub-lieutenant apart from myself. He too was a good friend but sadly he died at a young age. But unlike other small ships we had several lieutenants, R.N., proper pusser officers to supervise the training. Two arrived together and in the case of each of them a funny thing happened, so I shall slightly disguise their names: Lieutenants Taylor and Rundall. Early one morning two letters landed on the wardroom table with easily identifiable and identical handwriting, one for Lieutenant Taylor and one for me. In each case, mainly for the purpose of secrecy, the address to everyone in the armed forces was simply the ship or unit's name followed by BFPO, standing for British Forces Post Office, a sorting office, and a number. I at once recognised that they were both from a young lady in South Africa, whose attentions I had tried to deflect as being too predatory, but who, as it now seemed, hadn't given me up as a hopeless candidate for her affections; and I removed the one addressed to me before Lieutenant Taylor appeared for breakfast. He was clearly delighted to see his envelope and in due course he regaled us with an admiring description of his 'fiancée'.

Lieutenant Rundall had the visage of a basset hound and was universally known as 'Smiler'. He was a competent and dutiful officer but he was not blessed with a sense of humour and if he had been he would not have been able to show it. Twenty years later when I was head master of Lancing a request came from Commander Rundall, R.N., to pay a visit with a view to entering his son for the school. I said to Margaret Drew, my secretary – 'My goodness, I wonder if that's Smiler Rundall? It's not a very common name: I wonder…' and I described his

HMS Wrangler

appearance to Margaret. She always received visitors before I saw them, and when the Rundalls appeared on the scene her message to me was simply 'Yes, it is.' He had not remembered my name, an insignificant junior officer all those years ago, and I did not remind him. His son duly appeared, but I left Lancing shortly after his arrival.

The engineer officer was Lieutenant (E) Fraser, a charming Ulsterman with a quiet Irish brogue akin to that of south-western Scotland, a wartime officer from one of the old elite of Irish linen families with a dry sense of humour who would order 'a cauldron of steaming Harpic' when feeling exasperated. He was our liaison officer with the dockyard when we had a minor refit in Rosyth dockyard, his opposite number being Mr Rivolta. Fraser would be woken each morning by a knock on his cabin door and a call of 'Rivolta here'. I bought Fraser's 500cc Norton bike from him, my first motorbike and rather a dangerous one to start on, though much admired by pundits. It had no self-starter so you had to put it in gear and push, whereupon it tended to take off faster than I did, leaving me prostrate on the tarmac with sore knees and other minor damage. Fortunately it never went far before keeling over.

Fraser was excellent company, more so than Lieutenant Daniel, who had been commissioned as an upper yardsman (selected at a young age from the lower deck) whose regular party trick was to eat his wine glass after emptying it at the Rosyth Officers' Club. Our wardroom was completed by 'Jumper' Collins (a generic nickname in the Navy), a commissioned warrant officer, (T), our torpedo officer, a tough veteran. Although we were all British, we were as much as a mixture as the wardroom of *Relentless* with officers from four dominions as well as the Royal Navy.

The first part of the training of each group of boys took place in the Firth of Forth with Rosyth as our base, but after that the ship was free to go (within reason) wherever the senior officer proposed, in home waters. We visited Scapa Flow and Lerwick and Stornaway more than once, and represented the Navy at the peace celebrations at Aberdeen, and we circumnavigated Britain at least twice in order to drop off one class at Felixstowe and take on another. We did not call at many harbours on the way other than Plymouth, which had been heavily bombed and was consequently depressed, St Austell where the captain could visit his wife ashore, and the Solent; but I found it interesting to see so much of the coast of Britain and its islands. At the end of September I suddenly heard that I was to be released to go to Oxford. I

HMS Wrangler

attended the demobilisation centre at York and received my civilian kit including a rather bright blue pin-stripe suit, a trilby hat worthy of a prewar gangster, a superb tweed overcoat which lasted me for many years, a shirt, tie, underclothes, and a pair of socks and shoes, a civilian identity card and a form stating that I was an unemployed adult male.

8
Oxford 1946–49

My book *People in Places* describes the various institutions with which I have been concerned. It is a study of the relationship between institutions and the individuals involved in them (whether as drivers or passengers, so to speak) which enables them, if the recipe is correct, to create or maintain their own momentum as the forces which sustain and change human affairs.

My selection of institutions was, obviously, arbitrary. They are just the ones which I happen to have come across; and moreover I make no pretence at scholarship or originality. However, the seed of my interest in history having been sown at school, I was fortunate to be able to have it cultivated at Christ Church, especially by Hugh Trevor-Roper, Charles Stuart and Steven Watson. Hugh and Charles were members of a celebrated, or notorious, depending on your point of view, gang of three, the other member being Robert Blake. He was a PPE rather than a Modern History don, but his subject was nineteenth-century political history. Although, or perhaps because, he devoted years of effort to his distinguished biography of Disraeli, he was, and became increasingly, a staunch Gladstonian: indeed it was he who discovered Colin Matthew and managed to get him set up in Christ Church to edit the Gladstone Diaries.

A university is an institution where scholars can pursue their learning and students can gather to pick up the crumbs. Oxford and Cambridge are still loose federations of colleges, all of which value what independence remains to them in spite of having complacently relied since 1945 on government money, and in spite of the modern urge for centralisation. Institutionally these colleges spend their endowments conserving their buildings and on their lifestyle, which is very nice for all involved in it, but has little or no impact on their function except in the provision of accommodation; and as most of the dons are now married, they don't even live in the colleges. Nevertheless, what makes the colleges tick is the quality of their individual dons. Each one of them fits into a very snug pigeonhole, for the descriptions of their field of scholarship and office (professor, lecturer, tutor, researcher, and many others) are detailed and specialised, yet they sit rather loosely in the institutional framework of a college. Colleges may have elaborately constituted hierarchies – at Christ Church the Dean and Chapter, for example – but to an undergraduate the college seems more like a loose collection of undergraduates each following his or her individual trail just as every individual don is doing for most of his waking hours. It is the place itself which creates the institution: ideally designed for each individual either to pursue his own line or to meet his fellows for conversation. In this respect nobody has been able to improve on the layout of the great monasteries of Europe which reached their zenith in the thirteenth century, not merely in their multiple functions in society but in the massive resources which were poured into them by an astonishingly wealthy society. As the monasteries declined secular colleges succeeded them, including schools like Winchester and Eton and grammar schools in every notable town (many founded by Edward VI), and numerous colleges at Oxford and Cambridge. Their purposes were different from those of the monasteries, but their architectural layout could not be improved on. Actually, Christ Church occupies the crossroads between the monastic and the secular; founded by Wolsey for a hundred canons and hijacked by Henry VIII to produce secular administrators for the Tudor state. St Frideswide's abbey church was now to serve the double function of college chapel and the cathedral of the new diocese of Oxford. With the later addition of two quadrangles to provide rooms for undergraduates, Canterbury and the splendid Peckwater, and a magnificent library, it was ideally designed for its new role.

The colleges provided the environment for students to educate each other. True, the most impressive (and daunting) experience of the week is having one's essay criticised by one's tutor, but conversation with one's contemporaries is a continuous process of discussion and argument on all kinds of topics. That is why so many students who have been accustomed to the tight institutional framework of school life find Oxford and Cambridge so liberating.

During the postwar years a few undergraduates entered Oxford straight from school, having failed to pass their medical tests for the armed forces; but they were a small minority. The postwar generation was remarkable in that it included people who had broken off their studies to join the armed forces in 1939, and had now returned to round them off by a final year or two at Oxford; and it was made up of men who had joined up every year since then, who had been released gradually. Some of them had had extraordinary experiences: there were one or two lieutenant-colonels – 'temporary' or 'acting' maybe, but having faced responsibility more daunting than most regular peacetime officers of that rank, who would have been not in their early twenties but in their forties. There was a major who had been Provost-Marshal of Vienna, with more dictatorial authority in that city than the Emperors of old. There were men who had been severely wounded, or who had survived as prisoners of war of the Japanese since 1942, including workers on the Burma railway. But most of them were simply people who had had several years of extraordinary experience in all parts of the world. Undergraduates educate each other, but this was a generation exceptionally well qualified to do so.

It took me a time to slip into Oxford's easy-going ways and also to appreciate that my contemporaries were more than delightful companions, many of whom had had some unusual experiences: they were also a select bunch academically: not quite as select as they are nowadays, maybe, but very different from the mixture one had known at school, or indeed in the forces. There were a good number from state schools, grammar schools, and some from abroad, including two from 'India', or actually India and Pakistan as they were just becoming, the first Rhodes Scholars following India's dominion status, one of whom was named Bhutto: they communicated with each other (as with everyone else) in English. The Rhodes scholar I best remember was George Cawkwell, an immense rugby blue and a classicist who became a don at University College.

This was an almost exclusively male society. Most schools were single-sex and the armed forces certainly were, so we were accustomed to that. The few women's colleges were therefore intensely selective, and necessarily had stringent rules about the permitted conditions of male infiltration. Most of us knew at least one or two female undergraduates, but on the whole girl friends came, or we went, at weekends

Many of my closest friends were members of the boat club, as I was. This surprised me, as I have explained elsewhere. One has so many acquaintances at an Oxford college that the people one describes as closest friends are mostly those one happens to be able to keep up with afterwards, even if spasmodically. Three of mine were Salopians, two of whom, strangely enough, I had met when they were in the Shrewsbury eight for the wartime schools' regatta in 1941: Cim Mellor and

Alan Palgrave-Brown. Cim and I rowed in the coxless four and the pair as well as the college eight, and we used to put the world to rights in endless chat. He was a mathematician and an idealist determined with a missionary zeal to influence the institutions of industry, and he spent the greater part of his career with the Metal Box Company, makers of millions of cans, which over the course of time became thinner and thinner. He is one of the unsung heroes who have contributed to the development of civilised attitudes in management and working practices over several decades. His thoughts were on the whole a bit too profound and abstract – or perhaps even idiosyncratic – for me, but we acted as good foils to one another. It was a long time before I discovered that he had hated Shrewsbury, his house Riggs Hall having included more than its fair share of ruffians at worst and philistines at best. He was definitely one of those who find their university years, after their time at school, a liberating experience: he had come up for two terms for a wartime course before joining the R.A.F. as a boffin. I had the impression that these short courses, although better than nothing, were no more than that, and had the disadvantage of delaying the opportunity for people to do what ought to be done. Cim's experience did not endorse that view: those two terms were a transforming experience for him, preparing him for what was to come. Ever since those postwar years we have managed to meet, even if at long intervals, take up where we left off last time, and talk uninterruptedly for as many hours as are available – never quite enough for me to feel that I have fully digested his current thoughts.

Alan Palgrave-Brown was an identical twin of Alastair. They had deliberately gone to different colleges at Oxford, but nevertheless know one and you knew them both. They always referred to 'we' as 'I'. Alan was at Christ Church, Alastair at Queen's, Alan had coxed the Shrewsbury crew, so Alastair coxed the Oxford one. They lived in some state in a beautiful house in Suffolk, owning a successful family firm of timber merchants. When my uncle gave me a magnificent forest in eastern Scotland, I learnt about the fiscal incentives for planting and growing timber, still as designed after the First World War to encourage people to plant a crop with so many decades between planting and harvesting that it had been more or less abandoned in Britain as a result of free trade in the nineteenth century. I learnt the characteristics of the main softwood crops. The system of taxation was complicated, but the elements could be grasped easily. What was essential was to understand the possible risks and pitfalls – which many people, beguiled by an apparent opportunity to make some tax-free money in a regime of penal taxation, failed to achieve, with painful results. Alan and Alastair asked my advice about investing in planting, which I gave to the best of my ability. They planted a huge forest near Beattock, mainly of Sitka spruce, and to cut a long story short this was thirty years later to pay for the swimming pool at Shrewsbury School. Alastair died in his late sixties but Alan lived on. He had a great fondness for Shrewsbury and we met there on several occasions. We visited the boathouse where my brother Peter had been so triumphant, and inspected Alan's name, as well as that of Cim Mellor, inscribed on the record boards in the crew of 1941. Although Shrewsbury was founded in the sixteenth century, Alan is taken to be the school's most generous benefactor in all its long history. I also used to meet him at Christ Church at the periodic college gaudies.

The third of my close Salopian friends was Tony Chenevix-Trench, who was to become Head Master of Bradfield, Eton and Fettes. I will refer to him in my chapter on Shrewsbury, where he and I were colleagues, but meantime I cannot do better than quote the foreword I wrote for his biography *The Land of Lost Content* by Mark Peel:

> I fell under the spell of Tony Trench's captivating personality and brilliant but lightly worn intellect at Christ Church in 1946. A large number of freshmen who had been in the armed services for a longer or shorter period of the war joined a few veterans, including Tony, who had come up to the college in 1938 and had now returned to complete their degrees. Some of them had reached high ranks in the army, and some had suffered appallingly in mind or body or both. Tony seemed to have been able to throw off his dreadful experiences as a prisoner of war of the Japanese, and was the life and soul of the College. He was splendid company, President of the Junior Common Room and a leading light in the revival of the Boat Club, the Twenty Club and several other entertaining institutions. He regaled us with delightful anecdotes and penetrating but generous observations on human nature.
>
> Tony decided on a schoolmaster's career and returned to Shrewsbury where as a pupil he had been a bright star in a luminous firmament. I was fortunate to join the staff there a year later, so our friendship ripened, as did our exchange of views about schoolmastering. His interest was in drawing out the best from

boys as individuals. That is what he meant when he said that he was an empiricist, and not (thank heaven) an educationist. Naturally, for one of his academic prowess, Oxford exerted a strong pull, but after a short return there he realised that he was a schoolmaster and not a don. He returned to Shrewsbury as soon as a good opportunity presented itself.

In spite of his personal doubts and reservations, it was not long before he became a headmaster. He was no administrator and, as he himself said, no politician. He showed wonderful powers of improvisation and ingenuity in getting out of scrapes as an individual, but in an idealistic and indeed in an innocent way he was, in his chosen profession, a man without guile. He had none of the cunning or calculating qualities required in politics as 'the art of the possible'. He had none of the politician's ability to gather and calculate support, nor to wait for the right moment to pounce.

The recording angel knows that Tony achieved a great deal at Eton, both as a school and for so many of its individual pupils who liked and admired him. Yet he left with an understandable sense of failure. Perhaps there was something deeper than his weakness in administration or politics, or his recognised personal shortcomings: was his reluctance to delegate or to ask for advice due to a deep-seated lack of self-confidence? I believe that it was, and that an appreciation of his personal humility is a key to understanding the man. In a character of many contradictions it was this quality which led to his erecting barriers against seeking advice or help.

Year after year a group of us used to get together during the Christmas holidays for what was ostensibly a shooting holiday in Scotland. Most of us were schoolmasters, including my brother Peter, then at Shrewsbury, and Michael Ricketts, then at Bradfield, and later Alastair Graham, then at Eton, but never did a word of 'shop' pass between us. Huddled round a log fire playing Battleships in the evenings, or clad in enough layers of clothing to make Tony appear almost spherical, we enjoyed a long series of uproarious holidays with one or two of our wives who were willing to venture forth; enlightened by Tony's turn of phrase and his fund of lightly, or sometimes heavily, embroidered anecdotes. He was a countryman and, incidentally, a very effective shot at wild pheasants, duck, pigeon and anything else we could by subterfuge entice him to aim at in the hurry of the moment, including I am ashamed to say at least once a blackbird.

It was the misfortune of Tony, and of Elizabeth and their children, that the devils of the Japanese captivity came to revisit him when he was still in middle age. But he bounced back astonishingly at Fettes, and he died, as perhaps he would have wished to die, at the helm.

I had at Christ Church a special friend in Robin Noel who had been in the Navy during the war, had been converted to Christianity and who was to become a priest. He was a notably tall and spare figure, an outstanding oarsman who rowed no. 7 or no. 5 in our college eight and no. 7 in the university crew. He was earnest in his calling but he was interested in his fellow creatures and their foibles and he had a delightful sense of humour. As with Cim Mellor, he and I clicked and we could happily spend any amount of time in each other's company, talking of this and that. He was in the tractarian tradition, and an admirer of the scholarship of his tutor Canon Dr Cross, the shyest and most troglodytic of all the dons (against some strong competition). He especially admired Newman whose parish church at Littlemore, still with its bells and lace and presumably its smells as well during services, I visited with Robin more than once. We used to fit in visits to nearby Iffley, too: what more magical introduction could there be to a small Norman parish church? Robin became more and more a high churchman and finally not only a Roman Catholic but a Roman Catholic in Rome, where he died quite young, still in his forties. I felt that 'there's some corner of a foreign field'. I was sad that he had left the Church of England, and sadder still at his early death, wondering whether his asceticism had contributed to it.

Another of my very good friends, whom I kept up with, was Dick Gould, who was a couple of years older than me and had been in the Greenjackets. He had been at school at Winchester – and captain of the boats there – where those famous regiments of riflemen have their depot. He was a stalwart oarsman, always in the 'engine room' of our college eight, numbers 4, 5 and 6. He was married to Erica just about the time he came up to Oxford, so he was one of the few undergraduates who did not live in college even for one year, but he was nevertheless a very clubbable man; indeed they were a very clubbable couple, and it was always a treat to meet his beautiful wife. Like me, he became a schoolmaster: he was interviewed for Shrewsbury, but he did not go there. I suspect that at that stage of his career he was one of those interviewees who fall naturally into the role of interviewer and tend to give headmasters, at first acquaintance, gratuitous advice about their jobs. Anyway, he fetched up at Wellington before getting his own headmastership at Stanbridge Earls, a school for difficult boys who for one reason or another did not fit in to the common mould. He was happy and fulfilled in his own kingdom, which he developed and expanded until it became widely recognised as a leader, perhaps the leader, in its field. This work demands a high level of tolerance and understanding, both of pupils and of course of their parents. One of my nephews went there, if not on my recommendation at least with my encouragement, and was sent one weekend on a religious retreat, presumably in preparation for confirmation. There he taught all the other retreaters how to empty a gas meter of its coins. Dick was not best pleased and reported the matter to my brother-in-law, who was furious that Dick should complain, and should even consider punishment, for such a trivial offence, and told me so. I said that robbing the meter was obviously perfectly acceptable, but Dick might not have approved of everybody being instructed on how to do it. My comment unsurprisingly fell on deaf ears; but happily for me the problem was not on my plate. Thirty or more years later the governors of this school which had made such an important contribution to education made some flawed decisions and, as a result, the school has closed.

Dick and Erica invited me to the celebration of their diamond wedding so that I could intone the Latin grace used every evening in Christ Church Hall. They must have chosen me *faute de mieux* because the grace was always intoned by a scholar and I was a mere commoner. There was some doubt whether we had given thanks reverently or with reverence – 'gratias reverentur agimus' or 'gratias reverentia agimus' but if anyone could detect the difference after a glass or two of champagne they were probably, or even hopefully, in a tolerant mood.

From Winchester, that engine of academic excellence, came not only Dick the captain of boats there, but also Tony Pawson, a virtuoso soccer and cricket blue, a member of the famous Pegasus football team, and later a champion fly fisherman; and the tall fast bowler Philip Whitcombe who had the misfortune to bowl Bradman for a duck and thus could never hope to be remembered for anything else. Even if you get the VC (one or two undergraduates of the postwar years had done so) you can always try to shut people up by saying 'I was only doing my duty' or 'I was only doing what anybody else would have done', however transparently untrue that would be; but if you bowl Bradman for a duck you cannot credibly say 'It wasn't a good ball, actually' or 'I did it by mistake'. I wonder whether there is a Greek word for a feat of prowess bringing unwanted fame. A 'paraprosdokion' perhaps gets fairly near that meaning for words, but not I think for action.

Roger Pemberton was one of those whose friendship I most valued, not least because he seemed to be able to turn anybody or anything into a subject of mirth by a gently satirical turn of phrase. He was the only person who had gone through the same three mills as I had, Scaitcliffe, Eton and Christ Church, and to all intents a fourth one because he was a Marine and I a sailor. So there were ties of friendship born of common experience. He kept up with Hugh Trevor-Roper more closely than I did and was more tolerant of his antics. Roger and I have kept up with each other off and on for nearly eighty years.

I could mention dozens of other acquaintances whose companionship I enjoyed at Oxford: Richard Hobhouse for instance who lived near us in north Wales, or my two room-mates, Dermot de Trafford, a delightful companion from an old Catholic family who had owned that part of Manchester, and Hilary Barber who had parachuted into Arnhem. John Bickersteth, a cousin on my father's mother's side from a clerical family, used to come and shoot with us at Hawarden when he was Bishop of Warrington in the Liverpool diocese, and was afterwards Bishop of Bath and Wells; Dick Homan and his first room-mate Jasper Hubbard (a man of markedly independent views who had been court-martialled for refusing to take a submarine to sea from Malta for reasons I never tried to explore but I'm sure were well meant) – all these were enthusiastic members of the boat club – and many others.

The Dean, the Very Reverend John Lowe, was a Canadian, and I think it is fair to say that none of the undergraduates could guess why he had been appointed. He presided at 'collections' in hall at the end of each term. The undergraduates were called up one by one and he pronounced a few formal words, or perhaps only one word, 'satisfactory', garnered verbatim on the spot from reports by our tutors. But he was a non-event in our lives. Two dons of the old stamp made it their particular endeavour to fulfil a pastoral role, to get to know us and to show tacitly that they would help if we found ourselves in trouble – the chaplain Eric Mascall and the philosopher Michael Foster, who was by nature a shy, retiring personality but manifestly kind and sincere. The old days when nearly all the dons lived in college and habitually dined in hall each evening were on the wane. That I suppose robbed the colleges of some of their colour and style, but on the whole we undergraduates were sufficient unto ourselves.

9
Shrewsbury 1949–50

I walk through the Moss Gates. I am struck by the statue of Sir Philip Sidney, gentle warrior, the memorial of Shrewsbury School's war dead of 1914-18; with the names of those who died in the Second World War inscribed in sandstone on a curved wall behind him, giving Shrewsbury's icon just a hint of affectionate shelter and protection. I turn right, down a broad leafy avenue, and see the façade of a magnificent Georgian building – somewhere between a huge country house and an institution: a statement perhaps of what the school is about? On the right is the School House, red brick, its architecture a nice mixture of formality and improvisation: the headmaster's study is just there, on the ground floor. I have time before my interview to wander for a few minutes. The central doors of the big building are open, and I get a glimpse through to the other side – but I'll go round. To the left is the chapel – oh, dear! Victorian Gothic, brown stone, not smooth but rusticated, ill-fitting with its Georgian neighbour, undistinguished, an anticlimax.

Later I learnt that the school had moved from its ancient site in the town to the spacious plain of Kingsland only in 1874. The architect chosen to mastermind the project was Arthur Blomfield. He destroyed the finer details of the magnificent Georgian building – hence its hybrid but still impressive appearance as I have described it. The plan apparently had been to build a Romanesque chapel – but sadly Blomfield managed to override that plan, too.

I work my way round the big building. Lo and behold! 'High the vanes of Shrewsbury gleam, islanded in Severn's stream' – surely this must be the viewpoint from which Housman conceived those lines. The sparkling horseshoe of the river enfolds the town, with the glint of St Chad's, St Alkmund's, St Mary's, and others I was soon going to be able to identify – and up there to the left is the Welsh Bridge, where the setting sun 'bleeds upon the road to Wales'.

A few minutes later I am ushered in to the headmaster's study. Jack Wolfenden is welcoming, and asks me questions I can answer positively. He wants a form master who is willing to spend most of his timetable

Shrewsbury 1949-50

teaching a group of twenty or more boys in their first or second year English, history, geography, Divinity and Latin – or, if not all these subjects, most of them. He realises that my ambition is to teach history, but I know very well that I must work my passage: I can teach a few hours' history to what we would now call the Lower Sixth, then called the XL, the 'Forty'. Well, that's a good enough start, I think; but I've done no Latin since School Certificate, other than the few passages of translation required at Oxford, 'Oh, you'll be fine,' says the headmaster, 'if you do some revision before next term.' He offered me the job and I happily accepted.

In those days there was always a little coterie of kingmakers, whether retired public school headmasters or Oxford or Cambridge dons, or some of them both at one time or another, whose self-appointed mission was primarily to influence the appointments of headmasters of public schools, and secondly to help schools to recruit undergraduates green from their universities who had expressed a wish to teach. The names of these kingmakers kept popping up on school governing bodies. 'You need someone who knows about schools... do try to get hold of X or Y...you'll be lucky, he's already on the governing body of A and B and C' – these men were so well known that they were referred to by their Christian names, like kings rather than kingmakers, because this conferred credit from the right kind of people on those who claimed to know them well. They were the senior statesmen of the system. When I became a headmaster myself I always gave them a wide berth. I thought that they were what might later, in a less respectful age, be referred to as 'a load of old farts'; but they were influential, and I was sure that my school could get on very well without them. On the other hand, in their role of recruiters of undergraduates they were efficient and useful head-hunters, who merely offered up possible candidates and – perforce – left the choice to the headmasters. As far as I was concerned, it was J.C. Masterman who suggested me as a possibility to Jack Wolfenden.

Jack had become headmaster of Uppingham at the age of twenty-seven after a few years as a classics don at Magdalen College, Oxford. He was there for the best part of ten years before coming to Shrewsbury. He was liked and admired. He was a little bit slick, and his public utterings were too contrived in style, but he was an experienced headmaster who understood and tolerated the foibles of his staff, listened to what people said as if it mattered and was a brilliant administrator. He succeeded H. H. Hardy, who had soldiered on through the difficult period of the war, but retired in 1944. Like all headmasters Jack had had to recruit a large number of staff after the war, as veteran masters retired and pupil numbers recovered. Wolfenden was criticised by some of my most respected colleagues for not taking enough trouble over the quality of this large tranche of masters, who were then *in situ* for the rest of their careers. There was some validity in this criticism, but the standard of teaching was nevertheless very high.

Shrewsbury was one of the numerous grammar schools founded in Tudor times with the profits accruing to the Crown from the dissolution of the old monastic institutions; in particular, at the end of that process, the chantries which had been endowed to say numerous masses for the dead in the hope of shortening the time spent by their souls in purgatory. The schools would educate laymen to play their part in the new secular society. Shrewsbury was well placed for the education of the sons of the gentry in the north-west, North Wales, and Ireland, just as Rugby covered much of the north of England and those of the Scottish gentry who wished their sons to be educated in England. Just as Rugby was reformed by Arnold, so Shrewsbury benefited from a series of three remarkable classicists as headmasters, Butler, Kennedy and Moss – Kennedy's name being famous as the compiler of the Latin Grammar used almost exclusively by British schools.

Shrewsbury's illustrious reputation as a, if not the, leading school in the classics was very much alive in the nineteenth and indeed the twentieth centuries. When W. E. Gladstone was an Oxford undergraduate in the 1820s he had hoped that he and his fellow Etonians could 'knock those Salopians off their perch' as winners of the most sought after university honours and prizes. They did not succeed, and a hundred and thirty years later that had not changed. The classical sixth and lower sixth were universally recognised as the elite of the school, a product of brains, hard work, aptitude, ambition and brilliant teachers. The veteran Jimmy Street had given way to Stacy Colman, to the flustered figure of Harry Dawson who by now taught mainly the lower sixth; and to Tony Chenevix-Trench who came from Christ Church in 1948.

Trench: 'What did you read in the holidays, Townshend?'
Townshend: 'I read Ovid, sir.'
Trench: 'Oh, good. Which works of Ovid?'

Shrewsbury 1949–50

Townshend: 'The whole of Ovid, sir.'

Two elaborate and carefully rehearsed rituals were performed by the boys of the classical sixth from time to time in the middle of a lesson. The unfortunate master had no chance of preventing or interrupting them. One was The Train which could be heard first in the distance, became louder and louder, and pulled to a halt in the station. Doors opened, passengers alighted and moved in all directions whilst others boarded the train. Doors slammed, a whistle blew, the train departed with much puffing, which gradually faded into the distance, growing quieter and quitter until the lesson was resumed as if nothing had interrupted it. The other ritual was The Shipwreck: in the panic 'women and children first' entered the lifeboats which rowed away from the sinking ship until again silence was restored and the lesson resumed.

By the time I arrived Jimmy Street had reached his pipe-sucking anecdotage: he recited passages of Homer so exquisitely that even those who could not understand Greek could appreciate the rhythm of the verse. Stacy Colman, although a delightful companion, was a much more nervy character and a stickler for the finest points of scholarship. He had spent some years as a don at Queen's College, Oxford between two long inningses at Shrewsbury. He had a delightful and calming wife, Sally. Tony Trench came as house tutor, that is to say assistant housemaster, to Tom Taylor in School House, which was much bigger than any of the other houses and was divided into two, Doctor's and Headroom. Like College at Eton it was, as Samuel Johnson said of a goose 'an awkward bird, too big for one but not enough for two'. The other houses at Shrewsbury were smaller because they had been been built by individual housemasters on land owned by the school, and could be sold on to their successors. The housemaster recouped a return on his investment by being allowed to retain a proportion of the total fee. This was similar to the ancient system at Eton, where masters had gradually taken over the licensed boarding houses run by 'dames' ever since the school had begun to expand beyond the original seventy scholars; but the Shrewsbury system, modern and deliberate, had come about *faute de mieux* after the whole of the school's financial resources had been expended in the 1870s in buying the Kingsland site and the huge 'school building', which had outlived its various uses, finally as a workhouse or 'house of industry'; plus the chapel and some ancillary buildings. This archaic fee system for housemasters was gradually reformed and modernised and by the 1950s had finally disappeared.

Shrewsbury 1949–50

The last of these boarding houses had been built by Basil Oldham before the First World War. He had appreciated the school's priceless collection of manuscripts and early printed books, incunabula, had influenced the governing body's decision to provide a proper home for them in the new school library, a dignified but modest red brick building, and now in his retirement he was in charge of the collection, which he had catalogued. He lived on his own, looked after by one or two servants, and regaled his younger colleagues with a highly imitable spate of conversation.

The old brigade, who had hung on beyond retiring age to help out during the war, had all but one retired when I reached Shrewsbury. In one case a couple had been agonising for months as to whether they should continue to live close to their friends but suffer living in a community in which they had lost their role; or move right away. In the end they decided to ask the advice of their old friend, Basil. He answered at once in just seven words: 'Whichever you do, you will bitterly regret.'

The sole remnant of that generation still on the staff when I arrived was an irascible aged bachelor named Mitford. We young colleagues enjoyed treating him with every charm as if he was an old pal, in order to put him to the test. At one masters' meeting he launched a vitriolic complaint that although the common room had been redecorated the pictures had not been cleaned before being rehung. Tony Trench at once reacted by agreeing that 'it would certainly be a mistake to put a dirty picture on a nice clean wall'.

As at so many schools there were some strong personalities among the masters. 'Juggins' Hope-Simpson was the nearest we had to a Mr Chips: a delightful cud-chewing bachelor always guided by common sense. A keen gardener (he had a cottage with a scree garden in the Lake District), he created the garden between the chapel and the road which ran east-west across the 'site' to the Port Hill gate – a notable improvement.

The Kingsland 'site' provided the best layout I have ever come across for a public school. Much of it had been more or less level, and was now fully levelled for football and cricket, although the ground fell away gently to the west where Kingsland House, one of the few buildings there, was still the headmaster's residence. The houses and other buildings were grouped mostly round the eastern and northern side, but the site as a whole was a single entity combining spaciousness with

Shrewsbury 1949-50

a sense of unity. It could not have been designed more efficiently for the circulation of people whilst retaining its sense of space. On the north side was the impressive steep bank above the Severn, over which a toll-bridge had been built so that the town now had a third, southern bridge in addition to the ancient western Welsh and eastern English bridges. The toll – a statutory penny for pedestrians – was collected by a bad-tempered man called Mr Dunne, who on one occasion provoked a group of boys to rough him up. They were severely punished and at evening chapel they collectively confessed their sin: 'We have done unto Dunne what we ought not to have done.'

The geographical relationship between the town and the school seemed to me to be ideal. It was an ancient county town of immense character. The school was no longer crammed into the middle of it, but the town centre was accessible by a few minutes' walk. There was a house of day boys, more or less specifically genuine residents in the town, accommodated in the main school building. The mayor and corporation had some residual – mainly ceremonial – relationship with the school, and the captain of the school was still expected to deliver a Latin speech of welcome to each assize judge, which included a prayer (always answered) for a school holiday.

I lived at Braehead in Kennedy Road which had been purchased by our landlady Hilary when she had had the misfortune to be widowed; an ample late Victorian building which housed Michael Powell, Michael Charlesworth, David Brown and myself, where we indulged ourselves in a comparatively carefree and hilarious lifestyle. Michael Powell was a modern linguist. He commanded the school Corps, and he coached the eight: one of those stalwart schoolmasters, half way up the batting order, steady, energetic and experienced who was soon to take over a boys' house and who married Hilary. Michael Charlesworth was an Old Salopian: he had been in Basil Oldham's house, to whom he paid court and introduced me. He was a historian, number two to the brilliant Murray Senior, which was helpful for me as number two-and-a-half; a football coach under the auspices of Tom Taylor of School House, and a knowledgeable and competent organiser who got roped in for this and that. Later he tried his hand as a headmaster and then returned to Shrewsbury as the headmaster's right-hand man. Finally he retired to a house near Porthill – sadly his wife had died quite young – where he achieved the status of Mr Shrewsbury: who had been around since God knows when, knew everything about the school there was to know, and recorded the significant and amusing bits in books. He was witty and entertaining companion: I became godfather to his son Martin and kept up with Michael until the end of his life in his upper eighties. He was quite a sardonic character who was not everybody's cup of tea, but he certainly was mine. David Brown had been brought on to the staff as still a young man to head the fledgling geography department: he did that job well and was a very companionable colleague. He soon got married and after a few years he and his wife decided on a change and ran a gallery at Nesscliffe, opposite The Old Three Pigeons, from which Rosamund and I once bought a very tall earthenware jug.

The mention of a pub reminds me of the fact that there were 57 or 58 of them in Shrewsbury, and Michael Powell was a connoisseur of beer. He knew the best ones for the wares of each brewer and we often used to visit two or three of them for a pint after an exacting day's work. Most people used to drink mild-and-bitter (a mixture half-and-half) or less often just bitter, out of wooden barrels of course, stored at 52 degrees and then tapped and left to settle by publicans who knew and cared; and consumed at just the right time. Wine at several pounds a bottle was a luxury for special occasions.

I enjoyed the spadework of my job, teaching a class in the fourth form which covered a fairly wide range of ability, at a stage where the boys who were less gifted academically could, if so inclined, keep abreast of their fellows by hard work. I had a few problems with the Latin but they were not disasters. It was a lively task and I found most of my pupils congenial. About sixty years later a retired solicitor turned up at one of our garden open days at Hawarden, said I had taught him during his first term at Shrewsbury, and gave me his name. He said I had bet him a pound he couldn't memorise Gray's *Elegy*, assuming that he wouldn't try, but a few days later he said he had done so and I had to find time to listen to him doing it. Slowly the image recovered itself in my mind – I could visualise him exactly, a small figure with his hands behind his back, darkish-haired, polite and precise, standing there in front of my desk in that classroom. He earned his pound. I also enjoyed teaching history in the XL. The next time I saw one of my pupils, one of the Merifield twins, was in 10 Downing Street during Ted Heath's premiership: he was number two to the Private Secretary.

The school had a wide field of recruitment from the north-west and north midlands of England, from north and mid Wales and from

Ireland: still a school for the sons of the gentry, and the sons of the younger sons of the gentry and their friends and colleagues, and a broad field of professional men, together with its nucleus of strictly local boys as I have explained. It also took a tranche of pupils from 'first generation' prosperous west midlanders, families who had made their money in industry and commerce in Birmingham and its satellites, fathers who had no Latin or Greek but wanted their sons to get what had been denied to them. Finally, about one boy in five came from the southern half of England, where there was some family connection or tradition: these boys contributed a sophisticated leavening of the lump.

Alan Phillips of Moser's Hall, which was in very good shape at that time, kindly asked me to be his house tutor (i.e. assistant), which I thought would give me some useful experience. Shrewsbury had an unusual arrangement by which each study of four or five boys would be made up of one person of each age-group. It worked very well. I got to know the senior boys who were mostly in the classical sixth, and going through their Virgil with them in the evenings revealed to my surprise that I could now actually understand the shape of the Latin sentences as I read them, in a way I could never do when I last tackled the *Aeneid* and the *Georgics* aged fifteen. This helped me in my effort to 'rub up' my Latin.

The headmaster and the commanding officer of the Corps, Mike Powell, wanted to start a Naval Section but hadn't found anyone to do it. They asked me, and said that if I agreed they would 'find me some good people' to give it a start. I had remained in the R.N.V.R. during my time at Oxford – the Liverpool Division (HMS *Eaglet*) as it happened, which fitted well – so I accepted and much enjoyed this project: I can remember some of the founder members to this day.

I also enjoyed coaching rowing at a humble level. The Severn was too serpentine for abreast races, and was not navigable above the weir, but bumping races were ideal for house competitions. The Henley eights coached by Mike Powell were of a very high standard, and Shrewsbury produced a good number of Oxford and especially Cambridge blues, most of them at St John's College which ruled supreme in those postwar days, its eights with their notable style with the long finish being much the best at either university. But Mike did not seem to have the hoped-for magic touch which could restore the ancient days of the Kitchin's crews which had won the Ladies' Plate in the 1930s. This was hardly surprising since they were competing with

Shrewsbury 1949–50

the best Oxford and Cambridge colleges. Only three schools had ever won the Ladies' Plate throughout its long history.

The proudly named Royal Shrewsbury School Boat Club owned some sculling boats and allowed me to borrow one. I did one or two memorable idyllic expeditions sculling up to and above Montford Bridge, periodically having to disembark and wade with the boat on my shoulders to the top of the rapids. Coming back downstream one had to turn round and face upstream to keep control where the current was rapid and the navigation tricky. One day the Captain of the Boats, Ken Masser, came with me. I next met him about twenty years later on a visit to Eton where he had joined the staff and introduced kayaking in Arctic waters – he remembered that summer day on the Severn.

The Governing Body was constituted in accordance with the reforms of the 1860s, including for instance a representative of the Royal Society, of the universities of Oxford and Cambridge, and in particular of St John's, the biggest of the Cambridge colleges, with which there was a historic link. It included two representatives of the county council, a rather different animal from the councils of today. They were the felicitously named Sir Offley Wakeman and Colonel Arthur Heywood-Lonsdale of Shavington who, although far from being a scholar (he was one of those many Old Etonians who had never mastered the difference between a full stop and a comma), was a man of common sense and good judgement.

One day during my first term the headmaster summoned me to his study. 'Willie,' he said, 'Arthur Heywood-Lonsdale tells me that the bigwigs of the county have commissioned a history of the Shropshire Yeomanry, but they have sacked the journalist who has written it and they have asked me whether I have a young master who might take it on. They're willing to pay £300. Would you be interested?' I had only a hazy idea of who the Yeomanry were but the task sounded interesting and as my salary was about £400 a year the money would certainly come in useful. Three hundred pounds was roughly equivalent of £15,000 today. So it was arranged that I should see Major Sowerby of the Regimental Old Comrades' Association which was overseeing the project, and Major Bernard Nicholls of C. Nicholls, a firm of top-end printers, who would see to the printing and binding. This I duly did and I went also to talk to Arthur Heywood-Lonsdale at Shavington: we walked what seemed to be several hundred yards through the straight passages of this vast house to a cosy little room with a fire where he told

Shrewsbury 1949–50

me something of the regiment in its modern and pre-Second World War state. The Yeomanry regiments had been founded during the 1790s as volunteer cavalry to repel the expected French invasion. They had first served abroad during the Boer War.

This task led me all over Shropshire, a county of great estates, most of which had been institutionally destroyed by the march of history, especially by the First World War. Many if not most of the ancient families had disappeared or metamorphosed into modern guise in humbler houses. Some eccentrics had vanished, like Squire Mytton, but some survived, hanging on by the bootstraps in decaying houses. One or two of those regarded the First World War, the 'last contest' as they described it to distinguish it from the recent one, as an extended opportunity for sport, although a dangerous one.

There was at this period a new move afoot to save some of the historic houses, like Attingham, although it had been stripped not only of its contents but also of its purpose. I was able to absorb at least something of the fading world in which the squire had commanded a troop of cavalry made up of his own tenants, each of whom provided his own horse, in an English county more varied than any other known to me. The characters and sentiments of Housman's *A Shropshire Lad* are now so dated as to be hardly read today, in spite of the quality of the verse with its classical precision, its gentle rhythm, its happy turn of phrase and its memorable imagery. But like every wanderer in those days I knew before I visited them that Clunbury, Clungunford and Clun were 'the quietest places under the sun'.

I spent hours and days poring over scrapbooks, regimental records and the back numbers of the local newspaper, the *Shrewsbury Chronicle*. The events of the Boer War were the most difficult to disentangle and record on clear maps, beautifully drawn by Elizabeth Friedlander, but the Italian campaign of the Second World War was not far behind them: there are an awful lot of towns and villages in the mountainous parts of Italy, the parts where it was easiest for the Germans to hold up the allies; and by then the cavalry regiment had transformed itself into two regiments of medium artillery, operating in different areas. In this Captain A. R. Hilton, MC, was especially helpful. A dozen years later he had fetched up in Guildford and he was good enough to send his son to Lancing, where I then was.

This book gave me my first experience of writing history from original sources. It did not, however, leave me entirely free to select the subject matter. All the trivial but remembered incidents and anecdotes of peacetime had to be recorded. In that sense this was more a chronicle than a history.

Bernard Nicholls was determined to make the hefty volume a showpiece. He persuaded Hans Schmoller to design the typography. Hans was a refugee who had been born in Berlin and eventually settled in England via South Africa, a true artist-craftsman in book design. Allen Lane had roped him in to succeed Jan Tschihold, the Swiss typographer who in two or three years had transformed Penguin from being merely 'cheap in price but not in content' to being a leader too in typography and design. Hans was head of design for Penguin from 1949 until his retirement in 1976 and responsible in his field throughout the long period of Penguin's expansion to its standing as a world publisher and a leader in book design: now there are series of postcards of Hans's work. He was a delightful person and in showing me what to look out for taught me in a few sessions all the basic principles of typography and a good deal of the vocabulary required by its practitioners. He contributed immeasurably to standards of modern digitalised printing; for, in spite of the new flowering in graphic design which the digital revolution made possible, it also provided printers with a simple code of accepted basic principles of typography for books – incidentally having a dramatic but unsung effect on reducing prices by increasing the number of legible words per page. Unfortunately these principles of design and typography have come under the most brutal attack by people ignorant of any aim but to break a mould and show off. Gimmicks in the shape of horrible mixtures of style and font appear on the same page; and books are now glued together so that one can hardly bend them open.

The Shropshire Yeomanry did not appear until 1953. It was a lot of hard work, and I felt that I had earned my money. It accustomed me to the problems of using original sources, and it provided me with a lifelong interest in typography. It taught me how to make an index, and when I had finished I couldn't bear to throw away the box of cards in alphabetical order which had cost me so much labour, nowadays rendered unnecessary by computers. But above all it revealed to me the county of Shropshire, and nurtured the seeds which were sown by that first encounter which hooked me in 1949 when, like Keats's Cortes 'silent upon a peak in Darien', I first gazed on Shrewsbury town from the foot of the school building.

Shrewsbury 1949-50

Jack Wolfenden left in 1950 to become vice-chancellor of Reading University and to lead the life of one of 'the great and the good' who guided our national attitudes through their voluminous Reports, with the prize of a life peerage, a valued reward in those days, not a method of filling up the House of Lords with 'potential' party politicians with no aptitude for politics. His regime at Shrewsbury had been short but fruitful. He was succeeded by a very different Jack – Jack Peterson, the model Old Salopian, scholar and athlete, a delightful personality. He had been a much admired housemaster at Eton for which he had been hooked (like Geoffrey Nickson and Philip Snow) by Cyril Alington, soon after he left Shrewsbury for Eton as head master. Perhaps Jack was just too nice to make a success of the job at Shrewsbury. But the real problem was that he was worn out by the long slow decline and eventual death of his beautiful wife from multiple sclerosis. A naturally modest person, he ought not to have been pressed to accept this ultra-demanding role, at least until he had a breathing space for recuperation.

I left Shrewsbury after only two terms under this second Jack because I was offered a job teaching history at Eton by Robert Birley to fill an unexpected vacancy. I said to Robert that I thought I would be more useful to Eton after I had done what would also have been more useful (or at least more loyal) to Shrewsbury, and stayed there for, say, five years. But he said that it was now or never: with the house system at Eton as it was, there had to be a smooth age profile in the staff. I felt that I just could not refuse this unexpected opportunity. So my spell at Shrewsbury lasted only four terms. In spite of my enchantment, I thought it would be impertinent to include a description of the school where I had stayed for so short a time in my book *People in Places*. But I have had a go at it now.

10
Hawarden

Visits from Manley to Hawarden by the older tranches of my first cousins and myself whilst our Great-Uncle Harry and Aunt Maud were there in the early 1930s were few and far between, and were daunting occasions because everything was so posh. We wore our best clothes and our hair was attended to prior to our appearance as if we were actors about to go on stage; which I suppose we were, representing people unlike ourselves. Uncle Harry was a kindly old gentleman with white hair. Aunt Maud, grand, remote and delicate, had to be approached in the library – the largest and most cluttered room in the house – by way of a veritable obstacle course of small tables and breakable ornaments.

After Great-Uncle Harry's death in 1935 and Aunt Maud's departure to Warren Hall nearby, Uncle Albert and Aunty Kith prepared for their move from Manley. Uncle Deiney had moved from Calcutta to London, so that lot of my first cousins now lived in Kent. Uncle Tom did not retire from Bombay to Hertfordshire until a few years later, so Hawarden instead of Manley became home to my Stamper cousins, Elizabeth, Henry and Christopher, during their school holidays.

The garden was excessively neat in our eyes under the care of Mr Cooper (who always said 'quite, quite' instead of 'yes'), with plastic labels, and more earth than plant showing in the manicured flower beds. We disapproved of this style and wickedly used to go round untidying things and removing the labels; this activity was known as 'laying foundation stones' for the new regime which we anticipated and indeed proposed to inaugurate. Bicycles were central to our activities, especially for daily trips to the village and for riding the dirt track downhill through the beech wood at hair-raising speed; at the bottom of which were our headquarters for pottery and for smoking. There was a good bed of clay there and we made our primitive trays and bowls and mugs for sale at the garden fetes, which continued as at Manley, in aid of the completion of Liverpool Cathedral. We bought a cherry briar pipe, an ounce of tobacco and a box of matches, all for five pence, from the tobacconist in the village, a small and in our eyes wizened figure scarcely visible above the counter, whom we knew as The Miser from some imagined similarity to a Scrooge-type character. There was just room for Elizabeth, Henry and me to conceal ourselves between the bridge parapet and the stream. I don't suppose it occurred to us that the smoke might be visible. But we were far out of sight of the house.

These holidays came to an end with the approach of the war, the migration of the Stampers to Hertfordshire, and the withdrawal of Uncle Albert and Aunty Kith from the Castle to Broadlane at the end of 1939. Six years later, with a shortage of labour and indeed of everything, they felt that they could not – or rather, probably, knowing Uncle Albert, should not – return to the Castle, and he therefore offered the opportunity of living there to my parents, who now had six children. My father had postponed his retirement during the war. As the second son he had been left Manley Hall, but he could not have afforded to live there: it had been on the market since 1936; so we would have had to find a more modest new home. With Uncle Albert's offer came a generous subsidy; for, although Hawarden unlike Manley had an estate to support it, there was very little net income to be had from that source in those days.

My parents accepted. Uncle Albert and Aunty Kith returned to Manley, and in September 1946 we set off for Hawarden. My father with Peter, Penelope and me came by car, trailer attached as usual. We camped by the roadside near Tattenhall in Cheshire so as to arrive early in the day and meet the others who were coming by train: our mother with Nanny Thatcher, Francis aged 5, Helen (3) and Andrew (1). Nanny came from the village of Cippenham, not yet fully swamped and swallowed by Slough, and had the instincts of a country person (the Thatchers' neighbours were Mr and Mrs Squelch: Mrs Squelch came to stay at Hawarden and, as it happens, her name is next to that of Harold Macmillan in the visitors' book). Nanny Thatcher was to become as much part of the family and as much loved as Nanny May had been, most especially by Francis as the eldest of the brood, until eventually she retired to a cosy cottage which had been a sort of wish-fulfilment icon to her and the children for years. She was a less sophisticated person than Nanny May but she was very strong on common sense as well as having a strong affection for her charges.

Throughout the war the R.A.F. had kept the immediate surroundings of the house tidy in a basic way, and the building itself as an officers'

Hawarden

mess had been well looked after. The furniture, pictures and other household possessions had been stored, mostly in the basement, and the Air Force had brought in their own standard equipment. But inevitably after six years there was some dilapidation, and the need for complete redecoration. Staff were difficult to come by, and the one or two residents we employed in succession in the early days were not satisfactory. The only exception was Mr Parry, who came after some years as handyman-chauffeur, 'doing' the boiler (shovelling coke) and odd jobs about the place, and looking after the cars. By then a smallish Austin had been added to the much-loved 1935 Vauxhall (which had been laid up for several years during the war). My father bought it, more or less on impulse, after petrol rationing had ended, from a one-man car-hire business he came across whilst visiting Penelope at Downe House, called Kumfi Cars, so it was always known as 'Comfy'. In our family of eight, plus Nanny, a second car was certainly useful, and spared the Vauxhall the duties of a runabout including, for instance, collecting cypress branches for sale, which once resulted in Comfy being attacked, with Parry on board, by a temperamental bull. This severely dented and almost capsized it, conferring on it the status of a war-wounded soldier. Parry as the driver, although a bit shell-shocked by the incident, was happily not dented and did not get the same degree of sympathy.

There were a number of old-fashioned small firms in the village to repair the house: Hawarden Electric managed by another Mr Parry, C. Jones the decorator and Hector Jones the plumber. But we were a hands-on family (in those days a 'roll-up-your-sleeves' family) and we did a lot of the redecoration ourselves, just as we tackled the jungle out of doors. My mother, never to be defeated but never having boiled an egg, did much of the cooking, to which she brought an original slant driven by the primacy of fresh local ingredients, spent a lot of time and energy with the three younger children (but not at the expense of the older ones) and worked in the garden as well as the house.

We had a succession of admirable daily helpers, a neat lady called Joy working with a comfortably bulging one whom I called Comfort. Then we had dear Mrs Coupe, a proper prewar housewife, and finally our two wonderful Italians, Carla and Maria, wives of workers at the Buckley brick works where in those years of full employment local men did not like the hot and dusty conditions. Buckley had quite an Italian colony, but Carla and Maria were from absolutely opposite ends of Italy and I never fully grasped how it was that they became a pair:

sophisticated Carla came from the French-speaking north and had already learnt to speak English: Maria came from Sicily of typical Catholic peasant stock and never learnt a word of English in twenty or thirty years (relying on her daughters for that). But they were both treasures, perfectly methodical in the highest household standards, skilled seamstresses and willing to turn their hands to anything required, including complicated bits of interior decoration.

The garden and the old castle grounds had been untouched for six years. Peter and I set to with our Scotch two-handled scythes and our father bought an Allen Scythe with very big wheels and a traditional and amazingly reliable petrol engine. The only trouble was that the clutch was extremely tricky to work, involving a quick jerk-down of the handles at the same time as you gripped the lever. It worked sometimes, and sometimes it didn't; in which case the scythe continued blithely on its way, destroying whatever lay in its path. Trees which had run riot had to be felled with an axe, or a cross saw with an operator at each end. Peter and I became reasonably competent with our axes. Band saws were just coming in from Scandinavia and were very sharp, but no good for anything larger than small branches.

There was a fine prewar Atco mower, and a cylindrical push-mower for small areas, but they were of no use until the jungle had been tamed. The latest invention was the 'rotary' or flail mower, nowadays universal, which relied on speed of spin rather than sharpness of blade, and which could tackle grass and weeds some inches high. My father bought one but needless to say the early models were nothing like as effective or reliable as the modern ones.

In 1954 Major John Sharpley became 'park keeper' and looked after the old castle and grounds for the next thirty years. Born in 1900, he had been an apprentice quarryman in Cheshire, and he always enjoyed moving big weights, notably stones, without assistance. He was also an expert locksmith and could make keys for the old-fashioned locks in the castle. He enjoyed making every kind of device from second-hand materials. He was a typical slow-speaking Cheshire man of traditional stamp, never flustered or hurried, always patient. He made special trailers and trolleys for various uses. He had joined the Cheshire Regiment in time to experience trench warfare including mining under enemy trenches in 1918, and by the age of twenty-nine he had become regimental sergeant major. He had thus been a father figure for countless subalterns including three generals, all of whom remembered him with gratitude and affection. During the Second World War he became a quartermaster, received a commission and retired as a major. He had a pension and wanted an interesting but not too demanding job in the countryside. He was paid a small fixed salary with certain duties but no specified hours. Looking after the old castle and grounds was an ideal occupation for him. A widower (who had remarried), he had two daughters. One was the well-known journalist Anne Sharpley; the other married an enterprising Polish refugee who owned a silk dyeing and weaving firm and was persuaded to send his son, the apple of his grandfather's eye, to Shrewsbury, where he thought all the Latin and Greek would be rubbish, rather than to a technical college where he could learn about textiles. He was delighted with the result, including the teaching of science. His education in textile technology followed.

John Sharpley was always going off somewhere to visit an old comrade who was ill or unfortunate. He kept the British Legion going in Hawarden during the postwar era when almost all ex-servicemen put their medals away in a drawer and wanted to forget the whole experience of serving in the armed forces. A conversation with John was always interesting and instructive provided that one was not in a hurry: there was no such thing as a short conversation with Major Sharpley.

Peter did his National Service in the Palestine Police, realising that after the war the armed services would be uninteresting, to say the very least. He was rewarded with some unusual and occasionally dangerous experiences, and became a strong advocate of the Arab cause. Unfortunately he came back with jaundice, the ultimate effects of which he never entirely threw off. However, for most of the time he was an energetic and physically very powerful practitioner in the restoration of garden and grounds from jungle. I went straight from the Navy to Oxford; and soon after I came down he went up, read zoology and got a rowing blue, before (oddly enough) going to teach at Shrewsbury School as I had done. The years are therefore telescoped in my memory as I describe our work of restoration at Hawarden, which took place in university vacations or school holidays.

The estate's five hundred acres of woodland had been raped of their best timber during the war and then left unattended. Birch, alder, sycamore and ponticum rhododendrons, together with such poor specimens of hardwoods as had been unwanted for their timber, had the freedom of the woods to themselves. It was not until 1958 that we were

Hawarden

in a position to undertake a big programme of replanting. The rhododendrons were painfully slow to get cleared, and then the ground had to be prepared for the planting of conifers. The planting of hardwoods – beech, oak, ash, sweet chestnut, lime and others – was not within the commission's agenda and simply didn't take place. The birch and sycamore seedlings which did grow profusely were treated like weeds. It was considered that hardwoods had no uses in the future, and took much too long to grow anyway. The Hawarden woods had been planted since 1747. Many of the hardwood trees were over-mature but, happily, there was a younger generation coming along, which are now in the twenty-first century at last worth harvesting.

Mr Allman was head forester, but Joe Davies who had come in 1926 was the veteran. He was a wiry man but his wife was so fat that she couldn't get out of bed. Then came the one-eyed Billy Crofts, who owned his one-up-one-down cottage at the Old Warren where his prized possession was a complete Crimean War soldier's uniform which an ancestor had simply taken off on his return home and left there – Billy wasn't sure which war it was; they were all much the same to him. Then there was Norman Jones, whose arthritis eventually became so bad that he couldn't be expected to get on and off his tractor during a day's work and for years used it, *faute de mieux* and at the estate's expense, as his personal conveyance. On one occasion when Norman was holding a post and Billy was hitting it in with a hammer, Norman's hand was injured. The accident was investigated and reported by Frank Mills (who had succeeded Allman) as follows: 'Norman shouldn't have been holding the post, but then Billy ought not to have hit him.' This seemed to satisfy all concerned.

Last but not least in the forestry department was Dan Evans, who lived close to the castle, milked the cow, kept a small assortment of hens and reared the geese for our estate party at Christmas. Five of Dan's geese would feed fifty or so of us, provided (and provided only) that the carvers knew their job, which Peter and I did, much of the best meat being 'underneath' a cooked goose (having been on top of a live one). Mrs Evans made the butter: it was not compressed like shop butter and it did tend to disappear rather fast at the table of our large family. There were a couple of pigs under Dan's care too, but truth to tell the bacon was never quite as satisfactory as the specialised Danish stuff was when it eventually became available again. There was very little game about, hardly a pheasant to be seen and the rabbits strictly controlled by Bert

Dingle the gamekeeper, but there were some wild duck in the autumn and winter, a few partridges on the arable land, hares in the grass fields and more than enough pigeons eating the crops wherever they could. Peter was the main contributor to this mixed diet, although I, too, much enjoyed this 'shooting for the pot'.

There were three gardeners, Mr Adams the head gardener, Mr Pridding number two, who was soon beguiled by the better wages for looking after a few flowerbeds in front of the offices at the aircraft factory; and part-time Mr Harper, an octogenarian former coachman who still wore his breeches and leather gaiters. These gardeners worked entirely in the 'kitchen', or walled, garden. This was justified by our sale of vegetables, fruit and flowers to local shops. We also had quite an industry in daffodils in April, picking thousands and bunching them by the dozen for the Manchester wholesale market. We could treat this as a business for tax purposes, and with income tax at 15/- (75p) in the pound it was an economical way of keeping things going. Later, Selwyn Lloyd as Chancellor of the Exchequer stopped 'hobby farming' by disqualifying businesses which did not make a profit.

Bert Dingle the gamekeeper was, to use the caption written by Uncle Harry on the photograph of Hurst, one of Dingle's nineteenth-century predecessors, 'a fine man of the old order'. His father had been brought from Suffolk to Fasque in Scotland by John Gladstone to manage the pheasants and partridges. John thought that the Scottish keepers were good on the high ground with its grouse and red deer, but he wanted to obtain record results with pheasants at Fasque and therefore imported two keepers from East Anglia – who delivered the goods. Bert was the son of the head keeper, and came to Hawarden with John's approval because after many attempts Uncle Harry could not find a satisfactory successor to Hurst locally. Dingle brought to north Wales his hybrid Suffolk-East of Scotland accent, a few odd phrases and a confusion between the meanings of uphill and downhill – because, he said, to get uphill to his house in Scotland you had to go downhill. He didn't think much of the woods at Hawarden: 'there's not a right tree among them', and he had the bad luck to come in the 1930s when money was short, followed by the war when any rearing of birds was out of the question. But he was, indeed, a wonderful gamekeeper of the old stamp, as I began to grasp when my father arranged for me to go round with him attending to his vermin traps. There were no short cuts to his methods of tempting foxes and rabbits, stoats and weasels, to put a foot wrong.

Hawarden

He walked a long way every day (and unlike keepers in Land Rovers he saw everything) and later he asked for a donkey to carry his traps. His best meal of the day was when he got home, in the summer at nine o'clock at night. He had a large family who formed a complete line of beaters on the rare occasions when we had a shoot, addressing each of his sons as 'son' because, my father said, he couldn't recall all their names. Peter, needless to say, was a good friend of his and wrote to him once or twice from Palestine, giving an account of wildlife there. The replies were dictated by Bert to Mrs Dingle – the second Mrs Dingle she was – 'Mrs Dingle does most of the writing'. She looked after the two broods of sons and daughters with competent equanimity.

The other members of the estate's outdoor staff were Messrs Pownall and Littler, fencers and ditchers, both getting on a bit by 1946 when we arrived. After its long period in the doldrums agriculture had been revived during the war, when every effort was made to produce all the nation's food in Britain. Good drainage is paramount but was difficult around Hawarden where pockets of clay, mainly on steep banks, intervened in the mainly light and sandy soil. We looked down over the flat dairying country of Cheshire. Drainage was a craft learnt mainly by experience, with certain agreed principles, such as that you should never attempt to dig a new drain less deep than an old one. All the drains and ditches were dug by hand and the traditional clay pipes inserted, to catch the water as well as conveying it – but not too much of it, because this light soil tended to dry out around the end of June in a hot summer anyway, just when you needed the fastest growth. This was still the age of laying hawthorn hedges, a task on which a man might cover about ten yards in a day's work, but which would then last for donkey's years if the hedge was properly maintained; but mechanical hedge-cutters were just coming in, which sliced off the hedges flat at the top and gradually over the course of years destroyed them, meantime denying the countless birds which nested in them the cover they needed from overhead predators. Peter Barlow came in as a young man to strengthen this small team, but mechanical methods gradually took over drainage as well as hedging and he later transferred to the building maintenance team – after a few years in the garden.

The estate was managed by James MacCallum, a dour Scot who, like Dingle, had been recruited from Fasque, where he had been assistant factor learning on the job in 1926, and recommended to Uncle Harry by John Gladstone. He was a man of few words, and anything he said was preceded or punctuated by a little nervous cough. If he did not agree with what was said, he made no reply but remained silent, causing just the impasse he desired in a negotiation. He was a stickler for detail, respected for being always fair, and he saw the estate through the interwar years when the decline of farming continued and the financial problems of the 1930s brought it to its knees. Many farmers were bankrupted (especially anyone who had borrowed money to invest in improvements) and MacCallum enticed new tenants on to the estate, including two prudent and reliable Cheshire families, the Newports and the Birkenheads. Legislation had been strongly slanted in favour of the tenant and against the landlord since Lloyd George's time at the Exchequer before the First World War, both for agricultural and residential property, and statutory rent restrictions had not been eased to allow for inflation; but MacCallum held the fort and undertook a major improvement scheme after the war, as soon as conditions made this possible, notably in adding bathrooms and more modern kitchens. The ugly brick enlargements on many of the estate properties, mostly out of sight at the back, were the fruit of his efforts, and although they were not much to look at they made it feasible for the estate to continue with improvements as the years passed.

James MacCallum became Lieutenant-Colonel MacCallum overnight when he took command of the Home Guard in 1940. Walter Mills, his clerk in the estate office, became Captain Mills and the adjutant (he had been the youngest soldier – a drummer boy, he said – to join the Army in the First World War, one of a number claiming that distinction). To have the estate office suddenly turning into something like a battalion headquarters added to its prestige.

James MacCallum mellowed when he reached the age of seventy, but he had known the estate so well for so long that the records were kept more and more in his head, and when he retired after about forty-five years as agent, rather than producing maps, he took his successor round and showed him the details of all the boundaries – here we owned a hedge or a ditch or a track, there we didn't, or its centre marked the boundary; and he explained all sorts of little details and anomalies. Fortunately the legal documentation was in good order, although it was sometimes difficult to run to earth – perhaps in a tin box under the bed of Armon Ellis, our solicitor, an exceptionally able man who had decided to stay in Mold in his small practice rather than aiming for London and the High Court. To say that Armon, together with the clerk, Haydn Rees, virtually ran the county council would be an exaggeration, or perhaps an over-simplification; but he was both a wise old bird and a big fish in a small pool.

Dorothy Hughes joined the estate office as number three, an unflappable and wonderfully reliable asset to the staff. Later she married Arthur Pownall, specifically the plasterer on the building maintenance team, although like all of them he could turn his hand to many jobs. It was Arthur's uncle who was the hedger and ditcher. His brother, Ron, joined the garden staff, and did all kinds of related work like planting 'farm woodlands' and spinneys and fencing them in timber; but he was, and still is in his retirement, an exceptionally skilled gardener, growing plants from seeds and cuttings and filling a greenhouse with solid walls of glowing begonias. His vegetables and soft fruit are always better than anyone else's. He is a widower but still occupies the west lodge, as he has done for very many years.

The building team were the most important of the estate's departments throughout the postwar period, with a daunting backlog of repairs and improvements to catch up with. A key member was the joiner: Arthur Owen, straight from an apprenticeship in Chester, joined Hubert Law and then took over from him in the early Fifties. He didn't feel like retiring at the age of sixty-five and when eventually he did so, he went on making things – windows and doors and suchlike – until his late seventies when he became ill; but every night until he died he still used to find himself working out in his mind how best to make something. His widow, Vera, still in 2015 lives in the house in the estate yard next to the old joiner's shop. Another stalwart was Jack Williams, the bricklayer, a master of his craft who would undertake fancy work when required, say round a fireplace. Sadly he died not long after his retirement. I have already mentioned Peter Barlow – 'not a lazy muscle in his body,' said James MacCallum – who joined the team after a brief start as a ditcher and a few years in the garden, and could turn his hand to more or less any job required. He is still fit as a fiddle in his mid-eighties and lives with his wife, Rene, in the old stable yard. Their son, Terry, is now a member of the smaller building maintenance team.

In 1953 my parents commissioned Mr Burge, a distinguished photographer from Birkenhead, to create an album portraying the estate employees, and in 2003 Rosamund and I repeated the project. This time the photographs were in colour, although we would have preferred black-and-white, and were taken by Camilla Watson. We included the retired members who had served a lifetime, and we added a few of the small independent business proprietors who regularly worked for the estate and knew the various properties well. For more than forty years after the war there was no method by which a small business could borrow money from a bank, but the politics of the 1980s changed that and gradually 'small to medium-sized' businesses became the salt of the national economy. It was therefore preferable to retain only a small estate building maintenance team, who were always on the spot and knew the estate and its people well, and to employ independent small businesses for the specialised work, notably electrics and plumbing. Most of these businesses were one-man-bands, because the creeping curse of government regulation made it more and more complicated and expensive to employ a helper; but as far as we were concerned they were none the worse for that.

Several of the old hands, now in retirement but still occupying their houses on the estate, appear in both the 1953 and the 2003 albums. There was one person who had come after 1953, worked a 'lifetime' and retired, and there were people who had given good service over the course of those fifty years but for one reason or another had left for other pastures. It was easy to recruit good people when employment was hard to find: a steady job with a regular even if comparatively modest wage was preferable to the risk of redundancy; but when the national economy was booming, wages especially in the construction industry were enough to tempt people away. Moreover, there was not much promotion available within a small entity such as the estate.

When James MacCallum retired in his seventies I felt that the estate still needed a resident agent: there were so many little (or big) things that might go wrong out of 'working hours' but I knew that we could not afford the salary of an able and vigorous chartered surveyor. I therefore decided to appoint a retired service officer, trained and accustomed to take responsibility, to administer the estate on a daily basis, with access to an experienced surveyor. I decided on Commander Bob Spedding; and Ned Cowell of the well-known firm of Meller, Speakman and Hall (which after various metamorphoses has now disappeared as an entity), who was suggested to me by my brother Andrew, himself a chartered surveyor. I still think that this was a good idea, but unfortunately things soon started to go wrong, and I have to blame myself for relying too much on this team whilst over-committing myself elsewhere. Both members of the team started to suffer from intransigent personal difficulties which gradually led to what might charitably be described as under-performance, just at the period when penal taxation of both income and capital was at its most savage. Big houses were being pulled down every week. Quite a few estates went under. But like many others we had been through difficult times before and were able to withstand a war of attrition; although it was a comfort to appreciate that nothing ever stays the same for long. And when Bob Spedding left I managed to recruit the kind of agent I perhaps ought to have tried to find last time round.

By a happy coincidence in his affairs with ours, I reached an agreement with William Hall that he should establish his own firm of chartered surveyors working from our estate office, beginning by taking on simply the role of our agent. Communications had improved dramatically and we could get along without a resident agent. The estate office in the village would continue to operate every day, and we had the services of an energetic and experienced agent who had a flair for spotting opportunities and for picking up the pieces where things had gone wrong. It so happened that his way of thinking as well as his strengths and weaknesses were complementary to mine, and that if we were willing to give up time to chatting about one course of action against another we usually arrived at a satisfactory decision. His firm now also manages two other estates in Wales and two in Cheshire, and he has been able to bring in his son Anthony as his partner, which ensures continuity for the estate. Anthony has been able to take over from me the tasks I found most trying, and Charlie has taken on the specific estate projects, so I have been able to retire to a consultant's role.

We were fortuanate to be able to recruit Jane Connah, now Jane Lloyd, to succeed Dorothy Pownall. As the work at the estate office has changed and expanded she has developed her role and is now our indispensable office manager. She familiarised herself with computers, and has updated the software and the way we use it to retain accurate records and to provide up-to-date financial information. The upper floor of the estate office used to be a store for the shop next door, but that has been expanded to include its next-door neighbour and the upper floor is now our business hub.

The building maintenance team now consists of three people, calling on local small firms which know the estate well to do the more technical work. Grant Leeding is the foreman who inspects and organises the work as well as doing a lot of small repair jobs. Terry Barlow is Peter's son, and Mike Cole came to us a number of years ago after a long training as a bricklayer. Terry is specifically a plasterer, but the two of them cope with a variety of tasks and have an intimate knowledge of the estate property. They are well liked and apart from playing their part in the major refurbishments which usually follow a long tenancy, they are on hand to deal with minor problems and emergencies such as a slipped roof-slate or a burst pipe.

It was not until after Allman retired as head forester in 1958 that we were able to embark on a positive programme of replanting. Mr Shaw, who had worked for the Forestry Commission, took charge of an enlarged team for this work. He was succeeded by Frank Mills, son of Walter, but he left with the object of attaining a job of higher status. There often seems to be a gap before a satisfactory successor to an old hand can be recruited, but eventually we fell on our feet when a Buckley dairy farmer, Robert Charmley, had to sell the family farm in order to divide the patrimony with his siblings. He didn't wish to manage somebody else's farm, as he knew that he would want to do things his own way, and since he was an educated and perceptive countryman (he had passed his A Levels from Hawarden Grammar School) we were confident that he could learn his new job quickly. We had the luck to find Ralph Wainwright, who had just retired from the Forestry Commission, but whose lifetime devotion was to trees and forests, to act as he did for many years as our consultant, and he trained Robert in the niceties of his new profession.

Ralph was a gentle, patient person whose slow and deliberate mode of speech reminded me of John Sharpley. He was generous with his time and had a host of friends – witness his eightieth birthday lunch in a hotel near Oswestry – and he would only charge the most modest of fees. He enjoyed being Robert's mentor and gradually the state of our woods improved. Computers made it possible to comply with regulations by mapping, in order to fell and replant, small uneven shaped plots. Robert himself was an intensely loyal person who liked everything to be done to a high standard: a conservative who deplored the permissive behaviour of the younger generation. He recruited and trained Chris Basnett who was to succeed him when sadly he died in his mid-fifties. His last plantation was named 'Charmley's Belt' by the president of the Royal Forestry Society when they paid a visit to see our woodlands.

Hawarden

The old forestry department became the outdoor maintenance department, responsible for the hedges, fences, ditches and tracks, and was joined by Rob Morgans who had worked for us as a teenager and became a regular, looking after the old castle grounds and doing outdoor jobs as and when needed. We had grown some Christmas trees during Robert Charmley's time to support the wage bill, as we could sell them through the farm shop, and we more recently developed our production of firewood, sold through the same outlet. We bought a stronger crane on our timber-forwarder so that we could move trunks of ancient fallen trees back to our depot, and invested in two stages of log-splitters, the larger of which could split these trunks for the attention of the normal sized one. It is very difficult to make a profit out of firewood unless you have a retail outlet.

The farm shop emerged from a pick-your-own strawberry patch. I started this project as part of our small garden centre in the era when pick-your-own was a popular afternoon-out for families. The garden centre, based on the old kitchen garden, did quite well for a few years, but it was unable to compete with the mass production of modern horticulture. It shrank whilst our farming business expanded, and finally closed.

We found it difficult to replace Bert Dingle as gamekeeper. John Newport helped, and then we had two Scottish keepers The first of them left because he preferred the empty Highlands of Scotland to the trespassed woods of the north Wales border, and the second because he was a rogue. Eventually in 1967 Peter found Ellis Davies, a true Welsh countryman who was not yet fluent in English but whose wife Doris came from the anglicised coastal town of Colwyn Bay. He at once got down to the task of bringing the vermin under control, especially foxes. There were fewer and fewer gamekeepers in our area and Ellis got calls from farmers who had lost their lambs and poultry keepers whose chickens had been massacred. Foxes from the Cheshire plain, refuges presumably from hunting country, worked their way each winter towards the wooded foothills of Flintshire, but few of them found asylum. Ellis could whistle up a fox by night: its search for a mate was rewarded with a bullet from a marksman standing with Ellis until at the appropriate moment he switched on his torch. On one occasion a farmer who supposed that the fox-call was created by blowing a special whistle asked Ellis if he could borrow his 'thing'.

Ellis's house was surrounded by all kinds of animals: an assortment

Hawarden

of dogs from Labrador to terrier, a few cats to discourage the mice, a sty of pigs, a cow and two or three sheep, a couple of ponies, geese, ducks and chickens. Soon he started to catch up hen pheasants in the spring, to collect their eggs and set them under broody hens. It was not long before we were reviving two or three pheasant shoots around Christmas and the New Year. An incubator was acquired, and chicks were reared under modern electric heaters. Beaters appeared on the scene – 'Ellis's men' as Doris called them – and thus began the formation of an excellent and challenging shoot with a team of supporters who came because they enjoyed a day in the country as beaters, many of them working their spaniels: indeed for some years no less five of the six-strong Welsh spaniel team were out on the Hawarden shoots on winter Saturdays.

Ellis, now in his eighties, still comes out on our shoots. He is a valuable stop, for he knows exactly where to stand to discourage cunning pheasants from slipping out in the wrong direction without frightening them. He was succeeded by Gerry Evans, a retired telecommunications engineer who acted as our part-time keeper for many years. He is an excellent organiser and he kept the team going. We have always been able to recruit young supporters to succeed those who retire as beaters and stops, and there are several pickers-up with wonderful dogs who ensure that wounded birds are not left around. Now Dean Eagles, a tree surgeon by trade but a sportsman up to the eyeballs, has succeeded Gerry as our keeper and the continuity of our little syndicate of friends seems assured.

Over the course of almost seventy years since the end of the Second World War the shrinkage of farming in our national economy has continued. Unfortunately the laws and taxes designed to benefit the tenant farmer had the opposite effect, because they drove landowners to take on their own land whenever a lease came to an end. Income tax, already topping out at 98 pence in the pound, was 15 per cent lower for a farming business than it was on a landowner's rents, and there were important advantages in the tax treatment of capital assets also. Like other landowners, we took land in hand whenever an opportunity occurred, because even when a tenant died he could pass his tenancy on to succeeding generations. During the same period the size of a farm large enough to support a family continued to increase in size. Everything was stacked against a capable industrious farm worker becoming a tenant: the farming ladder was simply removed, mainly by governments which were aiming to sustain it. Although there were some landowners who were keen and effective farmers, they were in the minority. Most of them farmed their own land because there was no alternative, and they did not do so nearly as well as a professional family unit would have done. This incidentally led to landowners absorbing the government subsidies which were paid in order to keep food cheap for the public. Then came the 'Common Market' and the European Union with its Common Agricultural Policy, keeping the thousands of small farmers in France and Germany happy but paid only too often in Britain to wealthy landowners.

We had a run of problems with our farming on the estate until we recruited Laurie March, who came with his wife Pip to Cherry Orchard Farm and turned our performance round. Laurie was keen to support the farm shop which had promoted itself from the strawberry patch to a small-scale grower of fruit and vegetables with a wooden hut as its office in place of a caravan. He came originally from Kent. He was willing and enthusiastic to take on any challenge – a flock of ewes, a suckler herd of cattle, and arable crops on our lower-lying land. We met regularly to discuss our operations and our plans, to try to achieve the delicate balance between inputs and outputs. We got planning permission to build a small purpose-built shop with a store behind it and a car park, on our busy local main road. Then, alas, disaster struck when Laurie, a passenger in a Land Rover on black ice, was seriously injured and indeed would not have survived had he not been exceptionally physically fit. It was a long time before he could return to anything like a normal life at Cherry Orchard, getting around in his buggy and cared for by Pip. Now they travel all over Britain with their eventing horse, which came quite near selection for the Olympics in 2012.

I was given the opportunity of entering into a partnership by John and Denis Birkenhead in their dairy business at Rake Lane Farm. Their father had been recruited from Cheshire by James MacCallum and the two boys, two years apart in age, had been used by him as his labour force since they left school at fourteen. My brother Peter and I, who walked after partridges and any other odd game which presented itself, knew them quite well. Their father had survived the Thirties because he had never borrowed money, and they had been brought up not to do so. They wanted the estate to provide some capital and some more land so that they could milk 120 cows with modern equipment. This suited us well because as partners (two Gladstones and two Birkenheads with a quarter share each) we would be farming the land rather than renting it; and government grants were generous for new buildings. Using two sets of farm buildings and two sets of grants, the cost was not formidable, and the partnership worked happily and profitably for many years: but it never came up to expectations because John and Denis were so cautious, and then after Denis suffered an accident the responsibility fell on John alone. Milk prices failed again and again to keep up with costs and eventually their two sons decided not to continue the business.

At this stage David Edge wanted to 'go organic' on his dairy farm at Cop House, but this meant farming less intensively and he needed more land. His grandfather John Davies, a first-rate farmer, had taken on the land in the park during the war, when it was farmed intensively and parts of it ploughed, so we knew him well. He was succeeded by his son-in-law Geoffrey Edge, another very capable farmer. David took over from his father, and I knew that he was gifted with the family steadiness and skill. He was keen that our land should be farmed organically, as I was. I had just planted a number of small farm woodlands, partly in order to enhance the diversity of the area and partly to screen the industrial development, notably at the Airbus factory, which had changed the nature of the once open countryside. So we formed another sort of partnership with David, and we have all been pleased with the results. The bird surveys done by the Clwyd Bird Recording Group have been most encouraging, and although there has been a lot of publicity to inform us that organic food is not more healthy than inorganic, what we care about is the countryside and the fearsome damage which has been done by modern farming methods.

The legislation of Margaret Thatcher's government ended the restrictions which had applied to farm tenancies, so it became possible to let farm land for any period on which landlord and tenant agreed. This has enabled us to let some of the land not required for our organic farm to our neighbour Geoffrey Bellis, who took on Park Farm where his son Lee lives, on the retirement of Graham Crow, who had succeeded his father there. Geoffrey supplies the milk to our now much-enlarged farm shop: it tastes very different from the usual stuff you buy.

Thus in the Edges and in the Bellises we have neighbours who are not primarily tenants of the estate but independent farmers owing their own land; and the same is true of both the Wrench and the Arden families, who occupy the other two substantial farms on the estate at The

Beeches and Green Lane, in both cases with some addition of land from farms with neighbouring land, now defunct primarily because they were not large enough to support a family. John Wrench, now at last retired as a nonagenarian, was awarded the MBE for his work in revolutionising the harvesting of Britain's most important crop, grass. He invented the modern form of silage, cut whilst still quite short and green, rather than after its seed-heads had formed, and turned for a matter of hours rather than days so as to retain some of its moisture and its maximum nutritional value. The revolution created by John has been developed by improved methods of wrapping and storage, but in relation to its effect on the production of food it ought to be in line for a knighthood (or perhaps a few million pounds in 'bonuses' if farming had been converted into a modern form of legalised theft?) rather than an MBE. The years pass, and now John's son has been succeeded by his grandson at Beeches Farm. The wings of the Airbus 380 pass over some of their former land on the first stage of their maritime route to Toulouse.

In addition to these fairly substantial and independent farmers, whose businesses were large enough in themselves to support a family, we have several tenants of smaller farms who by ingenuity and hard work have continued to flourish within a (literally) vital agricultural industry in apparently inexorable decline. The Newport brothers, Geoffrey and John, came from Cheshire at more or less the same time as their cousins the Birkenheads. John who was married lived at Hayes Farm, fifty acres of which had been taken over before the First World War to form a nine-hole golf course, but on which he still had the right to graze sheep. Actually the sheep both mowed and fertilised the course, but not all the golfers approved of the 'unhygienic' character of the greens. Baiting the golf club became John's lifetime hobby, and he was well aware that his tenancy could not legally be terminated. But in all other respects he was a competent, genial and sporting farmer. After Bert Dingle's retirement he became a sort of honorary gamekeeper with a sheepdog, and Peter and I enjoyed rough shooting with him during the postwar era. Geoffrey was next door at Oaks Farm where he lived with their elder sister Ida, the elder-statesperson of the family who had set up her brothers as Flintshire farmers. They worked as partners, but each carried out given functions on his own farm. Geoffrey had a wealth of farming wisdom and conversations with him were always interesting and often instructive. However, he was one of those people who could never finish a sentence. Often he would stop and start seven or eight times, enfilading his listener with interesting clauses or bits of clauses which gradually came to hang more or less together as contributions to his meaning. (I have known three clever men who had this mode of speech, the other two being Charles Mayes and Councillor Conway.)

Almost the whole of Hayes Farm and a small part of Oaks Farm were used after the retirement of the Newports to expand the golf course from nine to eighteen holes. This expansion, together with the attractive character of the terrain, has enabled the Hawarden Golf Club, which celebrated its centenary not so long ago, to survive as a club for primarily local people when there are too many golf clubs competing for members. The Oaks Farm, almost intact, has been taken on by Ian Jones who is a skilled engineer with a love of farming. He owned a remarkable business at Hendre which made spare parts for machine tools, but eventually the scale and standardisation of machine tools combined with air transport threatened to put him out of business, enabling him instead to indulge his passion for farming and for farm machinery. He does a good deal of technical contract work for neighbouring farmers, including drainage.

David and Peter Connah are cousins, but very different personalities. David lives at Daniel's Ash, the most ancient and remarkable house in Hawarden, named as the site at which St Deiniol planted his staff as he preached to and converted the people of Hawarden or, to give it its pre-Saxon name, Penarlag. The parish church lies just above the farm: over the course of centuries more and more pockets of farm land have been used for the interment of our forefathers. David and his wife Olwen, sadly now deceased, converted the house with its attractive ancient timbers as a 'bed and breakfast'. He continued dairying for a time, but recently has concentrated on sheep, being the farm shop's main producer of Welsh lamb.

Peter's holding is much smaller. He succeeded his father John, a D-day veteran reluctant to throw anything away which might come in handy, who left about forty milk floats of varying antiquity in his back yard, one of which served as his hearse on his last journey. But milk-rounds are shrinking in the face of supermarkets and Peter has successfully taken to breeding horses. Although he might be described as the archetypal Flintshire Man – he worked on our farm for some years and is very well known to us – he looks the part dressed as a cowboy as he shows off his colts at horse sales far and wide.

Hawarden

Another farmer who has successfully diversified in a similar area – equitation rather than horse-breeding – is Peter Harden, who has an uncanny way with horses and is taking on the former dairy farm, although they have given up one large field to be the new home of the Hawarden Park Cricket Club (founded 1866) which has outgrown its original site.

The enterprise of John Johnson and his family in creating 'Greenacres Farm Park', has produced another variation on the theme of farm diversification. Families and school parties visit this former smallholding to introduce children to animals. The Johnsons retired in 2013 but their business was sufficiently secure for them to be able to pass it on to their successors. We always enjoyed our visits there with our children and grandchildren and their friends.

I visited Hawarden three times each year during the school holidays while I was teaching in the south of England throughout the 1950s. My father was older than my mother but both parents retained their vigour through the advancing years, and meanwhile the young family was growing up.

My father as a magistrate became chairman of the Hawarden bench and, following Uncle Albert, as I myself was later to follow him when I succeeded Cennydd Treherne, he became chairman of the Representative Body of the Church in Wales. It seems strange that three members of one family should be elected to the same job, but it was surprising how difficult it was to find suitable people to serve on the main committees, and the newly created province of Wales, stripped of its endowments, still lacked confidence in its endeavour to go it alone. A senior clergyman once said to me that it was remarkable how much the province had to rely on 'a few families' and I suppose that in an uncertain world you are best advised to stay with the devil you know. W. E. Gladstone was one of the staunchest Anglicans of his day, and by disestablishing the (Anglican) Church of Ireland he provided a precedent for similar action in Wales. My uncle and my father were, after all, sons of a Welsh clergyman. My father was in office through the interim period when the poverty-stricken province began to stand on its own feet: it was he who signed the cheque for a couple of million pounds (a massive sum in those days) to buy Bush House, and lived to see its sale for nine times that amount, although it was David Vaughan and not Charles Gladstone who was the 'financial wizard'.

Mr Harris, the manager of Lloyd's Bank in Hawarden, was a member of the Representative Body's finance committee and a close friend and mentor of my father in this work. He and his wife lived in the fine apartment 'over the shop' in the days when people of the status now described as 'executive' put down their roots and stayed in their jobs for life once they had earned their promotion; and when banks treated their customers as friends rather than unsuspecting objects from which money could be extracted. If the bank's clients strayed over their overdraft limit they received as tactful letter rather than being punitively fined as criminals.

Mr Harris was one of the characters of the village, his head slightly sloping as he commented on any subject from the weather to the local wildlife. He had the gift of being slightly pernickety without being fussy or tiresome. He and Mrs Harris retired gracefully to The Laurels. His brother was a solicitor who built a spacious house at the west end of the village. Mr Harris was succeeded by Mr Alexander, a more frontal figure physically, but mentally more laid back to the point of laziness, occasionally disguised by severity. He was succeeded by the competent Mr McCann, the last of our proper bank managers, whose field of operations was being eroded by 'experts' in agriculture (we suffered at the hands of one from Colwyn Bay) and no doubt other areas of business. Messrs Alexander and McCann were keen to take me, as one of their presentable clients, as their guest at luncheons hosted by their regional board; which had no identifiable function beyond drawing a salary for consuming four heavy lunches per annum in Liverpool. The members of these local boards were well-heeled local worthies who had no conscience about the pointlessness of their role nor the drawing of a salary for performing it. This was all part of what nowadays would be deemed public relations, contributing presumably a sort of 'old boy' flavour to the character of the local bank. My host was always Lord Kenyon, a clever and scholarly man who kept popping up in this sort of role although more aptly employed in some of his other more sophisticated occupations. It was one of those lunches at which the host made a stab at carving, or at least partitioning, a massive joint of beef designed to put his guests to sleep for the rest of the working day.

Another important village character was William Bell Jones, postmaster: churchwarden, antiquary, local historian and photographer.

Hawarden

Uncle Albert paid the salary of an extra post office clerk in order that Bell Jones could complete his three-volume history of Hawarden. Only three typed copies were produced, but the one in the county record office at Hawarden old rectory is a valuable work of reference for local historians.

It was becoming difficult after the war to employ telegraph boys with their pillbox hats to deliver telegrams by bicycle one by one to the addressees immediately as they arrived at the post office; so Bell Jones took to bringing them round personally in his large and venerable car. My father asked him how he could possibly afford this service, to which he replied that he always saved them up until he had enough of them to cover the cost. He was succeeded by Idris Jones from west Wales, another important village character who would discreetly dispense news or advice to anyone who sought it – or offered him an opportunity to provide it – from the post office. He had a passion for large sports cars, changing one model for another with bewildering rapidity. When my father asked him jocularly how he could afford this hobby he said that Mrs Jones (always a querulous and occasionally a frightened passenger) believed that the sale proceeds of one always paid for the next, but in fact it 'cost him a fortune'. He was quite well off on a sub-postmaster's salary: when I once asked him why he had come to Hawarden and had become a postmaster so far from his native heath, he told me that it was solely for the salary – producing an income which would have been undreamed of where he had lived. He worked hard: he was up and in the post office sorting the letters by 4 a.m. every day. He eventually bought a Jensen, the first model to have a 'permanent' four-wheel-drive and consequently subject to idiosyncratic behaviour when cornering. Unfortunately it came to grief in a scrape against a stout stone wall with Mrs Jones aboard. That was the end of Mr Jones's sports cars, an interest which he had shared with my brother Andrew, and ever thereafter he suffered from this withdrawal.

Another important figure in village life was the rector, Norman Baden-Powell. He succeeded Saunders Rees, a high churchman and a passionate orator of traditional Welsh stamp, one of those preachers from whose sermons one remembers long gobbets by heart, such as the one on the Beauty of Holiness which Peter and I used to rehearse to each other for years – it ended by asserting that if you rejected the beauty of holiness you might as well worship 'in a tin shack on a hillside'. Saunders had succeeded the even higher Nathaniel Cork before

Hawarden

the war, who had been shipped in by Aunt Maud, and who was so spiritual that he soon succumbed to nervous exhaustion in his task running a busy parish. Norman Baden-Powell was refreshingly normal and a splendid rector for many years, although he did make a point of his high churchiness by always wearing a biretta, one of those four-cornered brimless hats pinched together like iced-gems on Christmas cakes which one associates with Roman Catholic clergy – although Norman's was black, not red. The only disaster during his rectorship was the elopement of his daughter with the son of the warden of St Deiniol's Library, but since they ran away and were no more seen there was not much to talk about. We used to go to the rectory to watch the Boat Race on television, a new gadget looked upon as not quite necessary for people like us. The rector's son Ralph was a close friend of my brother Francis.

Music in Welsh churches is sung with gusto and with pride evident in the facial expressions (occasionally even contortions) of some members of the choirs and congregations. The organist of the parish church was Emlyn Roberts, whose services had been enlisted by Aunt Maud during the 1930s. A music teacher at Chester College (then still a theological college), he was a gifted organist and choirmaster and, as an FRCO and ARCM, exceptionally well qualified. Like most church organists he had firm opinions as to what was good music and what was not. The psalms and canticles, sung to Anglican chants, were to be pointed deliberately with each note given its full share of time, rather than hurried along at reading or even at dictation speed as in plainsong. And the hymns 'Ancient and Modern' were not to be hurried, every word sung and savoured with the respect due to the often convoluted morality. So the parish church music carried a rather lugubrious flavour, but nevertheless was of fine quality. Those were still the days of male choirs, the boys, mostly from the village church school, singing treble and alto and the men tenor and bass. But Emlyn saw beyond this, and in 1973 he founded The Hawarden Singers, a 'mixed' (to give it the official description in concert programmes) choir of men and women. Its performances were of very high quality and it soon started performing abroad, giving our village, as we thought, international fame, although their triumph was to win the mixed choirs at the International Eisteddfod at Llangollen not many miles away. Emlyn received a Ph.D. to add to his honours: we were all proud of Dr Emlyn Roberts. As the number of boy choristers sadly declined, the choir retained its quality as it became 'mixed'. Two notable personalities took on when Emlyn retired in 1988. Hywel John, head teacher of our church school, took on the Singers from Emlyn in 1988, and an Oxford graduate in Peter Trinder became church organist.

The Bishop's leadership of the diocese was not impressive and he made no effort to find an adequate successor to Norman Baden-Powell. Rector Dickin was clapped-out to say the least, a clergyman burdened with a large family living in poverty in the days before the Representative Body had grasped the nettle and obliged parishes to contribute to the cost of their clergy, with a one-tone voice of exceptional gloom and foreboding. He came to us from Chirk and it was surprising how quickly the parish began to fall to pieces; but since he was by then close to retiring age it was possible for his successor, the determined and strong-willed Philip Davies, who came from nearby Buckley (formerly a part of Hawarden parish), had started his career as a joiner, and had a practical approach to decision-making, to pick up the pieces. Philip regarded the parochial church council as a king regarded a medieval parliament: its function was 'to hear and consent'. He ran the parish, firmly and fairly, for more than twenty years.

Wales, as part of the 'Celtic fringe' of Britain, was strongly non-conformist. This was the big disaster as far as Christian unity was concerned, and had led to the disestablishment of the Anglican Church on the grounds that it was receiving public financial support with a minority of members. Thus many of the notable Hawarden characters – members or officials of the rural district council and the magistrates' bench, for instance – were not within the pale of the parish church and its six daughter churches at Broughton, Sealand, Sandycroft, Pentrobin, Mancot and Ewloe (Buckley and Shotton having already been hived off as separate parishes). The Presbyterians and Methodist churches and the moderate Baptist denominations were not far away from the Anglicans in their teaching – essentially they were more 'reformed' or 'protestant' – but the host of more radically non-conformist chapels, often single congregations, represented a different kind of protest movement altogether, the roots of which have not attracted as much curiosity amongst historians as one might expect. Now they have almost disappeared, and the moderates, not being shored up by the Apostolic Succession, are very much weakened. The Church in Wales is often the sole survivor, and where it continues to flourish, as it does in Hawarden, it is an important institution in parish life. Thus, in a world

Hawarden

where many people seem to think that truth can only be perceived by means of 'scientific method', the rector and his clergy and the churchwardens and congregations still make an important contribution to the village and especially to its more vulnerable people.

Hawarden did quite recently have one famous row when St Deiniol's Library decided to rename itself as Gladstone's Library and the warden of the library wrote to the *Church Times* excusing this decision by referring to St Deiniol as an obscure Welsh saint. This fairly put the cat amongst the pigeons and rector Tudor Griffiths wrote an understandably furious response to the *Church Times* refuting this insulting (and indeed absurd) description. It is not often that any ancient Welsh saint, whether or not obscure, sets the stage for a village in Wales to wash its dirty linen in such a public theatre. The furore created by this incident was on quite a different scale from that caused forty years earlier by the elopement of the warden's son with the rector's daughter. It demonstrates that Hawarden still has its characters and, after all, good news is no news. Tudor, a dedicated rector, soon decided to move to the more 'evangelical' Cheltenham, a smart Gloucestershire spa traditionally favoured by retired Indian Army colonels, where Welsh saints are seldom mentioned. Now we have in David Lewis a splendid rector of more eirenical bent, determined that the congregation of the parish churches shall be inclusive.

St Deiniol's Library was (and is) the most remarkable institution in the village but until recently it still had something of the character of a Victorian retreat house, and since its residents came from far and wide its participation in village life was limited to visits to the Fox and Grapes for the kind of refreshment not deemed appropriate within its hallowed walls. It was founded by W. E. Gladstone as a residential library containing his own books, and although of very specifically Christian character it is open to readers of 'every faith or none'. The Reverend Dr Alec Vidler was the first of several wardens who was widely recognised as a distinguished theologian. His venerable beard and monastic habit served to exhibit his strong personality. After the war the library found its role as a theological college for ordinands who had missed out on their academic training whilst in the armed forces, under the remarkable blind warden Stuart Lawton, and his equally remarkable wife. He was a fine Old Testament scholar but above all a listener. He was followed by Warden Foster, an Australian and another Old Testament scholar of note, but the supply of ordinands was shrinking and the established colleges got first pick. Warden Foster became archdeacon of Wrexham.

A new dynamic was needed and it came from the Reverend Peter Jagger who galvanised the library into life, notably attracting readers from the United States, Canada and Australia. Peter was brought up a Methodist; a Yorkshire countryman and businessman, who became an Anglican clergyman without ever shaking off the flavour of his early years. His energy and determination and his disciplined life translated themselves to the library, and those who found the new regime rather too much for them soon disappeared. Peter was somewhat gullible in his judgement of his fellow men, taking on members of his staff and sub-wardens who seemed to him to tick the boxes but seemed to me to be tempted by the apparently laziest job available to a clergyman west of Suez, with no parish responsibilities, no sermons to preach, and food and shelter provided. Peter with his guileless approach was incapable of reading between the lines when a bishop thought he had come across a suitable placement for his idlest or most tiresome incumbent. The unsuspecting beneficiaries of Peter's innocence found themselves catapulted into something like the role of a junior prefect in a Victorian preparatory school. So the calm backwater of library life was occasionally ruffled by an interesting and complicated dispute which, however, Peter always won by attrition in the end. But he did learn his lesson. Having once appointed a former Anglican chaplain in Oporto as sub-warden (it was his right to make the selection), he later arranged a sabbatical term for himself as *locum tenens* chaplain to the Anglican community in Taormina, which certainly left him with more than enough time for writing an exhaustive book about Gladstone's early religious life.

Nevertheless, the library was usually humming with activity and many of the guests enjoyed their stay so much that they kept returning. Margaret acted as the efficient and welcoming housekeeper. We always tried to recruit trustees with distinguished academic reputations from far and wide, and valued them for their expert specialised advice. This enabled the library to keep abreast of the times as a national – albeit in miniature – rather than as parochial institution, and enabled us to meet some very interesting and stimulating people; but as a *quid pro quo* we expected them to attend only occasionally, and ran the day-to-day business through a small management committee which met four times a year on a date when everybody could attend: the warden, John Elphick our honorary accountant, Bruce Bickerton a chartered surveyor and myself as chairman. Peter bombarded us with bednights, his chosen statistical unit, and indeed he transformed the library into a lively and efficient institution and kept it so through changing times for eighteen years. He was never one to miss an opportunity. One night there was a small earthquake with its epicentre near the Lleyn peninsula: Peter spent the following days going round the building inspecting every stone for a crack which might give rise to an insurance claim. The concept of 'taste' never crossed his path, witness the décor interior and exterior. Unfortunately his health was never good and the time came for his retirement.

We felt the need for a more relaxed and sophisticated approach. Peter Francis who had been Dean of Glasgow Cathedral and 'turned it round' institutionally seemed the ideal person for the role, and he has once more brought about a generational change. Above all the library has become part of the village: local people go there either as readers or as volunteer workers or for coffee or a buffet lunch. He has also forged a link with the now University of Chester, originally a theological college and then a constituent college of Liverpool University. The library has become more at ease with itself and for its guests, and more confident in its academic credentials.

The library had originally occupied the old grammar school to the west of the parish church. To the east of the church stands the spacious Georgian old rectory, now the county record office. Geoffrey Veysey the first county archivist was a gifted local historian and a most likeable personality: he took responsibility for looking after the Glynne and Gladstone archives, mainly on behalf of the library where they had been deposited by the family. W. E. Gladstone's political papers were given by the family to what is now the British Library, and the ancient Glynne papers are deposited at the National Library of Wales at Aberystwyth, but the material at Hawarden is enough to interest international, national and local researchers on one subject or another associated with the founder and his family. *The Gladstone Diaries* were edited first by Michael Foot, but Colin Matthew soon took over, producing twelve of the fourteen volumes, the last of which, the Index, is an encyclopaedia of Victorian life. People come to the library from far and wide, some of them for instance just to consult Gladstone's annotations in the novels he read to contribute to their study of nineteenth-century literature. The library thus contributes a whiff of cosmopolitan character to village life.

Hawarden

The distinguished grammar school at the west end of the village was converted in stages beginning in the 1970s to become a large modern comprehensive school which has earned itself a good reputation. Halfway through the process it housed a secondary modern school under the headmastership of Ken Hibbert, a delightfully patient and tolerant character who had survived the trials and tribulations of a long-term prisoner of war, but was firm as a rock on matters of principle, and who died a nonagenarian in 2013, The grammar school was meantime for some years in Shotton. Then Chris Harvey in his long headmastership was responsible for building the success of the present school, with more than a thousand pupils. I was a governor of the secondary modern and then the comprehensive school off and on (more on than off) for twenty-seven years and saw how the interference of the local council, first the district then the county council, was the main inhibitor of educational progress. The local councillors were neither knowledgeable nor interested in education and the officials seemed concerned primarily with the delivery of inhibiting political correctness in the jargon of the day. Any senior teacher who failed to get a headship was compensated by being turned into an 'adviser' on his subject, so these admirable experienced second-line teachers, the salt of every school's staff, were removed from their proven occupations and sent round giving expensive advice which nobody needed or heeded.

During the Thatcher era some of the political governors were replaced by local businessmen, which was certainly an improvement, but the council retained a stranglehold by means of the chairperson, still an experienced councillor who knew his or her way through the bureaucratic maze, and by council officials who could produce inescapable reasons for not applying common sense. For many years the chairperson was Elizabeth Jones, a likeable and very conscientious councillor and a member of the parish church congregation, but she was not a reformer and her efforts were devoted to understanding and applying the methods, unfathomable by innocent laymen, by which the county council governed its schools. She was succeeded by David Butler, the first local businessman to occupy the chair, who was much more inclined to look for the best decisions educationally rather than the ones which fitted the bureaucratic and political rulebooks.

This situation was handled philosophically as an occupational hazard by the head teacher. After general elections one prime minister after another promised a 'revival' of local government: Tony Blair's government gratuitously provided local councils an additional £300 million for education, but the councils swallowed the whole mouthful overnight on increased salaries, and thereafter we heard no more of this revival. David Cameron was the latest (and perhaps will be the last) to give a similar undertaking, but this particular 'revival' of local government actually turned out to include stripping councils of what remained of their powers in the field of education: local government is all very well, as long as those concerned do exactly as the central government wishes. This has on the whole been a Good Thing for both the High School and the primary schools (three of them church schools) in Hawarden and its satellite settlements, but it did not happen whilst I was involved.

I had a number of good friends amongst the head teachers and their various staffs, at the High School notably Chris Harvey and two of his deputies. They accepted the activities of the county council as the law of the Medes and Persians. I was also a governor of the Rector Drew primary school. The 'old' stone and brick-built school of 1910 was demolished and its site occupied by three mock-Tudor houses. The new building, which looked as if it was constructed mostly of cardboard and had no classrooms as such, was built in Beefsteak Row, formerly the site of the poorest cottages in the village. Everybody except me thought that this was an improvement. The standards in the primary schools depend very much on the head, and also benefit greatly if they have a first-rate experienced teacher as their 'number two'. In this respect we were fortunate in Hywel John (a fine musician, incidentally) and Gordon Parry.

Opposite the High School are the Gladstone Playing Fields, with a car park, a pavilion and the scout hut, the original groundsman's cottage (now the office of the Hawarden Community Council) and a fine bowling green, all near its entrance. There are eight tennis courts and a skateboard 'park', and the three football fields are very fully used by the largest and most active of all the sports clubs in Hawarden.

The origin of the playing fields is a sad one. A fine house and more than a hundred acres of land were owned by the Toller family, but the only son was killed as a volunteer in the Boer War and the family was so shattered that their property was sold and the land bought for playing fields by the Prime Minister's two youngest sons, Harry and Herbert, the one a businessman who became a millionaire (not having been considered clever enough to go to Oxford) and the other Home

Secretary in Asquith's government and then first Governor-General of the Union of South Africa. Herbert died before the project was complete, so Harry dedicated the playing fields as a memorial to his brother.

The Tollers' house became a monastery and is still served by the Poor Clares and named Ty Mam Duw, the House of the Mother of God (the Virgin Mary), who devote their lives to prayer and good works. Not many villages can boast their own nunnery.

Halfway between the playing fields and the village centre lies Hawarden's Norman motte and bailey castle, known as Trueman's Hill, its site donated to the village as a playground by the 'young squire' who was killed in France in 1915. Thus Hawarden has two old castles. The one known as 'The Old Castle' may perhaps have been occupied by some hostile Welshmen whom the Norman invaders had neither the time nor the energy to dislodge; but they certainly persuaded the people of Hawarden to dig, for unlike the keep at The Old Castle, the motte at Trueman's Hill is entirely artificial. It is indeed a fine example of an early Norman castle, its impressive earthworks almost intact and its northward view over the Dee estuary still uninterrupted. The Hawarden Waterworks Company hit on the idea of constructing a huge brick-vaulted tank in the base of the motte before the First World War, but it is more or less true that unless you fell into it you wouldn't know that it was there. By Norman times the main road in to north Wales presumably went through the village, having superseded the section of the older Roman road which branches off the Chester road south of Aldford and leads from Broughton to Mold via the Dirty Mile: there was a 'cold harbour' at Dobbs Hill. Hawarden is one of the few Welsh villages which appears in the Domesday Book.

The tithe barn provides a fine church hall. At the east end of the village are the Institute and Gymnasium, adjacent buildings now run as a single entity. They were paid for by a series of magnificent fetes in the 1890s when crowds poured in to Hawarden station by excursion train to see and perhaps to hear Mr Gladstone, the Grand Old Man. After his resignation from politics he spoke on the virtues of home-grown food, encouraging his audience to cultivate allotments and sell their surplus products to enhance their incomes. He praised Hawarden butter, creating a nationwide run on the product of a few Welsh cows, and commended Mr Wilkin's enterprise in growing home grown fruit for his Tiptree jam, thus inadvertently bringing nationwide fame to an

Essex farmer. The Institute was to be a working men's club, including a library and reading room and a billiards table, and it at once became also the armoury and headquarters of the Hawarden Company of Volunteers commanded by Captain Hurlbutt. The memorial to the members of that company who died in the Boer War was later removed and kept at the County Record Office for many years before being returned to the former armoury, now the council chamber of the Hawarden Community Council.

The Institute and Gymnasium were in the doldrums for many years because they had no car park, but they were kept going by the faithful Mr Rolfe and particularly by two people who have given wonderful service to the Hawarden community for more than thirty years, Paul Temple and David Kay. Paul has been and still is the conscientious honorary secretary, and is also a server at the parish church. David has run the camera club and was a member of the Institute's council for many years. He is also an endlessly conscientious volunteer groundsman for the cricket club, and their scorer and honorary secretary. If it wasn't for him they couldn't get the pitches ready for their heavy schedule of weekend as well as weekday matches, which has enabled them to survive on their old ground until a new one can be established.

The Institute was revived by millennium grants for village halls, more or less obliging the county council to give planning consent for a one-way flow of traffic and a car park on the old tennis court and bowling green which had become redundant when the playing fields were opened in 1930. Once more the Gymnasium and Institute are now in full use for clubs and societies, amateur theatricals, dancing and parties, as well as being used by the community council. The constitution was updated and gives that council four members, a full representation but not a majority, on the council of management.

A mile east of the village is Hawarden airport. The aircraft factory was built in 1938 for the construction of Vickers Wellington bombers on the sites of Catherine Farm and Mary Farm and Manor Farm, and soon after the war broke out R.A.F. Hawarden, training Spitfire pilots, was built on the west side of it, sharing the runway. After the war the skill and materials used to build Lancaster bombers were diverted to making prefab houses, each house requiring three lorries to carry it to its site. Then de Havilland Comets were built there and eventually in the early 1970s came the first of the airbuses. Now the wings of all the airbuses are built there, the latest addition being the massive A380, and

Hawarden

taken to Toulouse for fixing to the other bits. After the war R.A.F. Hawarden closed (the latest of its buildings served as a resettlement camp for Polish members of the armed forces who were unable to return to their homeland and is now the Scout camp) and the officers' and other ranks' quarters were used by R.A.F. Sealand, originally a First World War station with grass runways on the reclaimed land of the Dee estuary, which became an important repair and renewal base for the R.A.F.'s radar sets. The facilities (or some of them) of R.A.F. Hawarden became Hawarden Airport. Truth to tell, it has not been a great success: every ten or fifteen years somebody takes the view that a commercial service could be run from Hawarden, connecting it with Liverpool, London or Cardiff. But these ventures never seem to survive for long. The most successful was the Hawarden to Cardiff route of the 1970s, which provided the civil servants of north Wales the opportunity of a day's jaunt to meet their counterparts in the south, but even they eventually ran out of subjects for discussion.

The Airbus factory is at Broughton, part of Hawarden parish, but is often referred to as being at Chester. However the meteorological station is on the airfield is still rightly called 'Hawarden Airport', and in spite of all the remarkable institutions in the village the only news that keeps Hawarden in the eye of our nation is neither W. E. Gladstone nor Emma Lady Hamilton nor Michael Owen, our three very different celebrities, but the fact that yesterday it was the hottest or the coldest of the wettest or the driest place in Britain. The reason is simply that the airfield is below the level of high tides, technically known as mean high water springs.

When the River Dee was canalised in the eighteenth century in a vain effort to keep Chester open as a seaport, some of the land on which the commoners of the manor of Hawarden had grazing rights found itself on the north rather than the south side of the river. An act of the reign of George II created the Hawarden Embankment Trust to receive rents of £200 per annum from the graziers on the north bank to compensate the Hawarden commoners. The trustees still meet annually to divide the spoils between good causes in the old ecclesiastical parish which constituted or coincided with the Manor. Not until the 1970s did anyone have the bright idea of commuting the rents and transferring them to a registered charity, which has eventually enabled the trustees to dispense a worthwhile sum, although it is nowhere near the value in real terms of £200 in the eighteenth century. The farmers of the parish have by tacit consent a strong representation as trustees, but all the parts of the old parish from Saltney to Buckley are represented.

The Hawarden Castle School for Francis, then also Helen, and then Andrew, was started with a few neighbours, the first of whom was Elizabeth Bacon and later her two brothers Richard and Tim, with the tiny Miss Thomas as their thorough and traditional teacher. Then came the time when they went off to their boarding schools, my two brothers to the same preparatory school, Scaitcliffe, where Peter and I had been. Denis Owen, the stalwart number two in our day, had taken over from Ronald Vickers. although Ronald's son Richard was nominally headmaster and, indeed, devoted his career to the school. They were well taught there even if, as in our day, there were some eccentrics on the staff to add flavour, men much imitated by Andrew, who had a sharp sardonic wit and indeed type-cast some of them, introducing new adjectives into our family language. Mr Pike, the music master, became the type model for ostentation. 'Pikey', the adjective, came to represent the show-off, anything smart and new, especially flash cars. The Reverend Mr Kirkpatrick -'KP' – was also much imitated, a non-practising clergyman of perfunctory manner – 'Now, Gladstone!' – as if he ruled the world. Helen went to North Foreland Lodge, 'NFL', where my mother had been when indeed it was at breezy Broadstairs rather than the London end of leafy Hampshire. Francis became a broadcaster making documentaries, Andrew a chartered surveyor and Helen a children's nanny. Like Peter, Penelope and me they all continued to visit Hawarden regularly.

Francis was a producer of documentary films for television, first on environmental issues and then in medical subjects. He married Janet Schumacher but sadly, shortly after the birth of Melissa, she died as a result of a traffic accident. Melissa is a paediatrician married to Nick Beare, an ophthalmologist, and they have two sons, Arthur and Henry, and a daughter Florence. They have made their headquarters in Liverpool and Melissa has dedicated much time over the course of many visits to establishing criteria by which to measure the mental and physical development of children in Malawi in south-east Africa and, by extension, to other Third World countries. The benefits of her work continue to expand.

Francis later married Josephine Marquand, née Elwyn Jones, with multiple talents but first a botanist both scholarly and practical (everything she plants grows, to the envy of the author of these notes); daughter of the future Lord Chancellor, who almost straight out of Cambridge had been in Austria, an early opponent of Nazism, even before Hitler's rise to power and then, after serving in the Army during the war, a prosecutor at the Nuremberg war crimes tribunal. His wife was Polly Binder, an artist interested in folklore whose drawings of life in the East End of London and South Wales are documentary. Her impressions of young people in motion especially struck me with their lively and decorative character. Francis and Jo spent twelve years in Boston. Their son Elwyn, Edinburgh science graduate and expert on wine, now lives there with his wife Charlotte and their children Isla and Elwyn.

Francis continued to develop his interest in medical history, especially of anaesthesia, in which he became an expert. Later he and Jo moved from television to selling prints in the U.S.A., especially early nineteenth-century lithographs or modern hand-coloured reproductions, an interest which had developed from a project to search out antique books in Britain for American connoisseurs. They also became experts on Lewis Carroll, and wrote a scholarly book about him and, in particular, the individuals who appear as characters in *Alice's Adventures in Wonderland* and *Through the Looking Glass*. They were quite polymathic: Francis wrote a book on baseball. They made the west end of Hawarden Castle their home and gave its big rooms a striking and stylish character.

Helen was nanny with the Benson family in Chiswick, married Philip Young and happily took on life as a Norfolk farmer's wife at East End Farm in Ringstead. Their elder son James now runs the farm. His brother John, who got a first at Oxford, is a solicitor. Helen is a keen ornithologist: Peter, Pene, Helen and I all caught this interest in birds from our father. Of the six of us Peter and Helen became the most expert.

Andrew was the most commercially oriented of the six of us, although like his brothers he lived in a professional rather than a commercial milieu. As he embarked on his career he joked that he wanted to work in London, live in the country, and drive a Porsche. He was successful as a surveyor working for Cluttons and then in getting a sought-after job with Jones Lang Wotton. Then after a venture in Brazil (he was rather too early on the scene as a property developer there as things turned out) he became a partner in Humbert's. He married

Nicola Skewes-Cox and they had two daughters, Isla and Clova. After Nicola's father died they decided to migrate from Kensington to the West Country and he set up an office in Exeter, running his own firm. They lived in Nicola's family home on the fringe of Dartmoor above Ashburton. Sadly Andrew died at the age of fifty, the last of the six of us to arrive and the first to depart. Francis has written a vivid tribute to his life and character. (The origin of this was a speech at a family celebration: Francis has a gift for such occasions – I vividly remember his speech at the opening of the Isla Gladstone Conservatory.)

Peter and I became schoolmasters, he at Shrewsbury and I at Eton. Pene took a secretarial training. She kept a beautiful grey horse at Hawarden and became an excellent shot with a twenty-bore gun: I can hear the approaching beaters at Glen Dye shouting 'the Lady Penelope's clobbered another' – my senior readers will understand the context. Later she qualified as an occupational therapist and meanwhile kept up her viola playing which was one of her outstanding talents. She moved to Canada for some years, and then returned to London, before finally moving to the Lake District. She wrote two books, the first on the African explorer Alexine Tinne – a cousin on our mother's Crum side of the family. The book on Alexine was deservedly well reviewed. Penelope's other publication was the charming but more intimate *Portrait of a Family* about the Gladstones.

Peter had a distinguished career at Shrewsbury as zoologist, rowing coach and housemaster, and is fondly remembered by many of his pupils, especially for his ability to discover talent and build self-confidence in those who did not fit the orthodox mould. His approach to biology was lively, stuffed animals in a museum being replaced by a zoo, including badgers and then a fox which lived at home with him. The badgers travelled in his camper-van: I remember one arriving at Eton, when on disembarking it promptly sought out a drain in the gutter to relieve itself. The fox was trained to provide for itself and to live in the wild: it brought its litter back to introduce them to Peter in its old home -The New House. There was a rabbit called Mr Peapod who turned out to be a female and filled the garden at Ridgemount with generations of progeny, and a duck called Fizz picked up on the Henley towpath who provided evidence of a similar feat on the Lake at Hawarden in spite of having made its home in Peter's pocket; Fizz becoming the generic name of our population of mallards with just a touch of the farmyard in their ancestry.

Peter's supreme achievement at Shrewsbury, however, was to win the Princess Elizabeth Cup for public schools at Henley, and to win it no less than three times. The Ladies' Plate (the then equivalent) had been won by Shrewsbury in the 1930s. Of schools, only Eton and Radley had also ever won it, and there was a kind of folorn hope at Shrewsbury that the school might perhaps at some future date triumph at Henley again in this unseeded knockout competition open to every rowing school in Britain and overseas.

Peter did not want to stay on at Shrewsbury after the end of his tenure as a housemaster – and, indeed, what more was there for him to achieve? He was chosen by Peter Scott to start the new wildfowl centre at Martin Mere near the Lancashire coast. There he revealed his diverse practical talent for running a complete project more or less single-handedly in his own inimitable manner, beginning with the fund-raising and including driving the digger which excavated the ponds. He became engaged and married to Jeannie Roy and their eldest child Xenophon was born there, before they migrated to Fasque, where Cleodie and Fergie arrived. Again, what was there for Peter to achieve at Martinmere once it had been set up? He did not wish to become merely a warden and a guide.

All six of us were fond of Hawarden and continued to visit our parents there. Our father began to find the running of the estate burdensome and I took over from him in the late Sixties (his late seventies) while I was still in Sussex, making occasional visits. I found that I could board the sleeper at Euston at 11 p.m. although it did not depart for Liverpool until after midnight, and sleep comfortably enough on the train until about 6 a.m., get a lift to Hawarden from our village greengrocer who had bought the day's produce at the market, have breakfast with my parents, attend the estate office at some length and then inspect what had to be inspected, take a walk round the lake for recreation and catch an evening train back to Euston; thence to Victoria and Shoreham-by Sea; and so to bed. It was not an ideal system, but with correspondence and occasional telephoning it worked well for a year or two before Rosamund and I were in a position to move north. I was amused to find that, although I boarded the sleeper at Euston before midnight, the whole journey could then be accomplished on a cheap day return ticket.

Our parents decided to build a new single-storey house between the castle grounds and the village, but sadly our father died just before the project got under way. The first architect we commissioned to build the house for Isla turned out to be a dud, but we then found David le M. Brock, Professor at Liverpool University, who took on occasional commissions and designed a distinguished house at North Park. There was a single spacious high living room with a sun room and with the kitchen adjacent, and four bedrooms so that Isla could have her children and friends to stay. Aged nineteen she had married almost at once into a housemaster's house at Eton and then – when my father 'retired' – had taken on the family seat at Hawarden. Now for the first time she had her own house, full of light and sunshine, with her own possessions and her own fabrics and wallpapers, and could live her own stylish yet essentially simple way of life. In her studio adjacent to the house she designed and printed much of her finest artistic work, essentially for her own satisfaction and for her children, but also for a select band of clients. She made the altar cloth for Liverpool Parish Church (sadly it has not survived); and the altar carpet for Hawarden Parish Church, beckoning communicants, now after many years to be restored. She also designed the children's altar cloth, based on their own pictures.

Francis and Jo have become dedicated curators of Isla's work, of which the most tangible witness is the Isla Gladstone Conservatory. Liverpool planners were looking for a fresh start for the Conservatory in Stanley Park. The Park and Conservatory had been conceived as a major public amenity in the early years of the twentieth century; but the First World War and subsequent economic problems and then changes in social perception, including 'slum clearance', had diminished the Park's importance as an amenity. The eventual decline, neglect and dereliction of the Conservatory led the planners to consider how this remarkable building might be transformed for modern use and given a fresh start. Having seen Isla's work, learned of her having been tutored in Liverpool and heard about her botanical interests, they hit on the idea of naming the building after this female Gladstone and incorporating her design work within it. They knew that there would have to big changes to create a viable successor to the original Conservatory, so they were faced with the challenge of persuading English Heritage that this listed building of glass and cast iron should be sympathetically transformed in order to secure its economic future.

The 'Isla Gladstone idea' appealed to English Heritage. It preserved the surname of Liverpool's famous son, born in Rodney Street in 1809, who was to become the most celebrated statesman and reformer of the

Victorian age. Reconstructed in a different form, yet ingeniously designed to preserve much of its original character, the new Conservatory was dedicated to the women of Liverpool where Isla had found the help and support she needed to become a professional designer. Jo Gladstone was instrumental in the development of the 'Isla Gladstone idea' with Francis's help in its articulation. With the support of some loyal allies but in the face also of significant opposition, their extraordinary persistence was eventually rewarded by the completion of this unique and magnificent project.

11
Our Lancing Years, 1961–69

I became Head Master of Lancing in 1961 after spending just over ten years teaching history at Eton. I was looking forward to being an Eton housemaster but I had already become too encapsulated in my job: it was seven days a week living over the shop, and although the holidays were generous most of that time was needed for recuperation from the previous term and preparation for the next. It was a stroke of luck that I got the job at Lancing, as I have explained elsewhere. This is not false modesty: I have had my share of bad luck too. It opened up a wonderful opportunity both personally and professionally. I have already written a long description of the school as I saw it, and inevitably I have thus been drawn in to describing some of the individuals involved. On the whole, the problem with books of memoirs about institutions is, as Brian Young recently put it to me, that 'surely everybody knows that already'. Memoirs about institutions like Eton or Lancing invite descriptions of their best-known characters which tend to the condition of well-worn gramophone records and are best left to those who are gifted, as I am not, with the art of telling stories.

Being the head of a boarding school can be a totally absorbing occupation, but it helps to have a spouse and a family. I was lucky enough to acquire both while I was at Lancing. Fortunately, previous head masters had on two occasions before my arrival been obliged to quit their formal quarters. As has commonly happened at public schools, the head master's boarding house eventually became too large for him to be also a housemaster. When this took place at Lancing in the 1930s the then bachelor head master decided that he required not a more modest but a grander and even more cavernous residence. However, when the school returned from its wartime exile in Shropshire and found its feet again in its proper home on the Sussex coast, it flourished to the extent of requiring a new boarding house: and what could be simpler than to dedicate the existing head master's house to this purpose? So the head master moved again, abandoning the purpose-built residence adjacent to the school's two formidable quadrangles, which now accommodated a housemaster and more than fifty boys, and migrating to the old farm house on the land which the founder had purchased for his college.

The Old Farm House was less than two hundred yards below the main school buildings, set a little back from the drive which led up to the school from the main Brighton to Worthing road. The rambling house had been built in eight identifiable stages, at one of which the roof had been turned from east-west to north-south, leaving the old timbers intact inside the eaves. It was a relaxed, unspoilt, vernacular house, basically L-shaped. The windows of its long drawing room looked out over the Boat Field, the shape of a boat because it had been an ancient tidal creek on the estuary of the River Adur. Indeed opposite us on the far side of the drive, adjacent to the farm buildings and the new farm house, there was still a large pond. Further down the drive were a few houses for the non-academic college staff, including Frank Wood and Tom Deacon. At the bottom of the drive was The Sussex Pad and then, turning left on the main road, the rickety timber toll-bridge across the river leading to the distinguished small town of Shoreham-by-Sea: Old Shoreham with its Saxon church, and New Shoreham with its magnificent but unfinished Norman church, its harbour and its shops, the whole area bathed in the bright light of the South Coast seaside.

The Old Farm House itself was not excessively convenient for modern living because the kitchen was in an incipient third wing which if extended would have turned it from an L-shape to a U-shape, and was not adjacent to any possible dining room. But it was big enough for family meals, although it involved a good deal of fetching and carrying if we were entertaining guests, which we quite often were.

I persuaded Mrs Lintott, who had looked after us, a household of four bachelor masters, for some years at Eton, but had retired to her beloved Chawton in Hampshire, to come and see me in. She had been Mrs Warner in those days, but Mr W. must have moved out long before, presumably in order to avoid her rather strict and opinionated regime, and was never mentioned. Now she had married Mr Lintott, a small shy widower, because as she said she was sorry for him. This was an advantage both for him and for us, giving him the attention he needed and diverting some of her critical energy from me, and in due course from 'us'. Little Mr Lintott was perfectly happy to help with this and that, tidying up very small areas with very small tools. I am sure that if we had asked him to mow the lawn with his nail scissors he would affably and unquestioningly have made a start. Mrs Lintott was extremely efficient and did all that was required to run the household, and although she was indeed a strong character she was a pleasant and interesting person, proud that her family were neighbours of Jane Austen. She stayed for a time after I got married, and indeed was an almost indispensable help in our first year or two, but she had no intention of remaining when there was another lady of the house and we were fortunate in persuading Alice Caban, who had in earlier times been a children's nanny, to come and look after us and our young family.

Alice too had looked after us at Eton, having succeeded Mrs Warner there. She had looked after the Hedleys' children and had stayed on in the family as nannies often used to do, but when eventually they had dispersed Prescott Hedley asked if we might like to take her on. She was absolutely the ideal person to put up with four young, strong-willed bachelors in a tolerant, understanding, indeed affectionate and efficient way. Now her aim was the South Coast for retirement; but she agreed to come to us in the meanwhile, whilst she could look around for a small place to live, and she stayed for the rest of our time at Lancing. She was of course absolutely at home with small children, and she was a competent household organiser who would take on the cooking when Rosamund couldn't do it. She was a tiny rather rotund figure who told us that she had only weighed a pound or two at birth at Thaxted, and had been put in a glass container on a shelf in the hope that she might survive: which she did. She was a religious person – as fitted Prescott Hedley's family – but she hardly ever went to church, preferring to listen to Songs of Praise and join in softly with her hymn book to hand. Her housekeeping was methodical, and when our daily help asked her for more polish she firmly replied 'It's not my week for ordering.' Charlie and Vicky were truly fond of her (Robert was still a baby when we left) and fifteen years later when Vicky went to Lancing for her sixth form years she visited Alice regularly in her retirement quarters nearby.

The Old Farm House gave me privacy and the opportunity to meet Rosamund Hambro whenever either of us had some free time: which you can usually find if you want to. We had met before I left Eton. She was working in London in the Home Decorating Hire Shop in Walton Street, and came down to Lancing for weekends. She had previously been manageress (the only employee) of a toy department, but she had shot the manager of the store (by mistake) with a toy gun which fired a cork on the end of a string, and evidently he had not been amused. Sometimes I went up to London (I had jobs to do there, but could give up the evenings to pleasure) and sometimes we met halfway at Gatwick Manor where there was a restaurant we both enjoyed. Her mother was a war widow with a delightful small house in Sprimont Place in Chelsea and a cottage on Exmoor, where Rosamund had been brought up. Rosamund's sister Zandra was married and lived in what was then Rhodesia, now Zimbabwe. I liked all Rosamund's female friends, including Gina Hill-Wood who worked with her in 'Home Dec', who was to marry Richard Holt and whose family were to grow up with ours as long-term friends.

Rosamund and I announced our engagement on Independence Day 1962 with a view to getting married around Christmas time. But why wait for Christmas? We soon decided that we wouldn't, and arranged our wedding for 10 September, just in time to give us a fortnight's honeymoon before the start of the Michaelmas term. We were married in Chelsea Old Church. Charles Hambro was very kind to us. He gave Rosamund away and lent us his Rolls to 'go away' in. He gave her a diamond brooch which came off her dress the following year when we were at Henley Regatta, and fell into the road outside the passenger door of our car. We saw it, still lying intact in the busy road, some six hours later. The reception was in Park Lane and there were a few representatives of the media there. Needless to say most of them asked Rosamund what it felt like to be a head master's wife, to which the head master replied on her behalf in a head masterly way that if they couldn't think of a more intelligent question they should keep their mouths shut. One of them, however, asked her what she considered the duties of a head master's wife; to which she replied succinctly (and conclusively) 'Looking after the head master.'

It was evident that my predecessors had not been much interested in their surroundings. It is well known that Wykehamists are so clever that they don't even notice them, and John Dancy was one of them. The Old Farm House was decorated in porridge colour just as was my study at the school. We set about brightening it up, thanks to the wallpapers stocked by the Home Decorating Hire Shop, Rosamund being an expert hanger, and my mother screen-printed us the material for some nice curtains. We landscaped the garden, both above and below the house, and built a pond, with enthusiastic help from a gang of boys, at the lowest point. We created a croquet course rather on the lines of a

Our Lancing Years, 1961–69

golf course, which involved some pond-hopping, and we bought a Jacques croquet set from the sports department of Harrods. The assistant was concerned that we should buy mallets of the appropriate weight to suit our physiques and our style, but was baffled by our requirement that they should perform the function of what was known in those days as a mashie-niblick. But as far as the garden was concerned our stroke of luck was that my father's cousin Dossie Parish knew Fred Stern, by then created Sir Fred for services to gardening, author of *The Chalk Garden*. He kindly invited us to lunch at Highdown (where his first venture had been to convert a former chalk pit into a sensational garden) and he took us round and told us which plants which would grow well at Lancing, where rock chalk was only a few inches below the flint-laden soil. So we planted peonies, irises and hybrid musk roses. 'Dig a hole,' he said, 'break up the rock chalk and put it back in the bottom.' So we did. The members of the college domestic staff who lived in the houses lower down the drive walked past the garden every day on their way to and from work and often saw me working in the garden in the evenings. They were surprised to find a head master – or indeed any master – who actually did some work. This earned me unexpectedly (but deservedly, of course) their respect. We had wrynecks (now considered extinct in Britain) in the garden some summers, and nightjars in the woodland beyond.

Charlie arrived to our great delight in April 1964. It was soon after this that we persuaded Alice to come and help to look after him and us. Having siblings (amongst others) fifteen, seventeen and twenty years younger than I was, I had more experience of babycraft than my wife did. I was familiar with smells and nappies and the need not to cause injuries with the nappy-pin, to pull the baby's elbow towards the front in his cot, after having placed a cloth in the target area to absorb the his tiny offering when I held him over my shoulder after meals, administering a few taps on the relevant anatomical region to encourage the necessary belch. These were still the days when you had to boil nappies in a large metal container on the kitchen range, after which they were hung out on the line before being ironed ready for reuse. Throw-away nappies were just starting to come in when the younger children arrived.

I had a fine white 'convertible' V8 Ford Zephyr with red leather upholstery and a red roof, and Rosamund had a Mini which she had bought on a whim one lunchtime in London for £400 with a bequest.

Our Lancing Years, 1961–69

We had to change the Zephyr for a closed Cortina to avoid Charlie falling or blowing out, but the Mini lasted ten years until we had moved to Hawarden, a remarkable little car, although its wheelbase was rather short for potholed French roads when we economised on the ferry and drove it across Normandy, just where you don't want your lunch shaken down, or worse still, up.

Predictably, we had already decided to add a Labrador to the household. Leggie arrived as a puppy from Bradfield with their cricket team under the aegis of our friend their coach, then a housemaster there, Michael Ricketts. Leggie grew into a large fast dog who thundered over the Downs like an express train, never daunted by experience in his hope of catching a brown hare. There was a particular bush below our house round which he would often continue to chase a rabbit which we had already seen making off, dashing first in one direction and then the other, for a maximum of thirty-two rounds.

I have mentioned – and indeed described – some of the members of the teaching staff in another place. John Dancy had written me a very useful set of succinct character sketches of the masters together with notes on their strengths and weaknesses and in some cases references to their spouses, nearly all generous although I think I remember his describing one as 'a bit of a menace, actually'. One of the masters, he wrote, had married a Clarnico's waitress. I did vaguely wonder what the difference might be between a Clarnico's waitress and a waitress at some other café, but assuming that this was something I was expected to know I didn't make a fool of myself by asking. She seemed to be a well-educated person for a waitress – well-spoken and well-educated enough to make it slightly odd that John had pointed out that her previous career was not one which he considered would normally qualify one to be a suitable wife of a Lancing master. It was a long time before I realised that John, whose handwriting was not the easiest to decipher, had actually written 'classics mistress'. I suppose he felt an adjective was necessary, but perhaps it was merely that the classics in his eyes were especially admirable. Anyway, the masters and their families were an interesting, friendly, varied and delightful group of people. It may be that the useful and respectable profession of teaching attracts more than its fair share of actors and eccentrics, but that does not make it less interesting, or them less respectable. I don't think people who haven't taught in schools – comparatively large schools of course, and especially boarding schools – appreciate what interesting and wide-ranging communities they constitute. Indeed, people tend to use adjectives like 'narrow' or 'inward looking' or just 'boring', but really teachers are no narrower nor do they look inward or bore any more tediously than other professions. I will resist the temptation to give some examples.

My position as head master did give us the opportunity to meet some interesting people who visited the college. A few of them were already friends or acquaintances but the majority were not; nevertheless the opportunity of conversation with them brought something lasting to our lives in a less superficial way than, for example, an encounter with a radio or television interviewer or (God forbid) 'presenter' would have done: I had no axe to grind, and I wanted to understand and learn from them (as I hoped in a more limited way that the boys would) even if they only came to supper and stayed for a night. Even chance encounters can enrich one's experience and inspire one's curiosity.

Experience suggested to me that lectures to schoolboys on cultural topics are unproductive. A lecturer who draws a large audience of undergraduates at a university does so either because he has something new to say about a specialised topic, or because of an entertaining personality; or both. But these qualities seldom interest more than a small minority of schoolboys, the minority who are notable either for their intelligence or for their interest (often inspired by a teacher) in a particular subject. I therefore decided that I would only invite sixth form lecturers who had done or were doing interesting things, and that their brief would be to talk about themselves. In my opinion this would have provided some benefit to any sixth form at any school: but admirable – and indeed distinguished – as were the qualities nurtured at Lancing, there seemed to be two weaknesses: lack of style and lack of ambition. Now, whether style and ambition are qualities to be encouraged is a moot point. Perhaps we would be better without either of them. But that is not what I thought in 1960, nor is it what I think today for that matter. Therefore, I felt that people who had style or ambition, or both, and had (in my eyes) thus contributed something important to 'society' (by which I meant people in general), had a useful message to impart, and that (more relevantly) sixth form pupils in general were people who would be receptive.

The other side of this coin is that on the whole distinguished people, perhaps with the exception of politicians, like to get invitations: they like an audience. Even the president of a second-rank sovereign power, or a famous military general, whose command has decided the fate of millions, does not often find a large group of people who actually want to hear what he or she has to say. 'Celebrities' are a different breed: they sing for their supper. No supper, no song. But who wants to hear a celebrity? It goes without saying that celebrities are only celebrities because everyone who wants to hear them has heard them already.

President Kaunda of Zambia was in Sussex (probably in Brighton) for a United Nations or Commonwealth conference, together with dozens of other heads of state, all thirsting for anyone who actually wanted to listen to them. So I invited the President to come and talk to the school – simply about himself. Like most of the founding fathers of post-imperial Africa, he was a Christian (a Methodist, actually) and a former Scout, and he gave a very interesting talk. Admittedly his bodyguard almost shot the Captain of the School when he approached with a parcel to present as a thank-offering; but not quite.

I think the only other person I invited to address the whole school was Field Marshal Montgomery. He had visited the troops at Lancing College before D-day on the same day on which he had met Winston Churchill in Brighton and had proclaimed 'Prime Minister, I don't drink and I don't smoke and I am 100% fit'; to which the premier had famously replied 'I smoke like a chimney and I drink like a fish and I am 200% fit.' Monty remembered the occasion and, now long retired, he was delighted with my invitation: and true to type he chose as his subject 'Leadership'.

Knowing how much he had been disliked by officers but admired by the troops I told the senior boys that they might find his address naïve, but that they should observe the effect on the younger boys. The older boys reacted just as I thought they might, but the younger ones were leaning forward with excitement at the discovery that every one of them had a vital contribution to make in life and was capable of making it. This was a worthwhile experience for them, and a lesson in both leadership and history for the older and more sophisticated.

I wrote to thank Monty, whom I had always admired, and we kept up with him for a time. Retirement can be a difficult experience for eminent people, no more so than in the armed forces, a structured profession where on retirement you are firmly put on the shelf and expected to keep your mouth shut. He sent an interestingly subscribed photograph of his 1944 visit for the College, and at Christmas he sent us a card showing himself with Winston. The caption read: 'Leaving

10, Downing Street with the Prime Minister, he for the Commons and I for the Lords'.

All the other lectures which I arranged were for the sixth form, and were held in the room I had insisted on including for chamber concerts in the new music school. Hitherto there was no auditorium in size between the Great School where the whole school could assemble and the largest classroom, although the chapel or its crypt were alternatives for music. The new room could accommodate about 150 people comfortably and had a more intimate atmosphere for a speaker with an informal style. The College had been presented with the watercolour collection of Dr Morshead, who for many years had chosen to be the school doctor at Lancing although he was a skilled consultant and had enough money to live a life of leisure had he wished to do so. The chamber concert room thus doubled as an art gallery.

The most famous currently of the 'men of action' whom I invited to speak to the sixth form was Dr Beeching, who had been given the task of rationalising the railways. He has received a lot of stick in the press but he was an excellent choice for the job (he was the up-and-coming man at Imperial Chemical Industries, the biggest company in Britain) and he got rid of a lot of branch lines which had been built between about 1880 and 1910 and which ran at great cost with hardly any passengers but which nobody else would have dared to remove. Of course, if the railways had not been nationalised, these lines would have removed themselves by bankruptcy. He may have overdone things a bit in closing duplicate routes, but what point was there in keeping them when the concept of competition was taboo? He gave an entertaining and convincing talk, and we much enjoyed meeting him. I admit that I was surprised when he accepted my invitation.

I knew Brigadier Bernard Fergusson, who also came, quite well. He was a dashing soldier who had made his name in Burma by his crossing of the Irrawaddy, and I had persuaded him when I was at Eton to come and train the Corps in the way it was done. (It needed no boats and no ability to swim, although the soldiers took their rifles and ammunition with them.) He was a student of warfare – he had written a good short book on Prince Rupert who (like him in Burma) had a habit of taking the enemy by surprise and frightening them. Another friend of mine who gave a brilliant lecture, speaking for 45 minutes without a note, and not a word wasted, was Charles Douglas-Home, who had been a pupil of mine at Eton and who had risen meteorically to become editor of *The Times* when everybody still knew who held that position, one of unique influence. Maybe he inspired some of his audience with an interest in journalism – who knows? Sadly he died young.

Another successful lecture by my terms of reference was given by John Cooper, by then Lord Cooper of Stockton Heath, a leading trade unionist from south Lancashire, the very heart of Gladstonian radicalism where my great-grandfather had 'come amongst you unmuzzled' after his retreat from the University of Oxford which no longer wanted him. What I liked about John Cooper in the era when trade union leaders were becoming the 'overmighty subjects' of the realm (the National Union of Miners still nominated and selected sixty members of Parliament, who were directly beholden to it) was his reasonableness and his outstanding skill as a negotiator. I was delighted when he accepted my invitation, and he spoke – as he negotiated – persuasively about his career and his role. Whether this made a lasting impression on members of his audience I cannot say.

The only disaster – and it was a total disaster except in one important but unplanned respect – was the performance of John Wyndham, Harold Macmillan's private secretary, who lived at Petworth and was thus close enough for me to do my utmost to persuade him to come. He said that he didn't have any idea what went on in the minds of the young, and I replied that that didn't matter in the least – he should simply address them as if they were adults. (I learnt my lesson – not to press a reluctant speaker – but I learnt it too late.) He was a brilliant performer on television, answering sharp political questions with a mild and humorous air of aristocratic boredom whilst wandering around his farm and occasionally poking the pigs in his pigsty with his walking stick in the true Blandings style of Lord Emsworth. I was confident that as the person closest to the most stylish of our postwar prime ministers he would enliven the boys' interest in politics and perhaps even in a political career.

John arrived in a chauffeur-driven car and as soon as he was negotiating our threshold it was clear to Rosamund and me that he had over-fortified himself. He ate nothing for supper, during which I had time to consider whether to call the lecture off or whether to press ahead. I had learnt in the Navy that some habitual hard drinkers had the knack of pulling themselves together in a crisis and performing a tricky task as if they were stone cold sober – including a doctor who could perform an emergency operation when (metaphorically) half seas under – so I decided to avoid the embarrassment of returning our guest home unopened, so to speak, and hope for the best.

As soon as he opened his mouth his condition became clear to the boys, but with impeccable good manners they heard him through. He did tell one or two good stories about the tasks he had to perform in attendance on the Premier, including one about a fine Arab horse which had been given as a present and which he had to arrange to be transported to Britain. He discovered that this could only be permitted if the contents of the box were described as an 'ungulate quadruped'. This baffled both the customs officials and those responsible for the transport at every stage: this was vintage Wyndham. But the rest of his material was somewhat garbled, and when he came to the end he felt behind himself with both hands to check the position of the table which he could sit down on, and promptly fell to the floor between what in fact were two small tables which had been placed there, each with a chair, for his use and mine if required. He was gallantly rescued by the Captain of the School, who was in the front row prepared to thank the speaker, and by one or two others.

This of course was a pure music hall turn, requiring careful rehearsal to get it absolutely right, of the kind which seldom happens by accident. I only ever heard of one other occasion when it did happen by accident, and oddly enough the victim was Harold Macmillan himself. He sent his son Maurice to Eton where my father was his housemaster. They knew each other quite well – otherwise Harold would not have chosen my father for this responsible role; but he was nevertheless one of the most difficult parents my father had to deal with, because he always expected more of his son than his son could give, and blamed my father for not exerting enough pressure. But my father was one of those gifted housemasters who knows when it is best not to exert a certain sort of pressure on an adolescent. He also knew when it is best to give the person you are arguing with the last word. Harold was standing in my father's study, warming his posterior on the coal fire, and made to sit down on the fender after delivering his peroration. But it was one of those Norfolk fenders, with a gap in the middle, and he fell into the fire, having to be rescued and extinguished by my father. It was a coincidence that a similar fate which befell the future premier should also befall the future private secretary. Harold came to stay with us twice at Hawarden, once in 1949 and once in 1956 when he was Prime Minister: the difference was extraordinary. On the earlier visit he struck me as a pompous, monotonous and unconvincing speaker; on the second he was at the height of his powers, and he played his audience as a virtuoso conductor conducts his orchestra. He delivered one of the most brilliant political speeches one could ever hope to hear. I had made the effort to come from Eton for the weekend to support my parents on this occasion. Harold asked me why I hadn't entered politics and I told him it was because I wasn't clever enough to make a mark and didn't want to spend my life as a backbencher. He did not agree – there was a shortage of good people and he had to scrape the barrel to form a government. They needed more people like me. I dismissed this opinion at the time, but I do sometimes wonder.

Lancing Chapel also drew some interesting visitors: distinguished preachers were often our guests. The Archbishop of Canterbury came for the celebration of the centenary of laying the foundation stone of the Chapel, which was attended by representatives of all the Woodard schools. He preached what I found an impressive, even moving, and appropriate sermon. The provost told me it was a verbatim repetition of the words spoken some years before at the Durham Miner's Gala, when the archbishop was the bishop there.

Yehudi Menuhin, then the most famous instrumentalist in Britain if not the world, generously agreed to come and open the new music school which had been built on the north side of the Chapel, and to mark the occasion by a concert in the chapel in which he and his sister Hepzibah played the Mozart quintet. The concept of a new music school tickled him because he was a passionate believer in musical education, and was then raising funds for the endowment of his own now famous school. We knew that he would be a fascinating and delightful guest, but we also knew that he would be faddy, so we did some research on his dietary habits and introduced a whole small salmon which Rosamund had caught in Scotland the previous year and entrusted to a freezer in Sussex, together with some fresh fruit and vegetables and a range of very special 'home made' yoghurts. When we offered him the fish he turned it down and asked for yoghurt, as did Hepzibah; but when he then spotted a whole fish on the platter he at once changed his mind. 'A whole fish!' he exclaimed, as if he had never even imagined, let alone actually seen, one before; and they both partook heartily. The intense practice exercises and undivided concentration which he put in to the 'warm-up' period before the concert were impressive: it was clear that nothing he ever did was second best: as the concert itself amply confirmed.

The other star in the musical firmament whom we met at Lancing was Peter Pears, an old boy of the school and a friend of our musical director John Alston. He had suggested *Noe's Fludde* to Britten, who had written it with Lancing Chapel in mind. He radiated charm as well as an inspirational voice in those days when the Aldeburgh Festival was at the height of its fame. Later, with extraordinary generosity, he came to Hawarden and performed in the library at the Castle with Ossian Ellis accompanying him on the harp to support the finances of the St Asaph Cathedral choir.

Another special visitor was John Betjeman who was in his element. He stayed with Henry Thorold. He was excellent company and wrote me a charming and comical letter.

Rosamund had one particular old school friend in the area, Sally Elliott. She and her husband Teddy, a Cambridge engineering graduate and a pioneer in plastic coatings, lived at Roundabout Farm near Pulborough. We became close and indeed lifelong friends, and our families were more or less contemporary. And I had one particular school friend, Peter Hextall, a dairy farmer at Ashington, who with Barbara also became lifelong friends. Peter loved his land, which I suppose was just about big enough to earn them a living, and he was in the process of very deliberately withdrawing from the wider stage, but was active on his home patch, being for example chairman of the Steyning magistrates' bench. He had wonderfully thick hedges, home to a diversity of birds including three pairs of nightingales. He invited us to come and wander round his hedges in the autumn and shoot the odd pheasant, pigeon, rabbit and perhaps occasionally a hare or a partridge. We did this once or twice several years with Leggie: a rustic recreation from our routine activities. Peter was about 6 ft 7 inches tall, as were all their three cricket-loving sons. The impact of his strongly independent views and economic turn of phrase was gently moderated by Barbara. Their company was always refreshing and stimulating.

The University of Sussex was just getting started when we arrived, and we received a warm welcome from John Fulton its first vice-chancellor and thus, as the person who could set the tone, the nearest equivalent to its founding father. He was one of a band of remarkable people who became the vice-chancellors of the 'Robbins' universities, the first group of independent universities ever inaugurated in England, and who were mostly later rewarded with membership of another such group, life peers. The House of Lords has always been rather like a junk shop, with a more or less random variety of high-class articles in the front and a lot of equally varied rubbish tucked away in the back. The idea of improving the quality without having to add to the rubbish was a noble one, and for quite a long time a life peerage was a real distinction. Only when the upper house became a channel recruiting diverse people who could or would not conceivably have been elected by democratic methods – most of them (as it turned out) wildly unsuitable – for odd jobs in politics, with increased space in the attic for former politicians, did it become a totally indefensible institution. John Fulton of Sussex and Eric James of York were typical examples of the early batches, and moreover they were people of independent ideas. John decided the motto of his university: 'Be Still and Know'. I was (pleasantly) surprised that he felt he could choose a motto from the Bible, but he said that people who didn't read the Bible wouldn't know the context, so it would be acceptable to all. His professor of history was Asa Briggs, a brilliant catch: he became a long-term friend of ours, a true Gladstonian. He recruited Keith Middlemas, later to succeed him, as a lecturer: Keith and Susan became good friends of ours (he was a clerk of the House of Commons at the time) and were most stimulating company. Keith wrote many books but I think his magnum opus was *Politics in Industrial Society*, a study of the balance of political interests in the thirty or forty 'impoverished' post-Second-War years, and its moderating influence on the contesting power-centres, namely the state, the employers and the employees. His judgement was that this had worked well: a view held perhaps by very few people nowadays who remember the time when the whole structure fell to pieces around 1979, but forget to ask themselves how we (all of us) got along at all for the best part of forty years with a system that appears, with hindsight, to have been so dismal in its results. It is refreshing to read some modern history which paints the past as it really was.

Sussex people were wonderfully welcoming to us incomers, and as well as those we kept up with after we had left there were many hospitable friends – the Gorings, with a name to conjure with in those parts; the Donald Scotts: 'Which Donald Scotts?' one asked, for there were two, both educated at Marlborough and Christ Church; well, these were the Sussex ones; the Howards, with their magnificent house built in 1912, doomed to have only two years of life in the world which had created it; the Nathans, he twice widowed and now remarried, our close neighbours living just beyond the Ladywell.

The Chadwyck-Healeys lived at The Gote in the village of Street near Hassocks: Cherry who was chairman of our school council and Viola, he the proprietor of *The Engineer* and a former rowing star contemporary with my uncle Donald Erskine Crum. I met him often in his role as our chairman, but they were also personal friends. Oddly enough the Chadwyck-Healeys were not aware of the fame of their house as the most difficult address in Britain to which to send a telegram in the prewar era. I suppose that by the 1960s telegrams were becoming a comparatively rare method of communication, mostly used by then for 'greetings telegrams' of congratulations. Telegrams in their heyday could be sent by visiting a post office and filling up a form, but it was far more common to telephone your local post office with the text. The Demetriadis had lived at The Gote before the Chadwyck-Healeys. Thus the surname of the addressee was not the easiest start for a telegram, but once it had been settled one came to 'The Gote' – 'Give the address first, please.' It is explained that this is the name of the house. Then we come to 'Street' – 'Which street?' After that, 'Hassocks' – 'Did you say Sussex?' Then, finally, 'Sussex' – 'We've had that already, dear.' I wonder who lives at The Gote now. Perhaps they are Smiths or Joneses and anyway, like the rest of us, they no doubt have a post code.

Our immediate neighbours were the Hobbses in the 'new' farm house opposite, who farmed the land around the school. We invited each other to supper from time to time: the portions they dispensed were daunting, large plates loaded with meat and vegetables and especially with enough potatoes to feed the average family for a week; but they were excellent company, generous neighbours and tolerant of the occupational hazards of farming all round a large boys' school. This was a mixed farm with beef cattle and the emphasis on arable land growing corn, notably barley. The harvest was said to be the earliest in Britain, and was chosen by Massey-Fergusson, then one of the biggest manufacturers (known to Charlie as Mackie-Ferzucon) to demonstrate their next year's model combine harvesters, which therefore gathered Mr Hobbs's harvest free of charge. Charlie and Jamie Reeve were allowed to climb on them, and appeared in advertisements in the farming press. Mr Elphick was the only regular farm worker, looking after the cattle, a powerful though gentle person already in late middle age: I was astonished by the weight of the barrow-loads of manure he kindly brought round for our vegetable patch.

Our other friends who were pure farmers were the Hows, who farmed at Wiston below Chanctonbury Ring and sent their son to the school. Perhaps they were surprised to find a head master who knew something about their life. The first time we had supper with them we had roast chicken. Instead of carving the fowl in the orthodox manner, he simply chopped it in half crosswise across the breastbone, thus dividing it into two portions, one the front and the other the back. We were impressed. His son still farms there: I had the pleasure of meeting him recently for the first time since he was a schoolboy, at an over-sixties lunch for old boys.

Rosamund's cousins the Ellerts lived not far away but had ceased to visit the seaside and sold us their hut on Lancing beach, the 'Oreham Hut'. It was a delightful beach, slightly less accessible than the others in the area, and we could take the children and the dog for a run and a paddle if we had an hour or two to spare, keeping the buckets and spades in the hut. Leggie excelled himself on one occasion by deciding to lift his leg on the back of a deckchair on which an elderly lady was taking forty winks in the sunshine. She was woken by the unexpected shower but fortunately it was some little time before she looked around for the culprit. We were able not to identify ourselves as his owner without actually having to disown him. Sometimes we took a short cut to the beach across Shoreham airfield where an old right of way was still open. It involved going under two low concrete bridges which had been built to preserve the flatness of the grass airfield. We kept the beach gear in the hut but not the pram. On one occasion when we were taking the short cut homewards – the children liked to watch the Tiger Moths – I forgot that we had the pram on the roof rack and as we came out of the first of these low bridges there was one of those crunches of metal versus masonry which some of us have learnt to dread. I straightened out the chassis but the pram (a proper old-fashioned four-wheeler) always had a slightly eccentric gait from then onwards.

The Council wanted to build a concrete runway to inaugurate commercial flights from Shoreham to Bournemouth (from which there were cross-Channel flights) but this was strongly resisted by local residents. There was a public inquiry at which the Council hired Quintin Hogg (then out of a job because there was a Labour government) to represent them. I did my best to state the case against aircraft noise reasonably, but Hogg was a sarcastic bully and I realised too late that common sense and moderation were tactically worthless. At that moment Bill Tydd the bursar came to my aid and turned the case in our favour. Quintin, like Heseltine (whom I remembered as a boy at Moser's House at Shrewsbury when I had been house tutor), had a knack of rousing the crowd by forthrightness at a political meeting, and of getting headlines as the 'natural' leader of the party, but was never trusted with the highest office. The concrete runway was not built and the prewar canvas-skinned Tiger Moths continued to enliven the airspace in the splendid view from the college over Shoreham, the estuary and the coast.

The bursar combined the wariness of an accountant with the rigidly economical day-to-day management of the school property, hijacking the physical training instructor, Tom Deacon, as his maintenance and odd-job foreman. There was very little if any physical training as such. I cannot recollect the existence of a gym. Whether or not there was one, Lancing was not the kind of school where it would have been used with enthusiasm. The swimming pool had been built almost in Victorian times entirely on the initiative of the boys, and Tom's main and perhaps only task relevant to his avowed profession was to teach everyone to swim, including all the masters' children, for which he earned gratitude and admiration. He had presumably been appointed because H.M. Inspectors had decreed that every school should provide for the formal physical development of its pupils; but, anyway, Tom accepted willingly his alternative role, handling his staff with tact and efficiency. He ended every sentence with the words 'up from there'.

The only college servant who had been in office before the war, had followed the school to Shropshire and had returned with them was Frank Wood, the head steward, held in affection by all, ever patient, tolerant and obliging, who like Tom lived in one of the houses near the bottom of the drive. Having become accustomed to low wages in the 1930s when the school was in financial difficulties, he was willing to the bursar's satisfaction to put up with them in the 1960s; and the bursarial frontiers were not to be crossed. He was there at the high table every lunchtime, benignly responding to the requirements of masters who turned up late, or were in a hurry, or hadn't booked in, or wanted an alternative dish, or maybe were just sulking after a bad morning.

The two woodwork instructors were used by the bursar as he used

Tom Deacon. Carpentry was still regarded at public schools as a suitable subject only for those who were manifestly incapable of benefiting from academic study, although there were usually one or two clever boys who demonstrated that this was a misconception. Anyway, the instructors carried out their avowed task in a fraction of their working time and were invaluable to the bursar in repairs to buildings and furniture.

There was a little colony of men with mild learning difficulties living next door to the chapel verger, Bill Kentell who, with his wife, looked after their needs with the stern but conscientious virtues of his calling. Kentell was small of stature and severe of visage, strong in character and personality, with the dignity to perform his ceremonial tasks in the chapel services and to mentor the boys who wished to become sacristans or chapel guides in the conduct of the tasks they were to perform. He supervised the domestic life and routine of the team of cleaners and odd-job men who carried out many of the necessary unskilled odd jobs under Tom Deacon's tolerant eye.

The bursar's critics may have mocked this method of limiting the wage bill for the performance of menial tasks, but actually this was an admirable way of providing work and a sense of pride and purpose in a sheltered environment for a group of people who could not have survived in the wider world. Nowadays it is regarded as socially and politically correct to employ disadvantaged people. Of course, more of them were needed than would have been the case with workers drawn from the market, but that made the scheme all the more worthwhile. It was threatened when Jim Callaghan became Chancellor of the Exchequer and introduced the Selective Employment Tax. This short-lived and now long forgotten stratagem of benevolent socialism was designed to reduce the number of people working in services and divert them to manufacturing industry. If it had worked we would have fewer bankers now, and more people making British cars which nobody wanted to buy – a mixed blessing, perhaps. I wrote in protest to our local M.P. who sent my letter on to Jim and received a civil reply saying that the consequences about which I had complained were not part of what had been intended. The tax was refined, and the bursar's team survived. One of its members, Sam, was a keen fisherman who used to call on us on his way home and present us with a freshly caught skate. The skate is endowed with more than its fair share of bone and it challenged Rosamund's notable culinary skill. Actually, we had a mobile fishmonger who came to us all the way from Brighton, and was happy to sell us four herrings (those 'silver darlings' now virtually eliminated from the North Sea by the fishermen whose livelihoods had depended on them for centuries) for a penny each – an old penny; but his business did contract after a few years.

The college gardener was Mr Passey, who had been persuaded by the bursar to migrate from Shropshire when the school returned to Sussex after the war. Like many a sturdy Shropshire countryman he would work away at his task, in this case the lawns and paths, all day in his steady uncomplaining way. He was provided with a push-mower and a canvas sheet. A wheelbarrow was considered by the bursar to involve too heavy an investment, so all the mowings had to be tipped on to the sheet and carried away by hand. There was a broad carefully maintained gravel path across the lawn behind the upper quad, bearing a notice 'This Path Not To Be Used'. I asked the bursar why this path was not to be used and why it was nevertheless maintained, but I never received what I considered to be a satisfying answer to either question.

There was not a trace of any kind of flower or shrub in either of the quadrangles. In the upper quad the paths were in the shape of a St George's cross, and were not much used because most of the traffic (hundreds of boys walking to and fro every day) required paths in the shape of a St Andrew's cross, but they were obliged to keep off the grass. I admit that this monotonous tidiness contributed to an appropriate setting for the formality of the gothic architecture, and that actually the exquisitely knapped flint of the college buildings was not just grey but contained some white and a lot of honey-coloured stone, and perhaps I went rather over the top in planting a few trees and shrubs in the upper quad and revising the pattern of the paths. I had to promise the bursar that no additional maintenance duties would fall on Mr Passey.

The school buildings were maintained under the aegis of Mr Duke, proprietor of a building firm in Steyning, who could often be seen walking round inspecting defects with the bursar. Mr Hickmott, a true man of Sussex, was technically an employee of Mr Duke's, but he was fully employed as the foreman dealing with repairs to the inevitable multifarious minor defects of the fabric, and conversations with him about the maintenance of these flint buildings with their limestone quoins, roofed in Welsh slate, were always instructive. He also maintained the Old Farm House with its roof of old vernacular Sussex slate much of which, he said, was becoming 'nail sick', but it was some time before I could understand him because 'nail' in Sussex is pronounced 'narl'.

I was responsible for several additions to the old buildings to give the senior boys more studies, for which we enlisted the services of an admirable local architect, Mr Fleming. We discussed the designs and the economical use of space and I learnt a lot from him. I mastered the art of estimating the cost of new building work. By using some rules of thumb and making some informed guesses I could arrive by an hour or two's work at more reliable and accurate figures than architectural draughtsmen and quantity surveyors could do after spending days compiling a mass of detail. After I left Lancing I saw nothing of Fleming until many years later I met him one day in the Tate Gallery. I had one of those strange unexplained haphazard experiences which have occurred in my life only very occasionally: something made me think about Fleming in the train to London, although he had not entered my conscious mind for years: and within a few hours we met, and recognised each other at once, and had a very pleasant lunch together in the café. I have a kind of idea that when I said to him as we met 'What an extraordinary thing! I was thinking about you in the train today', he replied that had had almost exactly the same experience, but (again) after so many years I cannot swear to that.

The lane northwards from the Sussex Pad alongside the river to Steyning passed close to the tiny ancient bargeman's church of St Botolph, and then soon became a sunken lane (with no passing places) as it entered the delightful little town, which presented an alternative to Shoreham for shopping. Before St Botolph's was Pylon Corner on the left, reminding one that not all the structural landmarks of Sussex were medieval, where there was room for two or three cars to park before a walk over the Downs. There were many wonderful walks around Lancing, including those leading to Lancing and Chanctonbury Rings. The South Downs had not been ploughed for centuries until the Second World War, the chalky flinty soil being considered too infertile for arable crops; but the stored up fertility from hundreds of years of grazing combined with modern farming methods had demonstrated that corn could be grown profitably on these uplands, although those were still the days of rotations which included 'fallow' in their vocabulary. The Downs were never monotonous, with their ancient dewponds and prehistoric flint-mines and groves of yew, and above all the far-reaching views both to north and south: views of different character, gentler to the south with the Channel in the background, steeper to the north with its ancient agricultural settlements and woods. The valleys to the north were traditionally known as bottoms: north of Lancing for instance was Cowbottom Hovel and north of Chichester was Kingly Bottom. But the refined inhabitants of Sussex were beginning to find this ancient nomenclature distasteful if not quite indecent and in due course Kingly Bottom became Kingly Vale. I suppose that this was designed to help the tourist trade, and that a kingly vale might attract a more refined type of tourist than a kingly bottom.

In spite of its attractive beaches, most of the Sussex coast from Worthing to Newhaven had been spoilt by continuous rows of houses, known as ribbon development, in the 1930s, but one could walk mile after mile on the Downs hardly seeing a soul. Worthing was a pleasant town for shopping: we collected some watercolours from its galleries over the years. It was much favoured by elderly Scottish couples from the Empire – tea planters from Ceylon, for example – who did not wish to retire to the snow and ice of their native land, and I tried without success to encourage a campaign to annex Worthing to Scotland. Why not?

Brighton was only a few miles away. There are not many other towns which wear their character on their sleeve as Brighton does. How does it succeed, generation after generation, in being so bright and cheerful and stylish, and no doubt naughty, without ever treading over that narrow line and seeming to be cheap or vulgar? Of course the climate helps, but you can't put its attraction down simply to air. It was a good place to eat shellfish, and there was some fine French cooking too, enhancing the flavour of food in a subtle way which has nowadays edged out by the modern passion for massacring the flavour with spices. We also remember some entertaining evenings at the theatre.

As to theatre, these were the founding years of the Chichester Festival, rather given, admittedly, to doing things in new ways for the sake of it. It had a circular protruding stage, bringing the audience into the action in what I found a rather embarrassing way, but it put on some interesting performances. Also at that end of the county was Goodwood: Peter and Valerie Hadley entertained us there: he was one of Lancing's star classical scholars of the 1930s, and their son John then in the school was shining in that same firmament. Another summer entertainment, at the other end of the county, was Glyndebourne. We went there at least once every year, and enjoyed it rather as we enjoyed

Our Lancing Years, 1961–69

Goodwood, for we knew no more about opera than we did about racing. The Christies had created something very special in the milieu as well as the music. He had inherited pots of money, but he got it only on condition that he earned his keep in a reputable profession for a specified period, which he chose to do as an Eton master for ten years.

People from all walks of life wanted to retire to Sussex, which must have made it the most profitable county in Britain for estate agents and funeral directors, although it eliminated Cub Scout packs from the villages. When I agreed to the request of an old friend, who had dedicated his best years as the vicar of a Yorkshire mining town, to recommend him as a candidate for a living to the Bishop of Guildford, the bishop made me aware that he had hundreds of such applicants for every vacancy. In the diocese of Chichester there were even more applications. The vicar of Lancing had been appointed from one of these lists, a dream come true for his later years when he and his wife could slow down a bit; only to find that every day of his life was burdened with one or more funerals which he could not refuse to hold; a disappointed man.

We entertained our colleagues and the prefects to dinner parties and the new boys to tea parties, as well as a number of interesting visitors who came to preach sermons or give lectures or were governors of the school. Our visitors' book reminds us of periodic gatherings of the heads of the Woodard Schools known as the Southern Division, congenial occasions, and also of the Headmasters' Conference. But the position and character of the Old Farm House made it also an ideal family home. Vicky arrived in 1967 and Robert in 1968. None of our children were seriously ill except when Charlie as a baby got gastric flu one January in Scotland and had to spend a night in hospital in Aberdeen without his mother, which knocked him back. Our G.P. was Dr Riddle, the senior of three doctors who were retained, or partly retained, as the school's medical officers. He was a good old-fashioned doctor, gifted with common sense and natural aptitude in support of his training and experience. The huge roll-top desk in his surgery was crammed with unopened medical journals. Like all periodicals in those days they were rolled up in brown paper for the post, so the piles of them were more like piles of drainage pipes than heaps of paper. Dr Riddle made no pretence about keeping up to date, but he was a good and trusted friend and fortunately we did not suffer illnesses which might have required referral to a consultant.

Our Lancing Years, 1961–69

Brianne Reeve started a playgroup made up entirely of masters' children: Charlie and Jamie Reeve were bosom friends. I built a Wendy house and a small 'adventure' playground. There was a room beyond the drawing room with its door into the back yard, where I installed my carpenter's bench and tool chest, brought some two hundred miles from Hawarden by goods train at a total cost (including collection and delivery) of five shillings, nominally 25p nowadays. No wonder the railways were unprofitable and demanded subsidies from the government. In the house we had a simple model railway with plastic rails and a large clockwork engine and coaches which ran the whole length of the upstairs L-shaped passage from Vicky's room to the lavatory opposite our bedroom, Victoria to Waterloo. All the rooms still had over their doors the names of HM ships which they had been given during the war when the college was part of HMS *King Alfred* and the Wrens had occupied the Old Farm House; with the exception of one room named Ben and Lucy.

There was plenty for the children to do at Lancing, as there certainly was for Rosamund and me, but we liked to get away for a week or so during the Christmas and Easter school holidays, and for a full three-week break in the summer. We went to Rosamund's mother Baba's cottage near Exford at half terms and at other times when we could. Rosamund and her elder sister Zandra had been brought up on Exmoor, when Baba had lived in a house near the village. They had been sent to a small boarding school, Croft House, in Dorset near their grandparents, and spent their holidays at Exford, mostly on their ponies. (There was even a riding school at Croft House, known as the Colonel Torkington Memorial Riding School although the Colonel, husband of the head mistress 'Caesar', was still very much alive and kicking.) During the holidays Zandra and Rosamund were allowed to hire a horse box to go to a show only twice a year. These occasions were therefore very special, but on one of them the pony adamantly refused to go into the box. As they were struggling, Fred Marley passed by. He lived at Chibbet Ford Cottage, and every day he walked up the long steep hill to Chibbet Post and then down the even longer hill in to Exford for his shopping. He happened to pass as the girls were struggling with the pony, caressed it, took it gently round the neck and led it docile into the box. He was known to have a way with horses – he had taught his pony several tricks – and from that moment he and the Hambro girls became close friends. Baba moved to Quarme Kennels on the other side of the village, but when at a ripe old age Fred moved to a retirement home (the girls were now grown up) she bought his cottage at Chibbet Ford, refurbished it and slightly enlarged it, and named it Marleys.

There was a slate bridge for pedestrians over the ford, and there or in the field on the other side of the road the children could fish for little trout and sticklebacks. A heap of unwanted dry stone walling stone had been left against a rock outcrop just above the cottage giving us an ideal site and materials to build a den where we could cook over a camp fire, wet or fine. The ancient Landacre Bridge barely a mile away was an ideal place for picnics and playing in the River Barle; and there was a nice little beach at Lee Bay near the Valley of the Rocks. There were plenty of long walks for us. Rosamund still had old friends in the area, and there were always people who remembered her affectionately at the meets of the staghounds. My great-grandmother had lived in a thatched cottage in Porlock (its site now occupied by a petrol station) and had hunted with the staghounds, so I knew something of Exmoor and was able to keep my end up.

We visited my parents at Hawarden every school holidays and in the summer we spent three weeks at Glen Dye, a glorious sporting lodge in the Scottish Highlands, which my bachelor uncle had given me together with its grouse moor at an age when he could reasonably hope to live for seven more years (which he did – just) and avoid what is now called inheritance tax. Glen Dye, perched on a rocky terrace above the tumbling river, was large as sporting lodges go, a wonderful place for children to enjoy themselves and with plenty of room for us to invite our friends, especially those with children contemporary with our own, and to share our good fortune with our relations. The house was never occupied except during the summer. Long winters of snow and ice saw to that, and there were no four-wheel drive vehicles other than fairly basic Land Rovers. Nor was there anything like a 'subscriber trunk dialling' telephone service, and the nearest shops were in Banchory nine miles away. Electricity was produced by a turbine at the sawmill, and although there was an efficient lade to provide a good head of water, and the sawmill was not worked in the evenings, the best the system could do was to provide lighting for the lodge, the gamekeeper's house and the farmhouse. We always knew when the Buchans were boiling their kettle for their goodnight pot of tea, because the lights at the lodge dimmed and flickered. There was a fierce wood-burning stove to provide hot water for the bathrooms each evening. Living adjacent to the lodge there was a fairly basic caretaker: the second keeper's wife. For who would choose to live in the glen in the winter unless their calling strictly demanded it?

We used to put an advertisement in *The Lady* to recruit two young ladies to cook for us for the three weeks, and almost without exception we found willing and competent people, some of whom we kept in touch with for years afterwards. These holidays were nevertheless still hard work for Rosamund, and to some extent for me, but they made a splendid and almost total break from school life, enabled us to have most of our closest friends to stay, provided uproarious fun and laughter, and refreshed us for the challenges of the coming new school year. My three brothers with their families, and my sister Penelope, joined us in the shooting, as did Zandra's husband Micky. (Only Philip, Helen's husband, did not come: a Norfolk farmer has other things to do in August, even if he has time to shoot a few native partridges in September or October.) Our brothers and sisters and most of our friends had children, so there were almost as many mouths to feed in the early evening as there were at the grown-up dinners. The only cook who managed single-handedly was Debbie, a New Zealander, who was notable for travelling light: she had only the clothes (a shirt and a short skirt, to all appearances) she stood up in and a plastic bag containing a pair of sandals. It is commonplace nowadays for young people to travel the world with no more than a knapsack, but Debbie was one of the first to realise that it was as easy to buy stuff as it was to carry it around. She cooked for us for three years, became a friend of the family and came back to Hawarden for a time to earn her keep by doing any odd job that we needed. I remember teaching her in one easy lesson how to do air-layering in the garden, and she produced from one shrub a long (and still surviving) line of deliciously scented pink and white azaleas of American origin. Eventually she returned to New Zealand to inherit the family farm.

We lived luxuriously, but subject to a simple formula. No lunch other than sandwiches was provided on weekdays, so the cooks could get a rest between absolutely punctual bacon and eggs at eight o'clock for breakfast and absolutely punctual dinner twelve hours later. But on Sundays we had a fourteen-pound sirloin of beef for lunch, and I prided myself on the rapidity with which I could carve it: the undercut first, cut crosswise in thick slices, each slice divided according to the total number needed; then turn the joint the right way up, and cut fairly thick slices lengthwise. One slice of each for everyone, usually about 20 to 22 portions. Dinner was also standardised – a main course (including venison twice a week, and salmon or sea trout at least once if anyone had caught one) and a traditional pudding such as apple dumplings. There was dry sherry before dinner every evening (a popular drink in those days) and then draught beer (the ladies were not much considered in this respect, it must be admitted) and port one night (the lodge had an exciting residual cellar including several shelves of 1908 port – an exceptionally long-lasting vintage whose life may have been prolonged by a cellar slightly below the desirable 52 or 53 degrees Fahrenheit); and claret the next night. Those who wished for some pre-fuelling used to visit the Feughside Inn, where there was a petrol pump and supplies of motor lubricant – topping up the car with oil frequently was a prudent precaution in the Highlands in those days – for the traditional reason of getting oil. Occasionally as a special treat we had smoked salmon as a first course for dinner, always a fish which somebody had caught last year and which had been kept for us in the smokery at Montrose. On one occasion we came in and found that my brother Francis's setter Kerla had got on to the table a few minutes before dinner and had neatly swallowed every one of the twenty-two portions.

After dinner the washing up was done communally with a singsong in the pantry, whilst a smaller team set about less noisily using the methods of mass-production to make tomorrow's sandwiches for lunch. Everybody got four venison sandwiches, a slice of anchor cake (thus named for its capacity to immobilise the consumer) and an apple.

Alice came to Glen Dye with us whilst the children were still tiny, but she retired and we needed somebody younger to keep an eye on them. We enlisted a domestic agency in Sussex who were confident that 'our Miss Buggy' would be ideal. 'Our' Miss Buggy sounded like a well-tried hand, and we expected a perhaps slightly formidable personage of advanced middle age, but Valerie turned out to be a glamorous dark-haired young lady who had by no means even begun the run-up to middle age; capable certainly, but formidable – no. Her father had been an accountant in the south of London and her parents had decided to make the change from a tedious urban professional life to the idyllic leisurely occupation of running a village shop in rural Sussex. Needless to say they had jumped out of the frying pan into the fire and were evidently suffering from stress. Valerie did not relish the role of an

Our Lancing Years, 1961–69

unpaid shop-assistant-cum-therapist, and was looking for an alternative. She matched our requirements ideally. Capable, charming and enthusiastic, she came to Glen Dye for more than one of our summer holidays, and also came to help us to settle in at Hawarden where, as may be imagined, there was some competition between handsome young men with sports cars for her company during her leisure hours.

My father died in 1968, just as he and my mother were planning to move to a smaller house, and we felt that the time had come for us to live at Hawarden, where we moved the following year.

12

Some Hambros and Some Beatons

Rosamund's parents were Robert Alexander Hambro, known as Alec, and Barbara Jessica Beaton, known as Baba. They were married in 1934 and Zandra was born in 1935. Rosamund was born in September 1939, a week after the outbreak of the Second World War. Alec was a land agent with Fox & Sons and they lived in Throop House, a modern 'Georgian' house at Holdenhurst near Bournemouth. Alec was one of that generation to whom we owe so much: he had joined the Dorset Regiment's Territorial battalion before the war. They were sent out to North Africa as part of the Eighth Army in defence of Allied control of the Middle East and thus essentially of the Suez Canal, and he died of wounds in Tobruk, under siege by the German Afrika Korps in 1943. He had been in command of the Reconnaissance Company of his battalion, always in the forefront. Baba was thus left a war widow with two young daughters, and moved to a rented farmhouse, Berrycroft, at Ashbury in Berkshire, the first home which Rosamund remembers. Rosamund did not remember her father.

Baba's elder sister Nancy married Sir Hugh Smiley, Bt., of the Grenadier Guards. Hugh had inherited his family's fortune and they lived in a state of some extravagance before the war. They had one son, John, and lived at Froyle House in Hampshire, an ancient house which was later the home of the McKenzie-Hill family, of whom Victoria ('Tory') married Xenny, elder son of Peter and Jeannie Gladstone. This is one of those peculiar and remote family connexions, in this case linking Rosamund's family with mine, which are more significant than might be expected because of their sentimental associations; I shall mention several of these fortuitous family links.

After the war the Smileys went to Bentworth near Alton, a beautiful small house kept by Nancy with her characteristic style and neatness, where Hugh did all the cooking with similar meticulous features. At the dinner they gave at the Cavalry and Guards Club to celebrate their golden wedding all the food and wine was to be pink. Hugh's big disappointment was that the peas (and only the peas) were green. Hugh did not think I had made an entirely sound choice in proposing to marry Rosamund because as a child she had not been taught to put her toys away neatly in the evenings, and warned me of his worries in a more or less tactful way. Actually, a more meticulous person in this respect than Rosamund would be hard to imagine. But it did not seem as important a criterion for a happy marriage to me as it did to Hugh. Everything in the elegant little house at Bentworth – and it was as full of things as it reasonably could be – was always in exactly the right place.

When I had started teaching at Eton, ten years earlier, Geoffrey Nickson grabbed me to coach his house rowing crews, and he also asked me to look after his house on the odd days and nights when he was away. 'The Captain of the House', he said, 'is John Smiley: everything will be perfectly correct.' John is Rosamund's and Zandra's only first cousin. He inherited his insistence on the highest standards from his parents, but without any hint of pernicketiness. He was to become the perfect Grenadier Guards officer, lacking pomposity but always insisting that only the best was good enough, leading by example and therefore inspiring confidence and handing on the traditions of the Foot Guards, the elite of the British Army. He and Davina live in the Corner House at Chobham. Their three children, Melinda, Christopher and William, live diverse, happy and successful lives and it seems that the nine grandchildren are set to follow suit.

Nancy's and Baba's elder brother Cecil, who had already made a mark as a designer and a photographer, joined the Royal Air Force as a camouflage officer during the war and was sent out to North Africa to camouflage aircraft and military installations from enemy planes. He also found a role as a war photographer there, and recorded vivid scenes of desert campaigning, although the most famous of all his war photographs was taken before he joined up, of a child in a cot, injured in the head during the London blitz. Cecil's life and achievement is too well known, not least through his own written works as well as his art, to need any comment here; and he seems to be one of those rare figures who never go out of fashion. Indeed, two major exhibitions on his life and his work were held in 2014. Perhaps the fact that he was never trained (after Harrow he couldn't remember what subject he had read at Cambridge, and went down without a degree), but endowed with enviable natural talent and perfect taste as well as originality. He visited us occasionally at Hawarden and took a delightful set of photographs of our children when we were strolling round the Lake. We visited him several times at Reddish near Salisbury, the kind of small perfectly proportioned house people call a 'Queen Anne gem'. To meet and talk with him there amongst all his own things was a treat of rare order. I had the privilege of acting as one of his executors, with Hugo Vickers, when Hugh Smiley declared himself too long in the tooth to continue in this role.

Alec Hambro's father Angus was a younger son who made his career in politics. He married Rosamund Maud Kearsley and they had two children, Alec and Peggy. Peggy married Selwyn Jephson, and lived at Merly House in Dorset. Angus was a captain in the Dorset Yeomanry, but too old to serve in the Second World War, and he was a Member of Parliament for Dorset from 1910 to 1922 and again from 1932 to 1945. He organised the legislation which enabled local councils to build houses: the very first council house was built in Dorset: Zandra remembers the occasion when he took her to see one on an estate in a village.

Angus's wife Rosamund Kearsley died young and he remarried Vanda St John Charlton with whom he had four daughters: Patricia (Tish), Elizabeth (Libby), Jean and Mary. They moved to The Hill House in Milton Abbas and were immensely kind to Zandra and Rosamund.

The senior branch of the family no longer lived in the vast house in the valley on the site of the old abbey buildings at Milton Abbey with its fifty bedrooms and eleven large reception rooms, which was to become a school under the headmastership of Hugh Hodgkinson, a retired commander in the Royal Navy, and a member of the family, who realised that it could flourish as a school for boys who were not quite up to the standard of Common Entrance of the leading public schools. He possessed the ideal talent for this project and the school quickly became esteemed in this role. When I was head master of Lancing Hughie and I saw a good deal of each other. Eventually the governors made one of the classic mistakes to which governing bodies are prone, wanting the academic standard raised. Hughie left but needless to say this proposed change was not a success and the school after a long dip recovered its original successful character.

Peggy and Selwyn Jephson had one daughter, Judith, who married Richard Chetwynd. Tish, the eldest of the four daughters of Vanda, married Jack Woodruffe, a director of the Bank. They were to retire to Phesdo at the foot of the Cairn O'Mount in Kincardineshire, which I had inherited in a derelict state: John Gladstone had purchased it as a dower house, but there had never been a widow in the family and it was already in poor condition in 1926 when my Uncle Albert inherited it from his bachelor cousin John. There was (literally) no market for large houses between the wars (no house sold for more than £3,000 in the 1930s) and by the same token it was impossible to find tenants for them, though Phesdo was a YMCA hostel for a time. When economic recovery eventually dawned in the mid-1960s, Jack Woodruffe as a retiring banker and Tish, wanting to live in Scotland, asked me about Phesdo and I offered to give them the house if they would fully restore it, which they did. Their son Simon whom I remembered as a clever boy at Eton joined the bank. After Tish died Jack married her younger sister Jean.

The next of Rosamund's aunts, Libby, married Sir Brian Bonsor, whose elder son Nicholas I also remember as a boy at Eton, a distinguished oarsman there, who served with distinction for many years as an M.P.

Jean, who became a lady-in-waiting to the Queen, married first the Reverend Andrew Elphinstone, younger brother of Lord Elphinstone, a bachelor and laird of the estate of that name in the County of Forfar or Angus. Like its little northern neighbour the County of Kincardine, also known as The Howe of the Mearns, where the Gladstones owned Fasque, Angus had a couple of traditional names to choose from. The two counties, The Mearns in the north and Angus in the south, shared the splendid agricultural belt which ran from Stonehaven in the north, where the Highland boundary fault runs into the North Sea, as far as Forfar in the south. Andrew and Jean lived at Maryland at Worplesdon, just north of Guildford. He was the clergyman of the family and he agreed to marry us in Chelsea Old Church by permission of the rector. By this time Baba was a parishioner, living in a delightful small house in Sprimont Place, off the King's Road.

The youngest daughter was Mary, who married Bill Seymour, a prolific author and expert on the historic battlefields of Britain, who was a chartered surveyor and resident agent for the Crichel Down estate in Dorset, a name known nationally for having won a famous case against the government, compelling it to offer back for re-purchase by the former owner property which it had requisitioned during the war and no longer required. Oddly enough, the two High Court cases which were quoted time and again in connection with the occupation and ownership of land (the Agricultural Holdings Acts) for more than thirty years after that were the Crichel Down case and Gladstone v. Bower, in which I had won a case enabling me (as a result of the erroneous but enforceable drafting of the relevant Act) to evict the incompetent Mr Bower from part of Manor Farm at Hawarden. Most of Manor Farm had been requisitioned by the Royal Air Force in 1940 in order to build its hangars and numerous other installations and buildings; and on the other side of the lane houses for its officers. When the Air Ministry tried to sell the installations on the market in 1953 my father objected that they had contravened the Crichel Down Rules and they backed down, but they kept the officers' houses for R.A.F. Sealand a few miles away until the 1980s, after which they started selling them off. But we discovered this and eventually, after endless prevarication and three visits to Whitehall to see ministers we were referred to the Parliamentary Ombudsman who found in our favour. Thus we were able to buy back the houses under the Crichel rules at their then market value, refurbish or rebuild them, and sell them at a profit. So we were very much concerned not only with Gladstone v. Bower but also with the Crichel Down case, which gave me some ground of conversation with Bill, as if the battlefields of England were not enough. Mary as the youngest daughter was not much older than Zandra and Rosamund, almost like an elder sister when they were at the Hill House.

Zandra and Rosamund were fond of their grandfather Angus and remembered his jokes; and of their step-grandmother Vanda who regarded them very much as members of her family. It was Angus who, then in a wheelchair, gave away Zandra at her marriage. Zandra and Rosamund went to Croft House School in Dorset in order to be close to the Hill House. Zandra profited from the education it provided, doing well in her exams, but Rosamund was left to herself to do more or less what suited her and did not benefit much under the headmistress 'Caesar' Torkington. But both of them made some close and lifelong friends there.

One of the worst shocks Rosamund suffered during her childhood was to discover at the end of a term that her mother had moved house: she never saw her old home again, never even saw her own room with all her things in it.

I have mentioned Zandra's and Rosamund's life on Exmoor in the chapter about our Lancing years. When Baba moved there from

Some Hambros and Some Beatons

Ashbury they left behind one old friend, Rosamund's nanny W.C. Still, who continued to write to Rosamund for many years, but their cleaner Mrs Bennett came to Exmoor with them. The girls, Zandra at twelve and Rosamund only eight, were packed off to their boarding school. Baba moved to Exford as secretary to Jimmy Walker (Sir James Heron Walker) who owned a variety of properties in Somerset, at Monkham, which he had previously used as a guest-house. The girls' ponies were taken by train to Dulverton in padded goods trucks, but Rosamund's refused to get into a horse box at the station so she had to ride him in the evening all the way back to Exford, an experience she did not forget. The highlight of their summers there was visiting Saunton Sands, which Zandra regarded as a paradise. We went there once or twice with our children but preferred Lee Bay in the Valley of the Rocks, a much smaller but attractive sheltered sandy beach.

Baba and the girls were snowed in more than once at Monkham. When they moved to the smaller and more suitable, and more delightful, house on the other side of the village, Quarme Kennels, approached by a very steep narrow lane, it was even more likely to be blocked by snow. The postman had a pony, but sometimes even he could not get through. When Zandra and Rosamund were grown up Baba moved from Exmoor to Sprimont Place in Chelsea, where Rosamund and I often visited or stayed with her. She had been loyal to Jimmy Walker for many years, and they remained friends, but he let her down. Soon, however, she managed to buy a tiny house at Chibbet Ford near Exford, which had belonged to the Marleys. I have mentioned that Bob, a genius with horses, had become a lifelong friend after gently persuading one of their ponies to get into the horsebox to go to one of the two annual shows for which the cost of a horsebox was allowed.

In the early days Zandra and Rosamund used to rent the little house next door from Miss Hellens, where our children could sleep in an attic, when we went to stay with Baba, but after a time Baba managed to enlarge her tiny cottage, partly by paring back the cliff behind it, so there was room for us all there even when we had three children, as I have described under our Lancing years. We enjoyed many walks – Baba was not easy to keep up with.

Sadly, shortly after our move to Hawarden from Lancing in 1969, Baba became ill with pancreatic cancer, and in spite of treatment at the Marsden Hospital in London, and although she had been very fit and active, there was no effective cure and she died aged only sixty. She

Some Hambros and Some Beatons

spent her last months at Hawarden and her body lies in Hawarden churchyard.

Zandra was living in what used to be Southern Rhodesia, before its Unilateral Declaration of Independence or 'UDI' (by Ian Smith), by the time Rosamund and I were married. She had married Micky Lamb, who was farming there and had made a very successful expedition to England to find his bride. They were married in Milton Abbey. Their three children, Alec, Zara and Roger, were all born in Rhodesia, Roger within a few days of Charlie's birth in April 1964. By this time they had decided to leave Africa, where there seemed to be little chance of the white regime surviving for long, and as far as possible to get their assets back to Britain. They bought an attractive old mill house at Purton in Gloucestershire (the Purton near Stroud, not the one by the old Severn bridge) where Micky started very intensive pig-farming on the Rhodesian system. This enterprise was destroyed by fire before there was much opportunity to test it in a very different climate.

The Lambs moved to a lovely Cotswold house not far away at Frith where they had about twenty-five acres of grassland, ideal for Zandra and the children's horses. Micky tried to create a pond for fishing but he had not calculated with the tendency of water in the Cotswolds to find its way underground through the chalk. Like ourselves they were a hands-on (as nowadays described) family, and there was much clearance of scrub with bonfires. Mick's main alteration to the house was to excavate a wine cellar, from which mercifully the wine did not descend into the lower regions as the pond-water had, and he turned his hand to doing up and selling houses, using Alec (who was not academic) as a labourer. Alec did eventually qualify, by his own initiative and persistence, as a stone mason, but his gift was mainly for doing more general maintenance work and at one stage he spent six months at Hawarden with our estate building team, making friends with Arthur Owen and Peter Barlow. I didn't really feel that Micky had tried to make the most of Alec's talents and we encouraged him to take on a number of jobs requiring a variety of skills from start to finish. However, he has spent most of his adulthood abroad, mainly in the 'Pacific basin' and he now works as a tree surgeon in Australia with his Cambodian wife Heng and their little boy Angelo.

Zara was the most academic of her family, and successful at school. She soon got married but in recent years has been able to make the most of her ability and do all the computer-work and accounts as well as the administrative and secretarial work for small businesses which are fortunate enough to employ her. Her son Jasper is a mathematician at Clare College, Cambridge.

Roger was clever but mildly dyslexic: he went to Milton Abbey School and then to the University of Birmingham where he achieved a degree in engineering. He was poised to play a part in the widening of the Queensferry bypass at the time of the bank collapses in 2007–8 when the work was cancelled, but he managed to get an important job on a long-term major irrigation scheme in New Zealand, where he quickly made a number of friends. He had the unpleasant experience of being in Christchurch at the time of the earthquake which destroyed many buildings including the cathedral. He got out of his office safely but hastily, leaving his coat hanging over a chair with his passport and other documents in his pocket. He had hoped that the family would follow him and settle in New Zealand but it was not to be. His four sons were brought up to be as tough as he was – he was a fell-runner – and the older ones trekked and camped in the Norwegian snow with him. But disaster struck on a family holiday in Morocco where both he and his wife died in separate accidents. The four boys, Angus, Montagu, Henry and Felix, were rescued by their mother's sister Charlotte and her husband Rupert Sebag-Montefiore who not only went immediately to Morocco and brought them home, but committed themselves to look after them as part of their family in their lovely Hampshire house, their own children by then being grown-up. This extraordinarily generous commitment gave the boys the best opportunity that could possibly have been hoped for to re-establish a sense of stability in their shattered lives, the four of them living together with affectionate adults '*in loco parentis*', who immediately found suitable schools for each of them. The two elder boys are gifted academically and got grammar school places. The two younger ones went to independent prep schools.

Micky, as his early career in Rhodesia suggested, was an adventurer. Unsurprisingly he bent some of the rules, as did many other Rhodesians under the new regime of Zimbabwe, in transferring his assets to England. What better method than gold Krugerrands – as long as somebody could remember where they had been hidden. In addition to his enterprise restoring and selling houses, he speculated on the futures market, being convinced that provided one stuck absolutely rigidly to a rather complicated code of practice rather than speculating in the hope of maximising profits one would survive in a volatile investment field;

Some Hambros and Some Beatons

but of course one has to be very watchful – miss a trick and you're done for. And when your escape route doesn't work things become difficult; but Micky, an opportunist, having missed a trick, would and did by the skin of his (or a colleague's) teeth, find another way out.

He took to hang-gliding but decided it would be convenient to chop the metal frame of his glider into sections which could be carried on his car's roof rack and rejointed for a flight. He spent some days with his hacksaw in my workshop at Hawarden. Unfortunately he came to grief and landed in a tree, but fortunately he was spotted there by a passing lad, which saved his life. He recovered and was able to lead an active life, but he was never quite the same. He crashed his car on a blind bend and was in a coma until, very sadly, he got an infection and died in the Erskine hospital north-west of Glasgow. I was asked to look after his affairs, which I did under the auspices of the admirable Court of Protection, an essential institution happily known to few. Thus passed out of our lives a friend who was always good company with his unforgettable chuckle, a 'yaffle' which seemed to owe something to the green woodpecker, bursting with one unorthodox idea after another, a genial nonconformist and a keen sportsman.

Frith was too big for Zandra, especially with the children now grown-up, and she moved to a smaller house, The Sleight, in the village of Coates near Cirencester, well-placed for her to maintain her interest in hunting and riding which has now persisted almost into her eighties. She met a delightful Irishman Philip Hyland, like her (by now) a Roman Catholic, and in due course they were married. After twenty-five happy years Phil died and not long afterwards Zandra downsized to a small house in Cirencester. In spite of its strategic position as a major route junction since pre-Roman times it has remained one of the smallest of well-known towns, with a population of only 18,000: so she is in a quiet location near the site Roman hospital on the outskirts yet also bordering on the abbey park near the town centre, with pleasant walks for her terriers almost from her doorstep.

Neither Angus Hambro, the third son of his parents, nor Alec (his only son) made their careers in the merchant bank for which the name Hambro was so well known, but Charles, Rosamund and Zandra's uncle, who was the senior partner of that elite body, was immensely kind and generous in many ways – and gave Rosamund away when we were married. The merchant banks of the City of London provided virtually all the loans for commerce and industry in Britain and many in

Some Hambros and Some Beatons

other parts of the world, in the days when Britain was still Top Nation and bankers were gentlemen; until the Big Bang in the 1980s ushered in the free-for-all which over the course of the coming years virtually put an end to the merchant banks of London and spawned its unique recipe of arrogance, greed, fraud and misery which eventually came home to roost in the banking collapse of 2008.

The Hambros are descended from Calmer, a member of a German Jewish family from Hamburg who moved to Copenhagen in the 1770s, became Christians and therefore in accordance with Danish law changed their name. His baptismal name was intended to be Calman Hamburg but the clerk's handwriting must have been illegible because it emerged as Calmer Hambro. He set up business as a clothier, and it was his son Joseph who was sent to Hamburg to be trained as a merchant and who established the firm of C. J. Hambro and Son in 1800.

The Kingdom of Denmark included Norway to the north and part of the Duchy of Schleswig to the south. Hamburg, the most important port in Northern Europe, situated at mouth of the Elbe, was then a free port, an independent sovereign state in its own right, and an immediate neighbour of Denmark, which itself had a powerful navy and controlled the entrance to the Baltic. Britain had every intention of keeping her Baltic trade open and opposing Denmark's efforts to benefit as a neutral power from embargoed trade during the French Revolutionary War; but the Tsar of Russia, an autocrat of course, tried to establish the 'Northern League' with Denmark and Sweden, to side with the French. It was this that led to the first Battle of Copenhagen in 1801 at which Nelson eliminated the Danish battle fleet and obliged the Danish government to sign terms of surrender drafted by himself under fire on his upper deck. 'Send for the sealing wax' he said when he had finished, but the unfortunate messenger's head was blown off on his errand and it was suggested that in the circumstances Nelson might dispense with the wax – to which he simply repeated his order – 'Send for the sealing wax.'

The Danes were not compliant for long and the objective of the Second Battle in 1807 when the city was burnt and its new fleet again destroyed were similar; but in the subsequent years the 'Continental System' by which the British government endeavoured to blockade the trade of Napoleonic Europe, was bringing disaster to the Danish economy. Joseph Hambro, however, not only survived the economic crisis, and indeed flourished, but also, presumably as a result of his training in Hamburg in international trade and finance, became a close adviser to the King.

After the defeat of Napoleon Joseph Hambro moved to England in 1815, where he became Danish Agent at Lloyd's, already by far the largest insurer of shipping in the world, and soon started raising loans to the Danish government from London, to re-establish the Danish economy – then in dire straits. Thus began the banking enterprise which brought the family fame and prosperity as merchant bankers, especially under Joseph's son Carl Joachim who at his own request was created a baron by the King of Denmark although titles were officially defunct. Denmark was a commercial and agricultural rather than a manufacturing country: how nice to think of a Hambro saving the King of Denmark's bacon.

All over Europe the political scene had changed: governments were raising money in new ways for new purposes. It is true that in many of its most manifest characteristics post-Napoleonic Europe after 1815 was a deliberate return to the old regime. Indeed the old regime appeared to survive even the turmoil of the Year of Revolutions in 1848. But in fundamental ways the removal of Napoleon ushered in a new Europe, not least in the way governments raised and used their financial resources. The old banking families of Europe, although certainly they had supported kings and queens for centuries, had been involved primarily with the merchants of the ancient trade routes. Now new sources were being tapped by new firms who became bankers to kings and emperors, not only of the most powerful and ancient dynasties (the Ephrussis, corn merchants from Odessa, were now the new bankers to the Emperor of Austria) but also to the would-be creators of modern nation states. The Hambros supported the King of Denmark's efforts to maintain his position in the face of a rebellion in the so-called 'Danish Duchies' of Schleswig and Holstein. Later they raised loans for the Duchy of Savoy in the person of Cavour, who did more than any other individual to create the modern state of Italy.

Loans raised for governments in the post-Napoleonic era brought to bankers profits which would have been almost unimaginable in the time of the old regime. Moreover, these loans did not have to be paid in gold, as had Pitt's subsidies to pay for Britain's allies' armies during the war. Britain herself, bled white by the cost of the long French Revolutionary and Napoleonic Wars, and torn apart politically by irreconcilable

Some Hambros and Some Beatons

differences between Tories and the reformers, took a long time to recover; but there were opportunities abroad. Indeed, Britain was the only European state which serviced its entire massive National Debt, representing the cost of these wars, by direct taxation.

Carl Joachim, then, founded the family's bank in London and arranged the Schleswig-Holstein loan to Denmark and the loan to Savoy. His mother had been mentally unstable and Carl Joachim showed signs of the same problem as a young man: it had therefore been arranged that the money he had inherited from his father must be invested in real property, in the shape of a large house, with the condition that it must be passed on to Carl Joachim's eldest male heir. Once he had established himself as a millionaire banker he could afford to buy one of the biggest houses on the market with a fine agricultural estate, namely Milton Abbey in Dorset with its fifty-bedroom mansion on its quadrangular plan reflecting the layout of the old Abbey buildings, the ruined remains of which had been demolished to make way for it. The estate included the picturesque village on the hill which had replaced the old village, likewise swept away by the previous owner to improve his park.

Carl Joachim was a model landowner, improving his tenants' houses and building a village school. He also spent vast sums restoring the Abbey Church, which had survived the Reformation more or less intact but had subsequently fallen in to a serious state of disrepair; his adviser was Sir George Gilbert Scott. Sadly, however, his wife died about the time he bought the estate, and he soon handed it on to his elder son Charles Joseph. After remarrying, he preferred to live in his house on Putney Heath but continued to visit Milton Abbey for the annual family party at Christmas and to mastermind the restoration of the Abbey Church. There his effigy might almost speak as does Wren's in St Paul's – 'If you desire a memorial, look around you'. It is manifest from the interior of the church and even from the text of the guidebooks that he is still regarded with admiration and respect: the Baron was the saviour of the church and the estate. The only memorial to Zandra's and Rosamund's father, Alec, whose grave is at Tobruk, is in the church. Zandra was married to Micky Lamb there. The Abbey as well as having its own small congregation now serves as the school's chapel.

Charles Joseph inherited Milton Abbey in 1877 and although he did not live permanently in the vast house he was the model Dorset gentleman: M.P. for Weymouth and then for Dorset South and Colonel of the

Some Hambros and Some Beatons

Dorset Yeomanry. He had no children and left the house and estate as required to his nephew Henry Charles, known as Harry. But the cost of maintaining the house in state was beyond both Henry's inclination and his fortune, and he sold the property to his Uncle Everard, Carl Joachim's youngest (and cleverest) son.

Everard Hambro went up to Cambridge, entered the bank and was soon made a partner. He succeeded his father as senior partner, had a host of friends including several of the most distinguished bankers in the City, and was a Director of the Bank of England. He was immensely tall and a gifted athlete. Together with J. P. Morgan, whose office was his neighbour in the City, he leased Gannochy, the well-known grouse moor in north-eastern Scotland on the northern fringe of the County of Angus. Gannochy marches with Fasque, owned by the Gladstones, at their south-eastern and south-western extremities respectively. It became the much-loved sporting resort of many members of the Hambro family and their friends. Angus, Everard's third son and grandfather of Zandra and Rosamund, was named from the family's association with Gannochy.

Everard coaxed King Edward VII to Milton Abbey more than once to shoot pheasants. He was a generous philanthropist and he had a large, handsome and successful family. He and his brother Lewis Percival Hambro (the father of the Harry who sold Milton Abbey to Everard) were the founders of the modern and distinguished Hambro family, directors of the Bank, men of presence, gallant and distinguished soldiers, brilliant sportsmen and athletes, generous public servants and philanthropists. Their lives, together with a family tree (useful if incomplete) are described in the book *The Hambros* by Bramsen and Wain published in 1979. Angus's eldest brother was Charles, chairman of the Bank from 1925, two of whose daughters, Diana and Pammie, married the brothers David and Andrew Gibson-Watt, descended from James Watt of steam engine fame and now members of a notable Welsh family living near Llandrindod Wells, both of whom happened to be friends of mine, Andrew having been my contemporary at both my preparatory and my public schools; and David (who as a Conservative M.P. was Secretary of State for Wales) a member of the Church Governing Body and a keen forester. That Charles Hambro's son, another Charles, was also chairman of the Bank from 1972, and had a daughter and two sons, Charles and Alexander.

Some Hambros and Some Beatons

Returning, then, to Angus of Hill House, the grandfather of Zandra and Rosamund, his son Alec by his first wife Rosamund Kearsley married Barbara Beaton. The Beatons were an old and extensive Somerset family who have been traced back to Tudor times, many of them farmers, some substantially so and others described as yeomen, but no doubt they also had many other occupations. Rosamund's great-great-great-grandfather John was the one who moved from Somerset where his father, grandfather and great-grandfather had lived at Tintinhull, and he was clearly a rolling stone, moving from Reading to Calne and then to Newington in Surrey, Oxford Street and finally to Shoreditch and Hackney 'in the County of Middlesex'. He married Sarah Gove of Berkshire: perhaps he had moved to Reading with that in mind, but not very much except where they lived is known about either of them. They had a large family of five sons and three daughters. Their second son Henry Charles Beaton was the father of Ernest Hardy Beaton, Rosamund's grandfather.

There are two detailed family trees of the Beatons, one going back to sixteenth-century Somerset, and the other more simply tracing the more recent family of Zandra, Rosamund and John Smiley since 1770. Cecil was keen to discover whether there was any link between the Somerset Beatons and the celebrated Scottish Beatons, who included David, Cardinal Archishop of St Andrews, Lord Chancellor of Scotland and the prime influence in creating the Franco-Scottish alliances of the fifteenth century. His uncle James had been Archbishop of Glasgow and Lord Treasurer of Scotland. David was educated in France (although the family's Scottish roots have been traced back to the thirteenth century as the de Bethunes, landowners in Fife) before becoming Abbot of Arbroath, and he was later granted French citizenship: a Stuart thorn in the Tudor flesh if ever there was one. But the Chester Herald at the College of Arms, in spite of detailed research, was unable to find any connection between the Scottish and the Somerset Beatons.

Ernest Walter Hardy Beaton, born in 1865, was Rosamund's grandfather. He was a distinguished timber agent, selling timber worldwide to timber merchants through the international futures market. In particular he was a world expert on pitch pine, the most sought after of all construction timber, the exhaustion of which in the post-Second-World-War era is still lamented by anyone who wants strong, long-length, long-lasting timber for (especially) outdoor use. For many years there was a strong market in second-hand pitch pine – but now we have

Some Hambros and Some Beatons

reached the stage at which it is virtually unknown to practising architects, even those engaged on important conservation work. Ernest was an agent in the days when all the Siberian timber imported to Britain came through the Baltic market and most of the other imported timber from western Canada and the United States.

Ernest lived in Hampstead and had a wide circle of friends, a genial sociable man and a lover of cricket both as a player for the Hampstead club and at Lord's. He married Esther Sisson, daughter of Joseph Sisson of Penrith and of Elizabeth née Oldcorn. A family tree of the Oldcorns, who owned land at Greystoke outside Penrith, with notes in Etty's (as she called herself) handwriting, has survived. Isaac Oldcorn of Thwaite Hall (1739-1816) was descended from John Oldcorn a substantial farmer from Hesket in 1660. There were also Oldcorns in York, of whom Edward was a Jesuit priest implicated in the Gunpowder Plot and hanged, drawn and quartered in Worcester in 1606.

Ernest and Esther had two sons and two daughters of whom the second son, Reggie, died as a young man. Cecil was the oldest, born in 1904, followed by Nancy (1909) and Barbara (1912). Ernest died in 1936 so Zandra and Rosamund did not remember their Beaton grandfather, but Esther ('Ettie' or 'Etty') lived after that with Cecil in London and is fondly remembered by them. Her sister Cada Chatttock had two daughters, Tess who married John Ellert, and Tecia Fearnley-Whittingstall. We saw something of the Ellerts in the 1960s. (Their daughter was Georgina: Charlie and Roger were her pages at her wedding.) They lived at Oreham, not far north of Lancing. He was a stockbroker and managed Rosamund's investments: she still holds some of the shares he bought for her almost sixty years ago, a witness to his good judgement. They brought 'Aunt Cada' over to Lancing several times, now in her eighties and almost blind, but full of conversation. Ettie's and Cada's sister was Jessie Suarez, described in Cecil's book *My Bolivian Aunt*, who by then lived in Maida Vale – a riveting character as Zandra remembers, who had seen Colonel Fortescue in the jungle!

FOUR FERVOURS

BIRD LOCATIONS
NEAR ETON, 1910 – 1955

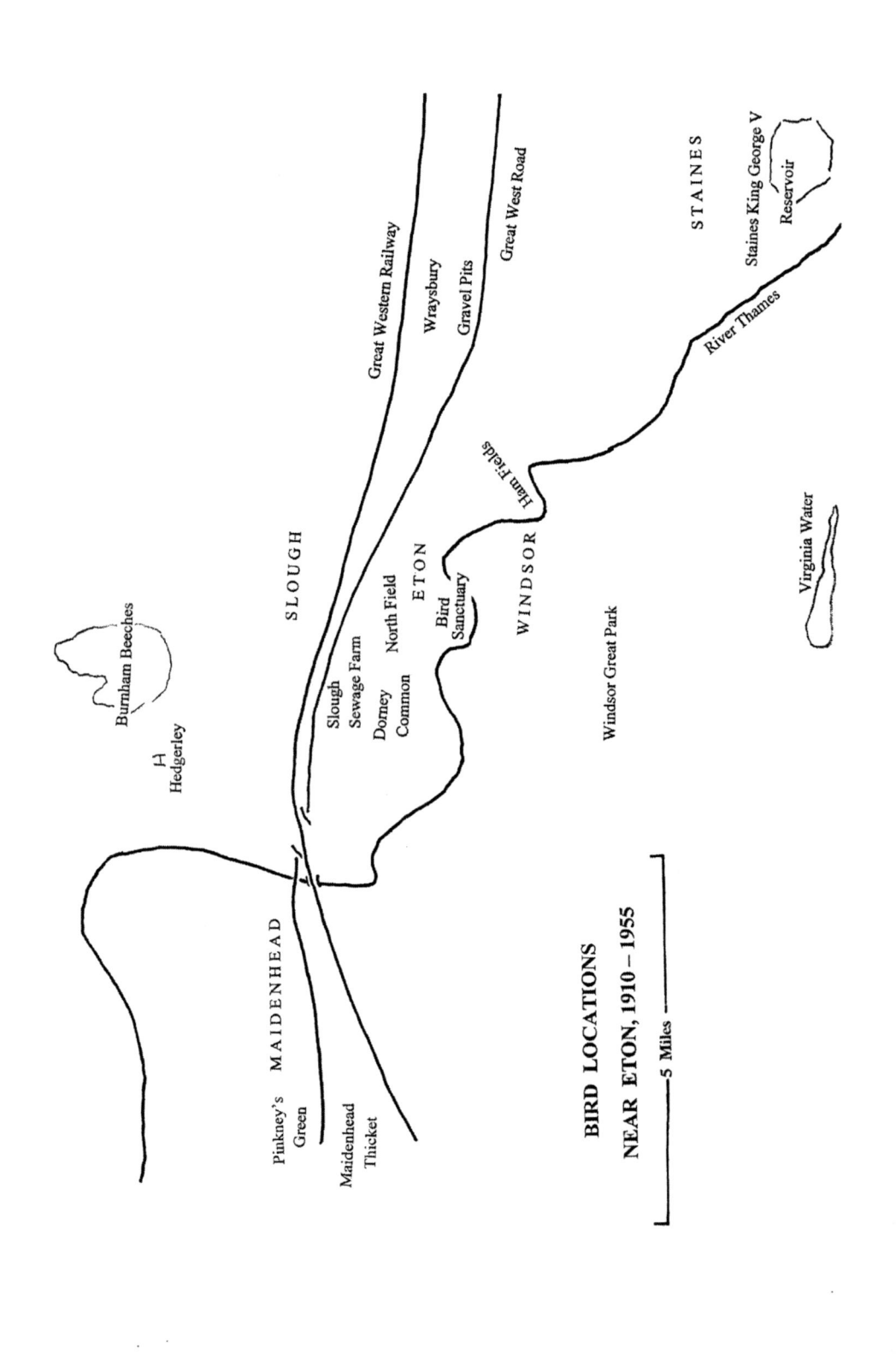

5 Miles

I
Birds

My interest in British birds derives from the fact that the area within a few miles of my childhood home, in what seemed to me to be a very ordinary and rather urbanised part of the Home Counties, was to my surprise correctly described by my father as one of the best in the whole of England for the remarkable variety of birds which lived in or visited it. He had a group of close friends who shared his interest, so that although communications were nothing like they are nowadays for attracting twitchers, a genre happily not then invented, news soon got around if there was a rarity to be seen. If my description of this area, and of a few other parts of Britain where in my inexpert way I observed the life of birds, is of interest, that is due to the sad fact that seventy years later so little of that rich variety has survived.

Modern farming is probably the biggest culprit; but there other factors too, which are not fully understood, or at least not frankly admitted and agreed to. On the other hand, the partial conservation which has gained ground over the last hundred years (since my Great-Uncle Herbert as Home Secretary in Asquith's Liberal government in the reign of Edward VII introduced the first and remarkably comprehensive government Act for the Protection of Birds), together with our awareness of the effects of climate change, have prevented or limited much wanton damage. We have already seen the advent or return of previously unrecorded or extinct species to Britain; and modern communications have produced a multitude of well-informed observers, leading to much more nearly complete records of rare visitors. Nevertheless, the losses are nothing short of a disaster.

When my father was a master at Eton, his colleagues included Eric Mayall, a wizard at finding nests. The only nest he ever failed to find was that of a wood warbler in Maidenhead Thicket after he had sat on a tree stump for some time listening to its alarm note (proving that he was close to the nest) and observing its activity. Only when he gave up and walked away did the bird immediately visit its nest in the very stump where he had been sitting.

Birds

Another colleague was Michael Bland, a charming but pernickety bachelor who lived at Baldwin's End and wrote the delightful book *Birds in an Eton Garden*. The boundary of his small garden gave on to the meadows flanking the Thames. He found all the nests by watching the birds while he was shaving upstairs before 'early school' each morning, although the most entertaining part of his book to me as a child was his chapter on cats, beginning 'All cats are bad but some cats are worse than other cats'. One morning (while shaving, of course) he saw two cats in the garden, took up a lump of coal from the scuttle, and threw it at the more offensive of them. It landed between them with explosive effect and each thought that the other had done it. He then witnessed a fight to delight his eyes. The loser eventually slunk away, the skin of its back peeled off like a glove. But to his dismay he saw the brute, a few weeks later, 'completely repaired'.

Then there was C. J. M. Adie, a bachelor housemaster with a much imitated slow nasal mode of speech. Once he stood up during a masters' meeting and made the following contribution to the debate: 'I suppose you couldn't .... No, I suppose you couldn't'; and sat down again. When he retired he built a house at Virginia Water. If it is still there it must be worth a fortune.

Another keen ornithologist was Eric Powell, a close friend of my father, a gifted watercolourist who later gave up teaching French and German and became 'Drawing Master', which is as near an art teacher as Eton got in those days. He had a magnificent five-volume bound edition of Gould's *Birds of Britain* and the three volumes by Archibald Thorburn, both sets in their different ways still highly esteemed by well-heeled collectors.

Younger than this group was Denys Wilkinson, who subsequently looked after the Ornithological Society and the bird sanctuary while I was at the school, and took us on expeditions: a truly delightful person who eventually retired to a tiny fisherman's cottage on the Gower Peninsula, the smallest house I have ever seen, with birds all round him. There we visited him and his family while on our summer holidays in Pembrokeshire.

The village of Eton itself was a remarkable place for birds – perhaps it still is. It is opposite Windsor on the Thames, twenty-one miles from Hyde Park Corner as its ancient milestone states. Windsor is built on a chalk outcrop but Eton is on a gravel bank a few feet above the level of the river – the name 'Eyoton' means on an island or eyot, pronounced 'ait'. Nearly all the boys' houses (there were twenty-five of them) had gardens, in many cases adjacent to one another, which attracted all the common garden birds, and in far greater numbers than is usual nowadays. Until the winter of 1947 there were masses of chaffinches: as was said by one who found birds boring 'All birds are small and brown, and most of them are chaffinches.' Chaffinches did not begin to recover their numbers until the 1980s, and there are still not many of them compared with the years before 1947. Nowadays there are many gardens without a thrush to be heard. In those days there were about two pairs of thrushes to every three of blackbirds. There were chiffchaffs, garden warblers and blackcaps, whitethroats and even a few lesser whitethroats, and in the gardens on the fringes of the village willow warblers and reed warblers calling in for a meal; robins and wrens of course, house sparrows round all the streets and buildings, hedge sparrows. Pied wagtails and nuthatches and spotted flycatchers and coal and blue and great tits found holes. There were green- and a few goldfinches and an occasional bullfinch, and once a hawfinch, as well as the chaffinches. There were tree-creepers wherever there was a large tree, lesser spotted and green woodpeckers, and in any garden with a pond a kingfisher would pop in now and again. There were swallows, house martins and swifts. We occasionally saw a redstart but never a black redstart until the blitz, when they discovered ideal nesting-sites in the ruined buildings of London. They spread out to many parts of the Home Counties where similar accommodation had been provided for them by the acts of another kind of winged visitor – from their own native Germany.

Wrynecks were common enough about the houses for people to become irritated by their repetitive 'pip-pip-pip', and they nested in one or two gardens most years until 1930, but successful breeding seems to have been rare. One year a hole in a tree in our garden housed a successful brood. My father reported this to Eric Mayall, now retired to Suffolk, who made the long journey to ring the babies with his young daughter whose arm was small enough to fathom the nest and bring them out one by one. After that there seems to have been a long gap until the Fifties when one or two gardens had them nesting again. The most remarkable of Eric's ringing successes was, however, that of a cuckoo in our garden, reared by wagtails which nested every year in a creeper on the wall of the house in an easily visible position. Many boys came to see the uninvited visitor, cared for by its foster parents, and Eric

Birds

ringed it. Two years later it was shot with a bow and arrow in (then) 'French' Cameroon. The native took the ring to the Roman Catholic mission, and the French priest sent it to London: he said that if the marksman had not been a member of his flock he would have stuck the ring in his wife's nose.

Once a red-backed shrike was seen in our garden but the only exotic rarities I remember were two short visits, by hoopoes. My earliest woodwork project was to make some nesting boxes for tits. The holes had to be exactly the size of an (old) penny; but however neatly one made the hole the tenants would rough it up.

There were rookeries in the old elm trees in and around Eton: it was calming to wake up to their cawing, an old familiar reassuring sound now seldom heard since the Dutch elm disease of the early 1960s, although a few small nesting sites survive in sycamores and very occasionally other trees including oak. Not only have jackdaws taken over from them, but for some uncomprehended reason even people who should know better call all corvids (jackdaws, crows and rooks) 'crows'. Rooks ate the grubs on ploughed fields. All over Britain in their tens of thousands they did good rather than harm. Innocent and gregarious, they have no feathers over their upper beaks and are a little smaller than crows, those friendless predators-cum-scavengers with their menacing call.

Eton was surrounded by very large fields, for the Lordship of the Manor had been granted to the College by Henry VI and its three open fields had survived (although no longer farmed in strips) as well as its South Meadow and its Broken Furlong – all teeming with skylarks and peewits. There were mistle thrushes; and fieldfares and redwings were quite common in hard winters. There were plenty of meadow pipits. Linnets were often to be seen in flocks when on the move, siskins less often. Yellowhammers were plentiful on posts or telegraph wires, corn buntings a little less so. These are just some of the species I recollect in and around Eton itself. There were a few sparrowhawks and in the trunks of the oldest elms lived owls and kestrels. Once we took a ladder to an elm along the boundary hedge of north field and found a kestrel's nest with its large clutch of brick-red eggs in the hollow top.

Along the river bank were willow and reed warblers, and sedge warblers rattling on in May until you got sick of them (grasshopper warblers were rare in the Home Counties) as well as yellow and grey wagtails and reed buntings and little and crested grebes, sand martins and common sandpipers, and kingfishers nesting in the clay banks of the river. In about 1936 a group of masters helped by a gang of boys created a bird sanctuary alongside the Thames, simply by protecting it from interference with 6-foot chestnut fencing. It covered less than an acre, just beyond the 'tin bridges' over the backwaters above the Windsor railway bridge. The concentration of nests of small birds in the reeds and other undergrowth and the willows was astonishing – largely as a result of cutting numerous narrow paths, since few nests in thick cover (except those of nightingales and hawfinches) are ever more than about a foot away from open ground. There were a few refinements such as a couple of small ponds to attract insects (there were plenty of frogs, too) but the mere fencing-off of the area against vermin and trespass and the cutting of narrow paths was enough to ensure success.

Just west of Eton and Eton Wick lies the village and manor of Dorney with its huge common. The west end of the common was often flooded, not technically a water meadow but in effect similar. I enjoyed finding peewits' nests, admiring their tactics of never landing near the nest so as not to attract predators, but running to it after alighting. When their eggs hatched (there were four, neatly facing inwards), the young could creep away into the cover of longer grass within twenty-four hours. There were plenty of yellow wagtails arriving from the second week of April. My triumph on Dorney Common was to identify a blue-headed wagtail and watch it from close range. There were a few duck around, but apart from mallard and teal I only remember pairs of shoveler here and there, not a rare species but one seldom seen even in small groups let alone in flocks.

The fields north of the common had been taken over by Slough sewage farm, which sounds unsavoury but wasn't. Slough was no longer a bog but a bustling new town, which owed its recent growth to the route of the Great Western Railway and the convenience of its flat but still uncultivated land as a huge vehicle park for wounded army lorries awaiting repair or writing-off during the First World War. Sewage in those days was treated by bacteria in circular tanks sprayed with water, which was then drained into earth-banked lagoons on these former fields at Dorney, and allowed to seep away. This created an ideal haunt for waders on migration, of which we saw a remarkable variety, especially in April and September. I remember being struck by the varied summer plumage of large flocks of ruffs and reeves, pristine in

Birds

April if fading in the autumn: it was a revelation to a young teenager that such exotic-looking birds appeared frequently in Britain. Snipe and redshank were everywhere, dunlin and ringed plover common, and often a few curlew, but Peter and I also saw greenshank, and occasionally the spotted redshank in its smart black plumage, and godwits both black- and bar-tailed; and green – and occasional purple and curlew – as well as common sandpipers, knots and golden plover. Peter was a much better ornithologist than I was: we saw other species too but I cannot trust my memory to mention the most unusual of them. The greatest rarity Peter identified at Slough was a water rail, a shy bird prone to slip away unobserved. (The land rail or corncrake had almost disappeared, driven out by modern reaping, certainly from the Home Counties: I only ever saw one or two; I remember one in Scotland in a rough field and another amongst the corn stooks.)

There was a second sewage farm near Old Windsor, namely Ham Fields, within an almost horseshoe bend in the Thames below Datchet. It was opposite Sunnymeads, a salubrious new settlement of bungalows for retired couples near the bank of the river, with its own station on the Southern Railway. This site would not have been selected if treated sewage was regarded as unhealthy. Ham Fields had a similar but lesser variety of waders, and many more duck, than the Dorney site. We saw garganey and occasionally gadwall there, shoveler and goldeneye, and a ferruginous duck – very rare, and not at that time an escaper from a wildfowl collection.

Ham Fields was close to the still increasing number of gravel pits around Wraysbury, which were packed with tufted duck and pochard – one could see so many thousands from the train that it was hardly imaginable that they would ever all disappear; but the growth of Heathrow (then known as Heston) has seen them off. These gravel pits were also inhabited by good numbers of the commoner surface-feeding duck. Just beyond them were the massive Staines reservoirs. Bird-watchers could get a permit to visit them, as my father did, often taking me. One needed a telescope. He had quite a large one, and I learnt to use it. With binoculars high magnification was usually sacrificed in favour a better defined image, as it still is now: 6 x 50 was preferred to 8 x 40; so a telescope was needed for any bird at all distant. Peter and I learnt to use the telescope to follow flying birds too distant for binoculars, a knack no longer necessary with modern binocular telescopes, although they do need a tripod and are awkward to hump around.

Birds

With an old telescope one had to use one eye to sight the bird, as one would sight a gun, and the other simultaneously to look through it. With a right master eye at the lens, one has to keep the target just to the left of the barrel with the left eye. This is useful with seabirds, which are often distant.

Staines reservoirs attracted a huge number of wildfowl, including species one would normally regard as sea or at least coastal birds, such as goosanders and a few mergansers as well as quite commonly small groups of smew. One could usually see a goldeneye there. All the common ducks were to be seen, and occasionally some uncommon ones; whooper swans and once or twice a Bewick's, although not as far as I remember very many geese. But the greatest rarity on the local scene was the great northern diver which turned up one year at Virginia Water after a gale and stayed for some weeks. Pinned to my prep school, I never saw it. Virginia Water had a population of wildfowl, but although the surroundings were more attractive we did not go there often because Staines accommodated so many more species.

Finally there were the Buckinghamshire beech woods only a few miles north of Eton. Burnham Beeches, dedicated to the recreation of the people of London, was famous for the visit of the President of the United States conducted by the British Foreign Secretary: Lord Grey of Falloden had taken Teddy Roosevelt by long-arranged appointment to see and hear the warblers one 'beech Sunday', the second Sunday of May, when the fresh light green leaves would be at their most exquisite. The other wood was Hedgerley, memorable for the corner where the wood warbler, with its distinctive song during its falling flight, nested each year. Most warblers tend to skulk and are identified by song rather than sight, so a beech wood with its comparatively sparse undergrowth is an excellent place to see as well as to hear, and thus to learn. But there was a thicket, too: Maidenhead Thicket, with little clearings and a few forest trees, with a denser population of warblers and many other species, but where it was more difficult to get a good view of them. This was a magical place, silent to the outside world but humming with bird life within. Never over the centuries had it been worth clearing for agriculture (subjected to 'assarting' as this was called in the Middle Ages) or indeed for planting as forest. But as part of the national effort to make Britain self-sufficient during the the Second World War most of it was grubbed up by bulldozers, which were just coming on to the scene, and ploughed. And then after the war motorways had to be built, and what more useless place could be found than the surviving part of the ancient thicket for a dual carriageway?

So, just about the time the governing body of Eton College sold the beech wood at Hedgerley which had been granted to them five hundred years ago by King Henry VI, because it didn't produce much income and was a nuisance to manage, the remnants of Maidenhead Thicket disappeared under concrete and tarmac. There were no sentimental environmentalists or historians to obstruct progress in those days.

My last view of the old thicket, before I left school for the Navy, was early on Ascension Day in 1942. Eton still celebrated red letter days in the church calendar with holidays, calling them in the school calendar 'non dies', non-days, when no work should be done, not even early school which took place on secular holidays like King George III's birthday. So my father and I got up early and met Denys Wilkinson at 4 a.m. On an exquisite May morning he showed us a whinchat's nest (the male was perched on the fence just above it); and then in the Thicket the nest of a hawfinch (a rarity), and of a nightingale. These are the only two species which do nest quite a way into a thick bush – a good arm's length. It seems appropriate that a bird so secretive that it will only sing in darkness should hide its nest from prying eyes more deeply than any others.

My father and I had a successful expedition one afternoon to see Dartford warblers on Chobham Common, which was admittedly more, although not much more, than 'a few miles' from Eton. We knew roughly where to look amongst the heather and gorse bushes, and lo and behold quite soon after we arrived we got a splendid view of a nesting pair. There is still a small part of the common left, although here too there was a handy strip of undeveloped ground for a new road, in this case the M3.

This visit to Chobham Common hardy deserves to be called an expedition, but during two summer holidays of 1937 and 1938 we did go on expeditions in Wales in the hope of seeing two of the then rarest species in Britain, the red kite and the chough. The kite was reduced to two or three pairs, all in Breconshire, and under constant threat from egg collectors. There were now two round-the-clock guardians, because the raiders had successfully started a fire to divert the solitary warden the previous year. My father knew of the clergyman who was supervising one of the habitats. We were to walk over the moorland for most of the day in the hope of seeing a kite, but if we failed he might be able to put one over us at teatime. 'Keep looking up,' he said. 'Don't look down to watch your step; and remember – look for the forked tail.' To me a fork was a thing you used at meals or in the garden, and I hopefully misidentified several buzzards before my father explained. We walked a long way and we did see a variety of predators and moorland birds that day: it would have been a satisfying expedition even without the kite; and we saw no kite. At teatime the clergyman, a neat figure small of stature, told us where to sit and walked up to a spinney above his vicarage: and sure enough, out flew a kite, its forked tail, slim profile and distinctive call all evident. I didn't see another until the 1980s when there were several haunts in mid-Wales. After a few more years one could be sure of seeing one or more near Plunlymmon, and at least once a year I used to take a long cut with that objective. Extraordinarily, a red kite had been caught in a carrion-baited crow trap at Glen Dye in Kincardineshire in April 1929, the first seen in Scotland since 1919 and the last for very many years thereafter The head keeper Duncan Fraser recognised it for what it was and told my uncle, who owned the moor. He had it stuffed, and there in the hall of the Lodge it has stood in its glass case ever since.

The year after our kite expedition our summer holiday was near Tenby and we made a journey westwards and then north along the coast of Pembrokeshire to search a particular length of cliff with our binoculars. We walked a long way, but eventually we were successful and spotted several choughs, with their unmistakable red beaks and legs, hopping around the cliffs. I did not see another until the turn of the century, by which time they had gradually spread to chosen areas northwards as far north as Holyhead. There I noted the spectacular vertical falls in their flight which I do not remember from those far-off days before the war.

Red kites are quite common now, having recovered their numbers in the Cambrian Mountains before eventually extending their range in all directions. Introduced birds have also established successful colonies in parts of England. A close friend of my father, Colonel Gilbert of Bishopstone near Hereford, tried to introduce some from Spain in the 1930s, but was not successful and was prevented from persevering by the outbreak of the war. Choughs are on the increase, but by no means common, as they must surely have been when their striking colours made them popular heraldic symbols.

Seabird populations were to the amateur observer much the same as

Birds

nowadays, except that the fulmar was more northern and localised. We saw the commoner gulls, and terns with their impressive vertical dives, puffins, guillemots and razorbills around Pembrokeshire and of course cormorants, all in plenty; but we were not very strong on skuas. During the war, parts of the coast were blocked off to the public, as were sensitive sites like Staines reservoirs holding London's water supply; on the other hand there were many other areas where unaccustomed peace and quiet prevailed. Even Eton itself with the lack of road traffic became more like the village it had been for centuries. Corn buntings and yellowhammers were common along the roads, their calls and songs once more audible to the walker or bicyclist. There were plenty of kestrels and sparrowhawks, but the larger predators were few and far between and buzzards were confined to remote moorland areas, although quite common there.

The most memorable bird expedition of my life was arranged by Kenneth Fisher, a biologist who was then head master of Oundle but had been formerly a colleague of my father at Eton, one of the group I have mentioned. His son James (who as a boy was in my father's house) was to become a famous ornithologist. Kenneth knew the remarkable Jim Vincent, who was warden of Hickling Broad in Norfolk, and arranged for him to take us on a three-day trip in 1941. He knew every corner of the broad and took us round in his quant, the local type of punt. He told me it might be a day or two before I could accustom my ears to hearing a bittern; and so it was: it was not until the third day that I heard one. The 'boom' is so deep that the human ear will not normally pick it up, but once heard it is never forgotten. Bitterns were very rare, but there were a number at Hickling. They had bred in Norfolk since 1911 and by the 1940s they were also breeding in Suffolk and Cambridgeshire, where there were large surviving areas of fen, but elsewhere they were rare, usually as winter visitors. Once I had heard one, Jim said he would catch it for me. He walked through the reeds holding his quant pole horizontally at waist height, and as he approached the bittern it characteristically froze, its thin head vertical so as to look like a reed. He gently pressed it down with the pole and took hold of it, one hand at its neck and the other holding its feet, and handed it to me with its sharp claws and its fearsome beak waving around. I held it in my two hands very much at arm's length, in which pose Kenneth photographed me before we returned it to its haunt. Once having become accustomed to the call one heard it all day in all directions. The next time I heard a bittern was, to my surprise, in August 1971 in Anglesey when we were on holiday on the edge of Maelog Lake, where there are several acres of reeds. It became evident that nobody else had heard it, and since its habitat was small I decided not to report it. I heard it again the next year or two, when we were in the same house. A few years later its presence became general knowledge to the ornithological world.

The other especially memorable event of that expedition was seeing the male marsh harrier, returning from the hunt, throw his quarry to the hen bird in mid-air, who caught it above the nest site. This is a spectacular sight at any time, but the species was as rare in Britain as the red kite, if not indeed even rarer. Volume 3 of *The Handbook of British Birds*, published in 1939, reports one to four pairs seen in Norfolk between 1927 and 1936, in 1937 four pairs seen but then four adult birds 'disappeared' and no young reared; in 1938 two pairs, but only one young reared. So they really were on the brink.

On the third day we saw the third species we had been hoping for, the bearded tit. Being so small it is hard to find in an extensive area of fenland, although it nests near the edge of its reed bed; but when you see it, both the bird and its nest are distinctive and iconic like the work of a Chinese artist; and being unaccustomed either to see or to be seen by humans they were likely to twitter around a small area until you wondered whether they were showing off.

Hickling was a haunt for many duck and, especially at migration times, for waders. There were reed warblers and buntings and a few grasshopper warblers, the first I had come across: their range has now much increased. There were masses of coots and moorhens, and each lunchtime Jim would gather a dozen or so eggs, always taking them from incomplete clutches to guarantee their freshness, and leaving one egg in the nest so that the unfortunate bird should not be discouraged. They were delicious boiled for a couple of minutes on our campers' stove.

I already had the enthusiasm and smattering of knowledge to be able to enjoy wandering with a pair of binoculars, which was just as well throughout my teens during the war when my parents could not get away and I was sent off on my own. I particularly remember visits to my aunt and uncle at Hawarden on the border of north-east Wales, overlooking the Cheshire plain, which was later to become our home. There were undulating meadows, mixed farming, parkland and mature woodland there. My most vivid memories are of the masses of willow warblers and the wonderful bird populations of big trees, especially oaks. The willow warblers had been common before the war, but had proliferated as a result of the increase of rough ground and unmown grass: you could never get out of the sound of their song which 'hath a dying fall'. Every big oak tree had its resident population, a proletariat of blue and great tits, chaffinches, robins and wrens, but also coal tits, gold-crested wrens and tree-creepers, often nuthatches and sometimes greater spotted woodpeckers, as well as its regular callers such as starlings, blackbirds, song thrushes and mistle thrushes and others more seasonal or occasional such as chiffchaffs and spotted flycatchers, although these last seemed to prefer holes in masonry rather than woodland. I do not claim that every oak tree had this entire collection, but the impression was of a plentiful and largely visible population, a bustling community of birds especially in the upper branches, such as one never sees nowadays. The taller hedges and rough areas were much the same, with finches and dunnocks and in the wetter areas both marsh and willow tits. We used to go further west on expeditions every year, especially to Llangollen, to see the pied flycatchers nesting under bridges. They like oak woodland and they did come to Hawarden during a few postwar years, nesting in boxes quite high up on the trunks of big trees, needing a light ladder for inspection. One of my delights was to find the nest of a long-tailed tit in a holly tree – in so shady a site, incidentally, that I swear the same branch, which had a nest for a number of continuous years, is still there, and much the same shape, seventy years later. Another special pleasure was to find a goldcrest's nest on a cedar branch. In the spring and early summer there were all the common warblers. The lesser spotted woodpecker was scarcer, but a regular resident. Of all the birds we miss nowadays the most notable was the call of the cuckoo, for it seldom now gets north of the Midlands: I remember a Canadian friend saying to me with astonishment – 'My goodness, that sounds just like a cuckoo clock!' (I did not feel I could explain, as he had just jumped off a wall into a bed of stinging nettles.) There were no resident woodcock, although they were not uncommon by the 1970s and '80s.

There were green woodpeckers fond of the anthills, and tawny, little and occasional long-eared owls, and barn owls roosting and nesting in the barns which gave on to open country, though one did not expect to see them out of doors by daylight. There were two wonderful rookeries in elm trees. Kestrels and sparrowhawks were common, but no larger predators. On the lower ground towards the River Dee there were coveys of partridges, not with twenty or more young as in Suffolk but commonly with eight or ten. There were hundreds of wheeling peewits, some snipe and a few little snipe, large flocks of redshanks and golden plover and occasional curlews in winter, for we were near the Sands of Dee.

During the early years of the war I became familiar with Glen Dye in Scotland. The best known of the eastern Glens, Glen Isla, Glen Clova and Glenesk, although their water comes from the Highlands, are south of the Cairn O'Mount. North of that you are in the Highlands proper, having crossed the Highland Boundary Fault. The smaller rivers, including the Water of Dye, flow into the Dee, and further north into the Don. The charm of Glen Dye is that it forms the complete catchment area, south and east of Mount Battock, of the tumbling and often savage river bearing its name. A mere six or seven miles from its source the Dye is crossed by a splendid single-arch stone bridge on one of the most important military roads constructed by General Wade to keep the Scots in order (the Black Watch were to be the police force) after the rebellion under Bonnie Prince Charlie in 1745. A few miles down the Glen, now a forest at this lower level, the Dye joins the Feugh which falls in to the Dee at Banchory.

In one energetic day you can walk the whole length of the Dye from the little burn issuing from Mount Battock. The upper reaches glisten with gold, mostly fools' gold but also some of the real stuff for those who have the patience to pan it (bearing in mind that in Scotland gold belongs to the Crown). It comes from the boundary fault, a steep cleft called the Gruiggal of Dye at that spot, near some still visible remains of the smugglers' old whisky road. On these higher reaches of the Dye you will see dippers, and teal with their large broods of tiny ducklings, little squiggling bunches nestling together in the water (as eider duck and scaup do on the sea coast). Even the ubiquitous pied wagtail is a pleasure to watch in these surroundings. Lower down you can observe the dippers running along the bottom. At the same season of the year you may see the ring ouzel, usually seen in Scotland above 1,000 feet, perched on a post or an old wall; and newly arrived wheatears darting low above the heather, outshining the resident meadow pippets and twites.

Ptarmigan are not seen below about 2,000 feet. Off and on there are

Birds

one or two pairs on Mount Battock, which rises to 2,500 feet, and for a few years there was a pair a couple of miles to the south on Meluncart, quite near the Cairn O'Mount road, which hardly touches the 2,000 mark – only, I think, when the Mount Battock birds have had several good seasons and declare their territory full. There are no other ptarmigan until you come to stately Lochnagar, visible in the distance on a fine day; and beyond it the Cairngorms. The ptarmigan are notoriously tame, although (or perhaps because) their camouflage, whether in winter or summer, is impressive. Golden plover and occasionally dotterel nest on the same high ground. Then there are the grouse, always a treat to hear and to see, each cock with scarlet comb and white feathered legs ostentatiously guarding his hard-won territory, the very model of a highlandman sentry. Lower down the banks of the river the black-game take over, in the forest and the forest edge. Very few people ever found a greyhen's nest, often concealed at the foot of a tree, until it became possible to monitor their positions by wireless. The cocks are strikingly black (or very dark blue) and white, when seen either at the leck in the spring (if you can drag yourself out of bed early enough); or when you have the good fortune to see a large flock in winter taking off one by one or in small groups against the snow, until you wonder how there can be so many in the whole of Scotland. The capercaillie did quite well until the 1980s, but they did fluctuate and became scarce every few years. If you could explore the woods and find out more or less where to look, you would have a good chance of seeing a cock on the ground at any time of year, and with luck you might see a hen in August or September, smaller and tawny and rather secretive, looking after her brood after they had left the nest.

Until predators made their remarkable comeback in the 1980s, the large moorland birds most often seen roaming over the heather were barn owls, so visible because of their white plumage. These nocturnal birds had to resort to daytime hunting whilst their chicks' appetites were growing, and they ranged far and wide from their nests. Often we would see short-eared owls, majestic and casual as they roamed low over the ground on the lookout for a meal. Nowadays there are more short-eared, but hardly any barn owls. Kestrels were common. One would see a merlin, often passing through the same area at approximately the same time on successive days, but it was some time before I was told by an expert that the cock bird tended to follow a more or less regular route over the moor each day when he, too, was hard put to supply a growing brood. On one memorable occasion we came round a bend on the moorland road and saw a golden eagle sitting on a post a mere twenty yards away. It was as surprised as we were: it was some seconds before it lumbered away. We used to see eagles, circling very high, on migration, mostly travelling westwards. For a few seasons there were a pair of peregrines nesting on the impressive rock outcrop of Clochnaben, but they were too much disturbed by walkers to this famous and accessible landmark to feel safe there.

    The expert who told me about the merlin, and who found a merlin's nest in a tree, right on the edge of the moor, and studied this unusual but not unique behaviour, was Nick Piccozzi, whose main task was the study of hen harriers, which had been extinct in Scotland except in the Northern Isles and Outer Hebrides until their remarkable but short-lived comeback. After a few years of recovery it became evident that male birds were in the minority, and Nick discovered and studied their polygamy. The male is the smaller bird in all species of hawks: it hunts different prey from the female, thus enabling the two adults' combined efforts to provide enough food to rear a brood of greedy chicks during their last week or two at the nest. The hen harrier nests on the ground, and tends to use the same site, or a site in the same general area, from year to year. The male, with a much more distinctive plumage, roosts in trees perhaps two or three miles from the nest: this remoteness is perhaps connected with its predilection for more wives than one, should there not be enough males to go round. This was seen as an advantage when these predators, not very long after their recovery, were again reduced to just a few birds: in those circumstances uneven numbers of males and females could be fatal to most very rare species. Yet with the hen harrier it was a mixed blessing. As the chicks grew in the nest, the female would wander off in search of young grouse, a species too big for the male's attention, then at their most vulnerable stage. Nick thought she found her young tiresome – greedy and aggressive – and amused herself by killing more young grouse than she need have done, leaving dead chicks around the nest site. This was infuriating for gamekeepers, especially in a year when there was a fine balance as to whether there would be enough birds to justify a shoot, especially a driven shoot. They had to sit and watch their livelihood being wantonly destroyed. In a bad year there were very few grouse chicks for the taking; and in a good year there were so many grouse that it was difficult to shoot enough of them in the short season to prevent the

Birds

disastrous ravages of disease resulting from overcrowding and starvation in the winter. But a marginal year was different. The destruction of just a few broods could tip the balance. The economy of country areas in the Highlands depended on the grouse. The shooting brought trade to the towns as well as the countryside, and ensured the employment of keepers, just about the only employment apart from forestry and marginal farming.

Anyway, a few years after the hen harrier's remarkable recovery, it was in trouble again, and perhaps nobody quite knows why, although a lot of people think (or say) they do; which is not the subject of this essay. A wide variety of other predators, virtually unknown in Britain for a century, are now quite frequently to be seen. One of the best known is the osprey with its sensational method of catching fish. We visited Boat of Garten two or three times to see the first pair nesting in Britain after it had been extinct. It has now spread as a breeding bird to many areas.

I saw crossbills but never mastered the woodland birds of eastern Scotland, nor became expert at the seabirds; but stomping the northern and western coasts in May brings many rewards apart from the scenery, including the magical motionless flight of fulmars, which I had first seen in Skye in 1946 while still in the Navy when their range was confined to the far north of Britain – when I also saw the dainty buoyant red-necked phalarope near Lerwick in the Shetlands, and gannets from the Bass Rock diving en masse. From the deck of a ship, well above them, which happens to pass near a shoal of fish, one has the rare opportunity to watch the gannets in their hundreds ruthlessly employing their binocular vision both above and below water. Many years later we watched a black-throated diver at its nest-site on the west coast. Only once did I ever see a red-throated diver and that was off Aberffraw beach in Anglesey.

Our bible was *The Handbook of British Birds*, written by four acknowledged experts, Witherby, Jourdain, Ticehurst and Tucker, and published in five volumes between 1938 and 1941 at the price for the set of £5, the equivalent of about £250 in today's values; but books, like food, are relatively much cheaper nowadays. Every species is illustrated in colour in the *Handbook* (the plates of geese were specially painted and donated by Peter Scott) and there are black and white plates to show comparisons – for instance of the wing-bars of waders, often the best means of identification. There are line drawings giving exact

Birds

measurements of rare variants by way of sub-species or geographically separate species, some of which classifications have since been modified, and in wide-ranging and oceanic species there are diagrammatic maps. There is a chart at the beginning of each volume of the Song Periods of British Birds, in some cases with dots, then dashes, at each end of their calendar as well as the continuous line of the main period of song: so if you think you have heard a Dartford warbler in January you can easily look it up and see if anyone else has. In the 1945 reprint of which I am a proud possessor – a handsome gift from my father – there are already just over fifty closely printed pages of additions and corrections (for example two additional sightings of the black-necked grebe, both in Cheshire). There is a magnificent Systematic List of British Birds at the end of volume five, and indexes of both Latin and English names. Yet this is a wonderfully accessible book. Each description begins with 'Habitat' and then goes on to 'Field-characters and General Habits' in which the passages in italics are often the key to identification – in most cases these passages are to be looked at first. After these two sections, each species is described under Display and Posturing, Breeding, Food, Distribution and Distribution Abroad; and finally there is an exhaustive scientific description in smaller print. Every paragraph is initialled by the one of the four authors.

You can't carry the *Handbook* around like a pocket book, but it is usually just as handy to look up a bird when you get home as it is to fumble with a small volume in the rain and the wind. The arrangement makes it easy to find what you want in a matter of seconds, and then to study it in detail if you feel the need.

There are a host of beautifully illustrated modern books on British birds, most of them giving enough information for the average enthusiast, and many of them single volumes; but I still find myself turning to the *Handbook* when I am in doubt or in need of confirmation. One only has to look at the books which were available before the advent of the *Handbook* to appreciate what a revolution it wrought in our knowledge of birds. Since then, that knowledge has been refined and expanded by thousands of specialised studies, yet as the general reference book it still holds sway. The one modern and generally accessible book of supreme interest – and this to many others than ornithologists, for it is an 'easy read' – which I cannot resist mentioning is *Bird Sense* by Tim Birkhead, published in 2012. It gives the answers as far as they are known to many fascinating questions which though fundamental

Birds

to an understanding of bird behaviour were not even being asked in 1938 when the *Handbook* began publication, as well as to some which were. You only have to watch a bird on the lawn, dashing from place to place – the early bird catching the worm – to wonder how it finds it. And nowadays we know that godwits travel eleven thousand miles on a straight course (a great circle) out of sight of land on every migration, and we're just getting an inkling of how on earth they do it.

2
The Landscape Garden

The words 'landscape gardening' cover a multitude of sins nowadays, including the white vans of small businesses, one-man-bands who used to be called jobbing gardeners, doing occasional or regular work for people who want their gardens kept tidy. But I have chosen 'The Landscape Garden' for my title, although my essay has nothing to do with this modern kind of garden maintenance; because I was fortunate enough to inherit a site which it seems to fit, and which I have had the opportunity to try to enhance and develop over the course of more than forty years.

I have felt myself constrained by two opposite forces. The first is the history of the mansion house and of the Old Castle in its grounds. The house is a 'historic house' known as Hawarden Castle and listed Grade I, rather unusually not for its architectural merit which is undeniably not Grade I, but for its historical associations. The Old Castle is a scheduled monument. The two most notable episodes in its history involved Llewellyn the Great, last Prince of Wales, on Palm Sunday 1282, and secondly the sieges, skirmishes and bombardments of the civil war which rent Britain in the 1640s.

The setting of these two buildings, in the shape of the garden and landscape around them, demands respect for their history. Being a historian myself, I believe that only history can explain what we and the world around us have become; so this historical constraint is no constraint to me.

The opposite constraint has been imposed by the rapidly changing environment of these two buildings in the form of a vast increase of population in the ancient and formerly agricultural parish of Hawarden, a trend which has accelerated in the last fifty years and continues to do so. More than 60,000 people live within a couple of miles of these castles. The old central part of the estate still consists of agricultural land and woodland, with the old part of the village to the north-west of it. This undeveloped land – the farmland has not been farmed intensively nor the forestry ruthlessly exploited – is now

The Landscape Garden

an oasis in the midst of an industrial and residential area. If this oasis with its historic flavour is to be conserved, it must respond positively to the challenge of a vastly increased population. Road traffic and industrial and residential development must be excluded, both actually and visually – as must, as far as possible, the noise they generate. Sadly, we cannot banish the effect of the street lighting which creates 'light pollution' or in old-fashioned phraseology 'obscures the luminosity of the galaxy'.

So there is plenty to be excluded. On the other hand, people who want to enjoy this oasis should be able to do so in a way which allows them to experience its relative peace and quiet and its fields, woodlands and wildlife. This inevitably reduces the degree of privacy, or rather the area with some degree of privacy, which those who live in the big house can enjoy, but I have tried to balance this by including in the immediate landscape of the big house (or, if you like, its own landscape garden) a few acres of parkland to the south of the house and the grounds of the ornamental lake which have anyway been enclosed as an entity since it was enlarged in the 1920s.

Thus several elements have been included within the landscape garden in a cohesive enclosure which I would like to call a paradise. Fortunately that word, although applied first and foremost in our national culture to the Garden of Eden, has been very widely used over the centuries to describe many kinds of beautified and usually enclosed spaces, not only of mythical or imaginary but also of very real and immediate character. The elements of this space are Hawarden Castle: the Old Castle and its grounds; the parkland immediately to the south; and finally, reached by crossing that parkland, the lake and the surrounding trees in its enclosure.

My father was a skilled and knowledgeable gardener, from whom I learnt much as a child and indeed as an adult. My mother was an artist, as well as being an immensely industrious 'hands on' gardener as my father was; but whereas he had developed his skill and his taste from his family and then from his colleagues and contemporary enthusiasts, she was more idiosyncratic, developing enthusiasms for particular kinds of plants – not necessarily rare or unusual ones – and then mastering the art of locating them in the right spots, cultivating and propagating them, and making some of them the subjects of her wonderful free-flowing drawings and screen-prints. She had strong ideas about garden design, which I admit did not always

The Landscape Garden

appeal to me, but which reflected her ideas in her own compelling way.

My Uncle Albert and his unmarried sister Aunty Kith introduced organic gardening when they came to live at Hawarden in 1936, and my parents followed suit. It has been gospel to me that the quality of soil depends on any goodness removed from it in the form of weeds or swept leaf-litter or grass-mowings or turf or ash from bonfires being returned as compost or leaf mould a few years later. We collect almost no grass-mowings now that it is possible to chop them so small in the mower that they will scarcely be visible if they are left where they are cut. We only sweep up leaves where necessary, knowing that trees and shrubs will gather them unto themselves as their essential diet during the autumn. For example, once azaleas have grown to about four feet in height they will create eddies to collect their own leaf-litter as it blows around in the west wind. Any leaves we do sweep up are used when rotted down to encourage the smaller peat-loving plants.

The bible for organic gardeners in those days was Mrs Balfour's book *The Living Soil*. We still have our copy and I am proud to think that we were one of the earliest gardens to have become 'organic' and to have remained so for nearly eighty years. This does not prevent us from occasionally restoring lime to the soil here and there where it is needed, or introducing organic fertilisers such as bone meal. Nor do we religiously avoid all 'non-organic' modern sprays for weed control in strict moderation where it seems sensible: not on beds, for example, but on gravel paths where necessary. But it is painful to see organic matter being carted away from gardens and treated as rubbish, probably mixed with rejected bits of plastic, rather than being recycled as living soil.

Similarly in the permanent grass of the old parkland we insist on natural manure being deposited or returned where it is grazed, and we have strict rules against blanket chemical spraying. Our fairly modest in-hand farming is strictly organic and 'eco-friendly' as is our tree-planting of spinneys and shelter belts on farms and our hedge maintenance. It is annoying to read or hear regular announcements year after year in the media that someone has discovered that organic food is no better for us than non-organic, missing the point that the intention is not merely to produce healthy food but first and foremost to conserve the planet and to retain or recover some of the diversity of our wildlife.

My father taught me the basics of gardening including propagation

The Landscape Garden

by cuttings. He was not an artist but he showed me that the best way to design a garden was by getting a bird's-eye view from an upper floor. This converted a two-dimensional into a three-dimensional view and created a stronger and more harmonious composition than one from ground level. My mother taught me the rudiments of how to compose a picture. Thus I developed for myself the concept that a garden was essentially a setting for a house, a composition, whether the garden was seen from the house or the house from the garden; and in each case from whatever indoor or outdoor position the beholder occupied. Only later did I appreciate that the garden must convey an interesting and ever-changing impression not just from various spots where one might stand or sit, but as one was moving through it.

These ideas about composition, had I known it, might be thought to fit better with Chinese and Japanese culture than with Western Europe. Oriental ideas of composition are, however, often static rather than '*mouvementé*', and they pay more attention to variations of texture as well as of shape than European gardens do. They are not necessarily concerned with the setting for or enhancement of a building, and if they are it is often a temple or a pagoda rather than, as is the case with European gardens, a residence. Their compositions are idealised, and designed to be seen from a special viewpoint or viewpoints. They are much less fluid than western compositions.

My ideas of composition, such as they were, were not remotely academic (nor original) but were born of my love of British landscape, which of course means landscape in a temperate and ever-changing climate: this was precisely the idea which, also, led me later to try my hand at watercolours, trying to pick up light and shade, the changing seasons, sunshine and showers, golden snow with blue shadows, ponds and lakes reflecting multi-coloured light.

Shakespeare's Julius Caesar prides himself on his walks and rides near Rome which he dedicated to public use; but what he seems to describe is more like a 'country park' than an urban park. Urban parks do offer some opportunities for landscaping, such as creating ponds, planting noble trees and opening vistas, but they are constrained by their sites. They have to make the best of what they get. But landscaping, first known in Britain in the eighteenth-century days of Humphry Repton and Capability Brown, is the concept of enhancing the setting of a great house in the countryside, a house in almost every case occupying a carefully chosen site – the very best available site on a landed estate.

The Landscape Garden

Gardening as an enhancement of a great house came before landscaping, and struck Britain from its Dutch and French beginnings in the seventeenth and early eighteenth centuries, although one can find it in Britain, here and there, earlier than that, in the form of the Elizabethan knot garden, for instance, as well as on the Continent. The objective of many early gardens was practical rather than decorative – to provide fruits and vegetables, often of exotic origin. But I think it is fair to say that that began more or less as it continued for generations, as a very deliberate addition to or enhancement of, rather than a setting for, a great house. It is a style which has survived in the Scottish 'flower garden' which is often out of sight, or almost so, from the house, essentially formal in style and composition. It is artificial – an 'improvement' on nature, not a reflection of nature. It is not exactly divorced, but nor is it married to the house. Even if it is close to the house it stands alone; and it has to be a different entity from the house's setting.

Later, in Victorian and Edwardian times, these intensely artificial gardens with patterned beds filled with colourful annual flowers did indeed complement or enhance great houses, including the terrace at Hawarden Castle, and including eventually houses like Waddesdon which were often even more a revolt against nature than the neo-classical monsters of the eighteenth century or the gothic fancies which followed them. Their landscapes were improved by natural-looking lakes and plantations after a study of their capabilities.

Some of our earliest and most magnificent, indeed palatial, 'artificial' gardens – at Hampton Court for example – are not set aside from the house but are in their own way landscape gardens too: they create views and vistas from the house, a setting for a house like a frame for a picture. The supreme example is Versailles, where the frame has become almost as important as the picture itself, for it leads the eye inwards and outwards to and from the immense palace which expressed the power of the monarchy. These examples were widely copied, even in very much more modest surroundings. The nearest my forebears came to this fashion at Hawarden was in the 1730s.

The Glynnes had bought the lordship of the Manor of Hawarden in 1653, but the estate was not large enough to support a squire in any style until the time of Sir John Glynne, of whom elsewhere. One of his early projects was to create a landscape garden around 1730 reflecting the style of the great gardens I have described and many others, gardens which did provide a setting for a house. The Old Castle as an ugly ruin

The Landscape Garden

was concealed by a surrounding line of alternate lime and spruce trees and, as if to draw the eye away from it, in the early 1730s Glynne enlisted John Eames, a famous garden designer, to create a massive earth-banked amphitheatre on a high natural mound to the north of the ruined Old Castle. On its axis Glynne planted radiating avenues centred on his house, Broadlane Hall, about a hundred yards south of the present Hawarden Castle. Fortunately we have an elaborate (although lacking both scale and perspective) print of this whole scene, embodying the Old Castle and the new amphitheatre with the elaborately patterned avenues leading from it.

But a mere twenty years later, when Glynne's wealth had increased by the reclamation of previously flooded land, he decided to pull the old house down and to build a brand new one further to the north, the present Hawarden Castle, later to be encased in turrets and machicolations and parapets by his grandson. So the axis of the avenues became redundant, and the whole lot were swept away, together with a few smallholdings and hovels to the south-west (remembered now only by a tiny field system and a very ancient pear tree) which interrupted the open landscape of his brand new park. The avenues were out of date anyway. The extensive park with its wide views had now become the desirable accompaniment of a gentleman's seat. The open rolling country at Hawarden was ideal parkland, which Glynne bounded in some parts by a stone wall and in others by a ha ha, an invisible boundary contrived so as to extend the open view beyond the park itself. There were no improvements within the park, apart from the removal of the two or three smallholdings, until the first stage of creating what was to become 'The Lake' nearly two hundred years later.

However, having built his ha ha where grazing land gave way to scrub, heather and 'booberries' (the local variation on the name for bilberries or wortleberries or blueberries), Glynne planted the Booberry Wood in 1747 beyond his ha ha, at the higher end of this scrubland, growing all the trees he required in what we would call a nursery, then called an orchard (which has given its name to the home farm, Cherry Orchard Farm); and this also enabled him to punctuate his park in the orthodox style by adding more oak trees to those already in existence.

Gardens were essentially, then, enhancements of or improvements to great houses, whereas landscaping provided a worthy setting for these houses. Landscape gardening, as opposed to just landscaping, came in during the nineteenth century, mainly as a result of the explorations of

The Landscape Garden

the generations of plant-hunters who travelled all over the world studying and collecting all kinds of flowers, shrubs and trees, including a vast range of rhododendrons to add to the 'ponticum' which had already been imported from Turkey in the eighteenth century. Actually, it was the prolific mauve-flowered ponticum, now such a curse in our woodlands and even hillsides, which was already tempting landowners to plant it along their woodland rides; but in later years, when it was appreciated how well many other varieties mainly from India and China would grow in Britain, and also how easy it was to hybridise them, the landscape garden, in the form of the woodland garden, came in to its own. True, some of the largest of these hybrid rhododendrons, splendid in flower, become very large and rather oppressive in a garden when fully grown. They should not be selected except where woodland is extensive enough to absorb them.

The Victorians were as inventive and skilled at the art of gardening as they were at so many other leisure pleasures from tennis and cricket to fly-fishing. They bought species rhododendrons and azaleas and produced hybrids galore and they planted them in already picturesque woodlands, on the banks of streams and in clumps alongside their inherited artificial lakes, producing this new genre, the 'landscape garden'.

Many late-Victorian and Edwardian landscape gardens, and indeed all kinds of large gardens, decayed after the First World War. Estates were broken up and most of those which survived did not have the resources to maintain their ambitious landscape gardens, still before the age of mechanisation. But some of the most splendid survived, like the Loders' huge garden in Sussex or the Marquess of Lansdowne's at Bowood or Lord Aberconway's sensational garden at Bodnant in North Wales. Only rarely, and not until a long time after the Second World War, were new gardens of this character created, one of the most notable being the Savill Garden in Windsor Great Park, conceived by an individual with an exceptional eye both for the potential or 'capability' of a site and the vistas which might be drawn from it, together with both the knowledge and the taste to understand the long-term effects of his planting. Few of these new landscape gardens are, however, settings for a house.

The garden I inheritedwas modest indeed in comparison with those I have mentioned, but it is not sour grapes to say that that had its advantages because it gave the concept of a paradise extending further than the original landscape garden, more of a sense of unity.

The Landscape Garden

The house built by John Glynne became, as I have mentioned, a castellated and gothicised regency mansion known as Hawarden Castle, facing due south over pleasant parkland in what people (even some educated people, like those who think that Upper Egypt must be north of Lower Egypt) would nowadays describe as the extreme top right-hand corner of Wales. It changed its name from 'house' to 'castle' when it was transformed in 1809 from being a plain mid-eighteenth century Georgian brick-built squire's house by Sir Stephen Richard Glynne, grandson of its builder Sir John. His wealth and social ambition, like those of his grandfather, had grown simultaneously. The undulating foothills of its parkland overlook the vast flatness of the Cheshire plain. From the Old Castle you can see Helsby Point to the east, where the Mersey estuary narrows and the Manchester Ship Canal begins, and to the south the Wrekin, a pimple on the horizon forty miles away.

In one outstanding feature the garden was ready-made, with a gift to the landscape gardener in the shape of the ancient ruined border castle built on an outcrop of rock not much more than a hundred yards west of this new mansion. The Old Castle had been the guardian of the ancient road from the English border along the coast of North Wales to Conway, the main seaport for those travelling on foot to or from Ireland.

The Old Castle is a picture in itself. How ancient it is as a defensive site nobody knows. A mesolith (a flint tool of the Middle Stone Age) has been found there. Bronze Age settlers left some bits and pieces close by. The layout has the character of an Iron Age promontory fort. But most of what we see was built in the 1280s AD, the era of all Edward I's magnificent castles of North Wales, although it is much smaller. It is designed on the Norman plan of motte and bailey, the motte a massive round tower with stone walls 14 feet thick at the base. The high windowed wall of the hall and much of the formidable curtain wall survive, in spite of the order of Parliament to 'slight' the castle after the Civil War. The castle itself stands athwart two artificial D-shaped mounds which accommodated the outer defences of the two successive entrances, the older one to the south, and the newer to the north giving access to a water supply adequate for horses and cattle as well as the human garrison, complete with the remains of its barbican and of its drawbridge pit. But what matters most to us is the Old Castle's magnificently picturesque composition from the direction of the big house to the east. It just looks as if it ought to be there: John Glynne, when he chose that site for his new mansion in 1750, chose well.

The Landscape Garden

The ugly rubbish of demolition in the 1660s metamorphosed into a picturesque ruin in the later eighteenth century. The Old Castle was becoming the subject of watercolour drawings, and a fine stone footbridge was erected over the old road to make it easy to visit the now romantic site. The screen of lime trees which had been planted to conceal it was beginning to look untidy, and those on the east side, together with all the spruces all round, were removed. The keep itself no longer looked like half a Cheshire cheese, for it was embellished with a romantic skyline.

Some repairs and much further removal of 'rubbish', mainly heaps of demolished stone, took place in the 1860s. Many barrow-loads were plonked in the deep ditch just next to the drawbridge pit, an archaeological sin committed in the name of the picturesque. The bailey had already become a flat lawn, suitable for archery, one of the few outdoor sports in which ladies – notably Catherine and Mary Glynne – could participate.

The concept of the nineteenth-century landscape garden had still not been invented, certainly not in intimate connection with the site of a great house; but some fine oaks and beeches managed to establish themselves, creating a natural vista from the house to the Old Castle and calming the starkness of the fortified site to the north and west. Wild daffodils began to naturalise on the mound. Who, if anyone, introduced them is not known.

The grassy slope between the old and the new castles was kept mown by the Victorians, but the garden itself came strictly to an end at the low wall at the west end of the terrace which had been raised in 1830 to give a grander and more artificial look to the south aspect of the house: a mount for the picture, if not quite a frame. Patterns of little flower beds with a maze of narrow gravelled paths filled the terrace until 1896 when they were simplified for reasons of economy. Whoever thought of the Victorians simplifying anything, let alone having to economise? But what they did by way of gardening, apart from growing fruit and vegetables in the walled garden to the north-west of the house, was indeed formal, and confined to the terrace. There is a grand photograph of Mr Gladstone in old age sitting on that low wall with the members of the first Colonial Conference, representing the self-governing dominions which Gladstone had done so much to initiate, statesmen from the Empire who had made the pilgrimage to Hawarden to meet the Grand Old Man.

The Landscape Garden

After his retirement in 1894, well into his eighties, Mr Gladstone would appear on the terrace after luncheon and raise his hat to the admiring multitudes in the park, who had arrived at Hawarden Station by excursion train in the hope of getting a glimpse of him. On a few special occasions, such as the fêtes to raise funds for the schools of the parish and the village's institute and working mens' club, he would speak from the terrace on non-political topics – such as encouraging smallholders to grow their own fruit and vegetables, not only for themselves but to sell. There are photographs of huge crowds, mostly male, half-and-half cloth caps and bowlers, straining to catch his every word. He never spoke down to an audience. It was said that he addressed a crowd of working men as if they were the House of Commons.

In the 1860s Mr Gladstone had built a new chunk on to the house to provide himself with a library and his family with a few more bedrooms, designed by a little-known architect in sheer mid-Victorian pick 'n' mix, almost as if you could order each differently shaped gothic window from a catalogue. Thus he added to the regency style of the 'new' castle, which was to be his family home for fifty years, its own (and his own) Victorian flavour.

A good deal was done to create a garden in addition to the terrace between 1918 and 1939 by my Great-Uncle Harry and my Uncle Albert, but apart from the 'tea house' and its concomitant extension westwards of the terrace wall, all the improvements were to the north and north-west of the house. The tea-house was a handsome small stone-built pavilion designed by Hal Goodhart-Rendel, which provides an important punctuation in the garden as a whole, emphasising that The Terrace Ends Here and facilitating the concept that the garden beyond this point should be a landscape garden.

North and north-west of the house Uncle Harry added shape and formality in the 1920s with a new front drive (since closed), a formal long herbaceous border surrounded by paving and enhanced by an old fountain from the village, and a broad gravel path leading to Eames's grass amphitheatre north of the Old Castle, which I have mentioned as the oldest feature in the garden. Halfway up this broad walk Uncle Harry punctuated it with a fine circular stone wall, a rotunda with paved steps and a formal rectangular pond.

Joining the craze for the wellingtonia, the English nickname for the massive redwood 'sequoia gigantea' of the American north-west, which was found to grow well in Britain, somebody planted one slap in the

The Landscape Garden

middle of Eames's amphitheatre, an extraordinarily insensitive act, whatever one thought of this ancient landscape feature. Of course, the axis of the amphitheatre had become meaningless when the present house was built a hundred years or so before, but how could anybody plant what would become an enormous tree right in the middle of its stage? But they did, and there it is, a focus for Uncle Harry's broad walk of the 1920s; for Uncle Harry ingeniously planted hazels and azaleas on the south-eastern fringes of the amphitheatre to make it look as if it had been designed to face due east in the direction of this new broad walk. That made sense of the amphitheatre again; but right in the middle, there the wellingtonia stands, testimony to the poor taste of its unknown planter, inhibiting any suggestion that this largest feature in the garden might be used for outdoor plays or concerts.

How far should one go in undoing what one sees as the errors of taste of an earlier generation? As to cutting a large peculiar tree, I have only done it once (at Fasque in Scotland) and I have regretted it ever since. Yet I wish I had taken the bull by the horns at Hawarden and removed that wellingtonia many years ago.

Uncle Albert succeeded Uncle Harry as occupant of the castle in 1935 and set about creating smaller more subtle spaces in the still rather dull open grounds north-west of the house. He had a mound of earth thrown up to create a shrubbery and to give the beautiful little water garden which Uncle Harry had created its own more intimate site. The mound was a good idea but the soil was of poor quality which has made it harder to get shrubs and small trees to grow well. Uncle Albert also created a north-south division of the area to the north-west of the house, by a fine stone wall from the west wall of the house as far as the west end of the terrace, and then by a yew hedge beyond it. He was not slavishly creating 'rooms' à la Sissinghurst, as has been done and often overdone in many modern gardens; but in the few years before the Second World War he was creating new spaces in their own right, relatively small but varied spaces which I have been able to develop in order to introduce to the garden, more or less at least as he would have wished, several features each with its own character, without disturbing the unity and simplicity of the whole.

Perhaps the first and most important concept for the person responsible for designing or developing the garden and surroundings of a big house is that of scale. A big house needs a big space, or indeed big spaces: a

The Landscape Garden

lesson known to the landscapers of the eighteenth century but often, alas, forgotten nowadays. A supreme example of sufficient space is Houghton, Sir Robert Walpole's seat in Norfolk, a house of the golden age before the ostentation of vast neo-classical palaces of the later eighteenth century burst forth in our landscape. Houghton was a statement – a grand statement – of who Walpole was, which however had to be placed in the undistinguished flat site where the Walpole family had resided since God knew when: a statement therefore not only about Sir Robert but about his ancestors, a statement both ancient and modern, of pride in the past as well as the present. The house, by Colen Campbell, sits triumphant on its billiards table, sufficient unto itself, unconfined, in perfect taste, harmonious in design; grand, even splendid, but without vulgarity, no single exterior feature exaggerated; even if indoors he did over-decorate his spaces, and then fill them too full of proudly collected chattels.

Houghton, in perfect taste, looks out on a broad, flat and seemingly endless grassy avenue, uninterrupted by one single feature, except that it is bounded symmetrically with woodland on either side. This lawn is just a flat green space, leading the beholder's eye until it disappears on the horizon; emphasising the right of the house to be the sole and unchallenged occupant of a visually unbounded space.

The grand stables and carriage houses are, as one would expect, set aside from the house with decent restraint. The walled garden, happily, is even further away, quite out of sight. There the Dowager Marchioness, not content with the huge garden she had embellished at Cholmondeley Castle in Cheshire, spent years creating smaller spaces. You could label this project as part of the passion for creating 'rooms'; but she did better than that, for the spaces and vistas are varied, interesting and unconfining. However, thank heavens nobody tried out this sort of project near the big house. The family know when to leave well alone.

Another even more famous and much more gigantic house, Chatsworth, is an example of the understanding of scale. Its spacious park, a single simple entity in tune with the scale of the house, rolls away in front of it, a setting which never draws the eye away from the house as the centrepiece in the landscape, yet is never bleak or boring, as the result of the judicious planting and maintenance of parkland trees: it is a full-time job for two well-equipped men to look after them. The terrace between the house and the park, surrounded by its pierced stonework wall, is simply too big to be planted with flowers or shrubs,

The Landscape Garden

which would appear fussy and insignificant. The Dowager Duchess of Devonshire, a lady well known for her originality, enthusiasm and taste, realised that only the largest rambling roses, pruned for simplicity, might make sense here: but, actually, so insignificant are they in relation to the huge size of the terrace that she might as well not have bothered. The extensive and original conservatories, gardens and cascades behind the house, still owing much to Paxton their famous sire, succeed in combining the scale required (no 'rooms' here) with variety and interest: they enhance the house rather than drawing attention from it.

Castle Howard is another palatial house, a statement of the standing of its family, where in a very different way – with decorative gardens and fountains in a huge flat space in front of the house itself – the importance of scale has been appreciated.

More ancient and more chaotic houses like Knole (well, there is nothing like Knole) still demand scale, but they can also accept more higgledy-piggledy garden features closer to the house, features which perhaps look as if they have grown, bit by bit, with the house. The character of the house announces this ancientness, by which it has grown and changed as the generations and indeed the centuries have called for modifications. There are very few medieval houses left in Britain. People used to demolish anything that was worn out or redundant (as the Scots still do if they can – they say the old house is 'done'), although ancient features do survive here and there, sometimes unrecognised by 'experts' for what they are. But where these ancient houses or parts of houses do survive, then the need for scale in their surroundings may be less important than with more modern or more unified 'trophy' houses. This is what justifies the creation of quite small, confined spaces and features close to the house at Sissinghurst, where an imaginative and original designer (a pair of them, if you include Vita's husband, Harold Nicolson) were able to mix small and elaborate and varied spaces or 'rooms' close to the house and to create a whole new and original and now over-imitated style of gardening. But they still allowed their lovely house to sit in its spacious and rustic surroundings: they avoided any hint of claustrophobia. You could get long views from the windows, and if you couldn't see deer in the park at least you could see cows.

National Trust gardeners do not always appreciate the idiosyncratic features, sometimes unusual or even eccentric, of the gardens they are appointed to tend. They spot a simple space as a gift, which they can

The Landscape Garden

exploit by tidying it up and filling it with flower beds. They tidy up the fields or parkland too, destroying the affinity of the countryside with the house. In the case of Sissinghurst an excellent example of this process was exposed by a member of the Nicolson family who lives there, in a recent television series: this is a danger in some other noble parks and gardens, because considerations like these go over the heads of the authorities who are ultimately responsible for the garden. A passion for tidiness coupled with the notion that spaces are for filling up can be a menace in almost any kind of garden.

This is not to say that the creation of small spaces each with its own character is not essential to the garden of a great house. A big garden aimed solely at scale and space is of limited interest. But it has the advantage over most gardens that there is space enough to include a variety of interesting and intriguing smaller features, capable of providing a memorable experience, even if only within limited seasons. It is difficult to create interest and intimacy in a very large garden without fussiness, and to avoid the pretentiousness of a public space. It is this unpretentious quality which leads some people to say that they prefer a garden of the comparatively modest size – such as that of Hawarden – to the Championship League.

Most of the smaller features which I have created or enlarged at Hawarden are within the general area selected for the earlier stages of this development by both my great-uncle and my uncle and my parents – that is to say the three generations of my predecessors – before Rosamund and I came on the scene with our young family in 1969. These smaller gardens are to the north-west of the Castle, between the vista to the Old Castle and the long south wall of the walled garden with its mature brickwork responding to the slope of the ground and its several sets of bee-boles and its two forged iron gates.

This long brick wall provides a perfect northern boundary. Even if I had created special spaces within the walled garden, always known as the kitchen garden, it would have remained separate. My parents continued to grow fruit and vegetables there from 1946 to 1969, employing three gardeners and selling the surplus mainly to discriminating shops in Chester. This commercial operation received favourable tax treatment in the postwar era, when income tax was at penal rates, namely 75% (and upwards for the really rich, if any). As the years passed and the standard rate was reduced to 60% the rules governing relief became more exclusive and our small business, which was never really profitable but enabled us to keep the kitchen garden in trim very cheaply whilst providing us with fruit and vegetables, was finally scotched by the production of vegetables by large farms using modern technology for mass production.

In an effort to keep up the garden affordably we set up a garden centre in 1970, but after a good start it, too, started to suffer from competition from large-scale mechanised production, and although we did try specialise in unusual plants which were not prone to this competition the demand for them was insufficient to meet our costs. We agreed that the manager Don Jones should run the centre as his own enterprise, but he did not succeed and eventually it closed. At that time we needed a new site for a tree nursery when the Forestry Commission's enforced postwar policy of growing only conifers was abandoned, and we used the lower part of the walled garden for our hardwoods. My brother Francis and his wife Jo, living in the west end of the Castle, took over the upper half as an orchard and wild garden. Yet again our little enterprise to grow our own trees was overtaken by mass-production and technology. I planted a pattern of yews to form a 'sculpture gallery'. The compartments are occupied by various pieces of timber, few of which could justify the label 'sculpture', representing this or that or merely being intriguing in shape, but although the yews have now grown into a fine gallery I have not got round to collecting any worthwhile sculpture to fill it, so I don't know whether this project has a future.

I renewed the big vine houses for the garden centre, but they did not really fit its needs, and since it was impossible in those days to obtain durable timber they did not last. I did not contemplate trying to return the kitchen garden to its traditional state, as has in recent years been done – at great expense – on a number of sites.

It was, therefore, the area between the boundary of the terrace with its extension by the new wall and yew hedge to the south, and of the kitchen garden wall to the north, that provided the main opportunity to create some smaller features and give the garden interesting variety; an opportunity first taken by Great-Uncle Harry and then by Uncle Albert. Interestingly Great-Uncle Harry, or rather his garden designers, did not know what to do with the upper part of this area, their best effort being to plant some yew trees; and in order to create space for a winter garden I felled one large, dark and ugly yew which had been planted in the 1930s to fill an empty space.

HAWARDEN CASTLE
LANDSCAPE GARDENS

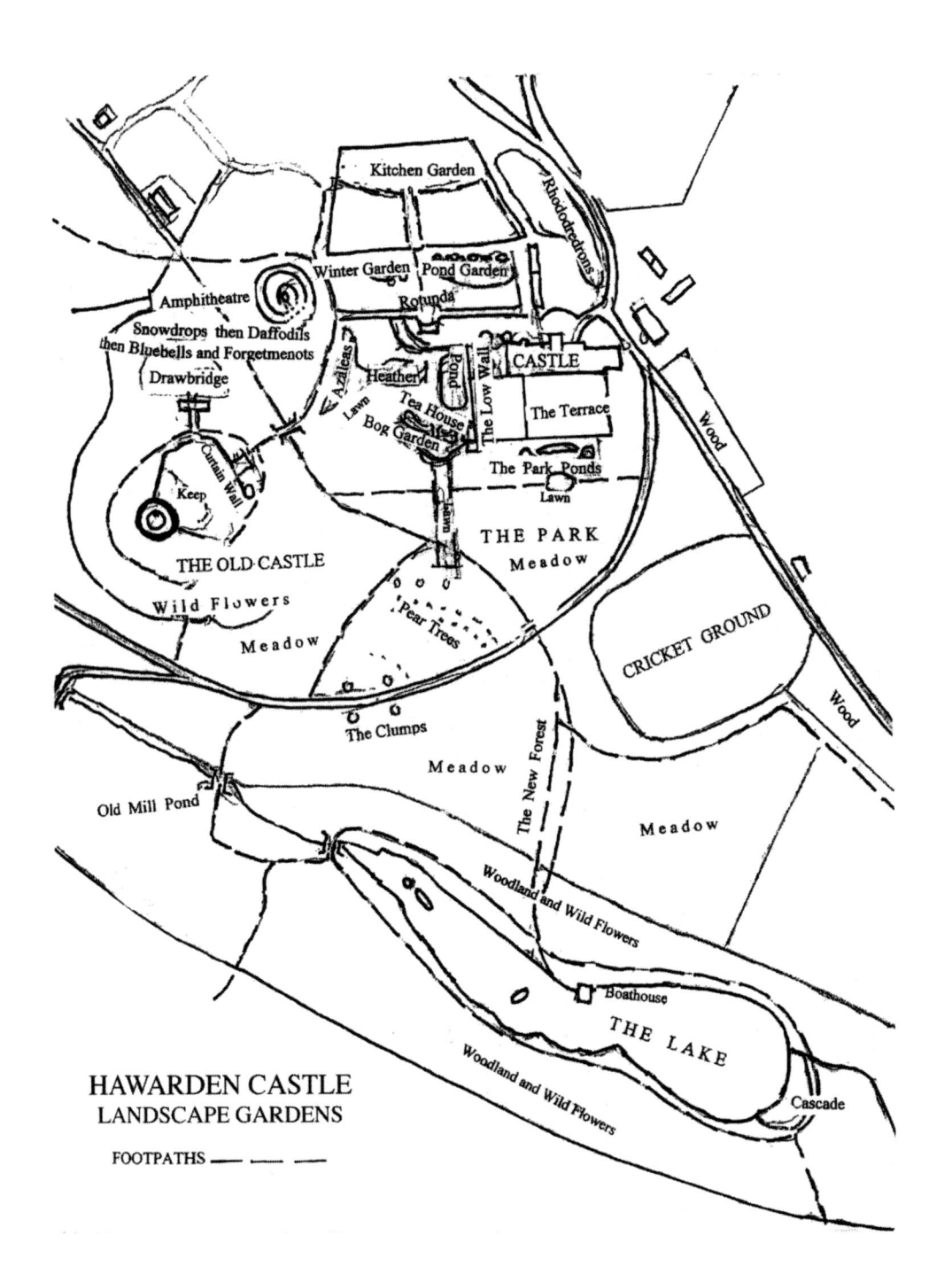

FOOTPATHS — — —

The Landscape Garden

I did not intend that this winter garden should contain all the winter flowering plants to the exclusion of other sites. It is pleasing to have a splash of colour or the waft of a winter scent at any strategic spot, particular at places people walk past often even in the depths of winter: jasmine perhaps on the south wall of the house, a variety of strongly scented viburnum in the long border which now includes some shrubs, a lone scarlet chaenomales here and there where it strikes the eye, and the Christmas blossom of the small oriental tree prunus subhirtilla autumnalis on the mound. But there is much to be said for having a particular part of the garden, if you are lucky enough to have the space, where an assembly of colourful or scented plants can cheer a short cold day. The stars of the show in my opinion are three. One is the red variety of the rhododendron nobleanum (although it is prone to be ruined by a hard frost); the pink version is more vigorous with larger flowers but it is smaller as a mature shrub and is not such a sensation as a large red one. Second is the yellow witch hazel hamamelis mollis with its very early and unusual yellow flowers and, especially, its strong scent – the old original is far superior to new varieties of lemon-yellow and pink, which lack scent and are boring in colour. It is a slow starter but once it gets going it can quickly grow to ten or fifteen feet high. If you can afford the space and the money it is a good long-term investment to get several plants rather than just one to make a real hit on a January day. Third in my book comes a carpet of hellebores: the earliest is 'niger', the 'Christmas rose', but there are many slightly later varieties which, if left to sort out their own lives, will produce a wide range of subtle colours and shades, and with a dose of autumn leaf mould they may produce seedlings. However many you cut, there are always plenty left, and the flowers make an attractive and unusual table decoration floating in flat bowls.

These are just my own favourites. There are other contenders for a prime place in a winter garden, notably perhaps chimonanthus the 'winter sweet' – tricky to start, and we already had a few of them in spots where their scent was most appreciated. There are other very early rhododendrons including dauricum and the common praecox which makes a fine purple show. There are a number of good varieties of viburnum. If we could get daphne mezereum to flourish here it would certainly have pride of place with its purple flowers and strong scent.

I'm afraid my idea of a winter garden is very different from modern

The Landscape Garden

assemblies of winter grasses, foliage and coloured bark one sees pictured so often in magazines in the sparkling grip of a frosty winter day. In wild places these individual species are of some slight interest, but even then they are greedy of space in relation to the pleasure they provide, and they lack scent.

A further qualification of my insistence on space and scale is that it may be possible to locate a very small but nevertheless interesting feature in such a way that it is hardly noticed as part of the wide scene. I made a herb garden, properly divided by box hedges, at the end of the wide path in front of the Castle just outside the kitchen door. I am not an expert at herbs, but it includes most of those commonly used in cooking, and it is right at hand for the cook. It adds interest to what one sees from the kitchen window, which is important, and it also adds interest for those who are sitting out of doors on the terrace in the summer, where the view is essentially a wide view without any other intimate features.

In spite of my arguments in favour of scale, shelter is the most important consideration for encouraging plants to grow. Scottish gardens in particular need high walls or massive yew hedges for shelter, but the ancient houses and castles which inspired many of these gardens get some of their sense of space and scale from their own impressive – indeed daunting – height. The best example I know of the National Trust misreading a garden is at Crathes Castle near Banchory. Requiring shelter, the garden adjacent to the castle is surrounded by walls and yew hedges. If you enter the garden from the front of the castle as was intended, you get a sense of space and of a spectacular and interesting garden view. Then, later, as you stroll downhill towards the right you find a number of surprises, some quite large (a rose garden, for example) and others smaller though devised long before the label 'room' for small spaces within a large garden was invented. Some of these spaces are complex in plan, some deliberately simple and restful, focused on a central feature; and as you go down further you will find some areas which are used wholly or partly for growing fruit and vegetables, some in beds or glasshouses or shaped as standard or espalier trees. So you have come down from the great garden in front of the castle into the quite intriguing, sometimes complicated and sometimes refreshingly quiet and simple minor parts of the garden. But the National Trust for Scotland obliges you to do the whole tour backwards. It sends you down to an insignificant lower gate designed for the use of the garden staff, to the least distinguished parts of the garden (which incidentally are suffering now from 'filling up' with new flower beds wherever the gardener can plonk them) where small lawns or simple designs at restful spots were; where you could pause or relax. You eventually find your way to the main garden, which you enter 'backwards' so to speak, unable to enjoy the sensational view from the front of the house or to follow this up by the intriguing exploration of the smaller spaces.

This is a spectacular misreading of the garden, which can only have been devised in order to herd the public round by the most convenient route.

There are, then, various ways by which a garden can benefit from the sense of space which the size of a big house demands as its setting. Where there are changes of level in the immediate vicinity of the house, or in other words when the house occupies a prominent position, that sense can sometimes be achieved by the distant views which this elevation allows: that goes, for instance, for Great Dixter, a gardener's garden if ever there was one. Great Dixter, indeed, provided an ideal site for a house and a garden designed as a single entitiy, although not with quite the same deliberation as at High Glanau Manor at Monmouth, which has been the subject of both written and televised attention in 2014. Here the house with its garden were indeed designed as an entity in the 'Art Deco' style which married the ideals of William Morris with the characteristics of Gertrude Jekyll's designs. The garden was vulgarised some years ago by the insertion of a turquoise swimming pool at a crucial point where it could wreak maximum horror on both the house and the garden: now it has been removed and the garden restored.

I will add a word of caution here about the restoration of gardens. Many 'historic' gardens which have been lost after generations of neglect have been recovered during recent years, but landscape gardens grow and change with the passing years and the concept of restoration does not suit them. If they have been neglected and are to be recreated they may require a different kind of 'restoration': not really a restoration at all but a new start on an old site. Indeed, if a house has been radically altered or replaced by a different and probably a smaller one, or indeed demolished, it is probably a mistake to think in terms of restoration at all. Maybe some old parts of the site can be re-used or recovered, even including some of the original features. But we should not shed too many tears if an old garden has been lost. Gardens are living entities as we are, and we don't expect to dress in the style of a hundred years ago, even if that was when our house was built. You can seldom say to a garden: 'Stay as you are.' Sometimes it is not a sin to invent a new garden for an old site. To talk of being faithful to history is rubbish in those circumstances as in many others. Indeed, the excitement of a landscape garden is the way it changes, if not from year to year then certainly from decade to decade.

I have carefully qualified my insistence that a sense of scale, a generous allowance of space, is a requirement of the landscape and the landscape garden which provide the setting for a big house – or indeed for any other large building, whether it is in contemporary use or a ruin. Indeed, many years ago I invented the phrase that a ruin needs to be 'come across', which was plagiarised by that stylish guide Henry Thorold – without acknowledgement. That flattered me by suggesting that he thought the phrase good enough to be worth taking over. I can almost claim that 'come across' in this context has now become a standard phrase to express an accepted view. But if it is, nevertheless we still suffer from not only the National Trust but also English Heritage passionately tidying everything up. The monks didn't have lawnmowers, so why should we?

I am not suggesting that romantic ruins should be allowed to decay under ivy and brambles, but simply that their surroundings should be in sympathy with their ancientness and disuse. Likewise, ruins of old gardens may be best left more or less as we find them.

So the first rule is to allow a building space in scale with its size, and to preserve both wide and distant views, often in the form of visually narrowing vistas, perhaps with a distant feature providing a remote focus. Following from this the features within a landscape or a landscape garden must be to scale, too: fine individual 'specimen' forest trees, for instance, which give the dimension of height to a composition whose first requirement is not height but distance. When you are young, trees grow slowly, but the older you get the faster the process seems. Beeches which seemed immemorial when I was young blew down in my middle age, gone for ever. Now that I am old, the seedlings which replaced them are big enough already to be features in their own right, although still far from their eventual magnificence. Sweet chestnuts, too, flourish here, although it is at least a hundred years before the trellis-like slant of their bark becomes remarkable in its own right, spiralling upwards There is a sweet chestnut selected as a self-sown

The Landscape Garden

seedling by Uncle Albert in 1937 which is already a fine tree, though it will improve for at least another century. Another, a kind of successor of the next generation selected by me in 1972, is already a fine tall tree, as are several oaks in the garden no more than 35 or 40 years old, although they do not begin to match our three veterans, the most splendid of which is about 450 years old. Select seedling trees need to be nurtured by every generation: self-sown hardwood trees always do better than planted ones.

These trees are already large enough to play their parts in the 'phi' factor, the Greek letter 'phi' being the maritime symbol for a transit, when two features on a chart are momentarily exactly in line, fixing a ship's position with extraordinary accuracy. The significance of this in landscape gardening is that of changing relationships, from left to right or from right to left, between the salient verticals of large trees, which form the frame of the composition as you see it at any moment, as you walk through the garden. The composition itself ceases to be static – it changes as you yourself move. In photographic terms it is the camera itself (in the guise of your own eyes), not its target, which moves. In terms of relativity this is similar to the exciting illusion of your train seeming to move while it is still stationary.

My third rule, then, is to try to arrange each feature so that, except in the case of the big open views and distant vistas, there is always an element of change in front of your eyes as you move. I have already mentioned the 'phi' factor, but equally important is the sense of discovery and, if possible, of surprise. Whether you are passing through a tunnel of heavily scented self-sown (but maintained by occasional pruning) azaleas, or entering the lower end of the pond garden through a narrow passage, you get a changing view all the time, and if possible now and again a surprise when you come across a completely new feature. This is made easier by the fact that most of the garden has to be on a large enough scale to suit the big house (and in our case the Old Castle), so that most of the smaller features have to be tucked away where they do not compromise this prime element of openness.

Great-Uncle Harry put in a rock garden, or rather a group of rocky features, to give shape to the bank of rising ground beyond his stone rotunda which punctuated the broad walk, and the rectangular pond which complements it. My father laboriously got some of the rocks removed in the immediate postwar era because he thought it would be impossible to maintain rock gardens, and those large lumps of stone

The Landscape Garden

have remained hidden in the bushes alongside the front drive ever since. But happily he gave up before he had removed many, and I was later able to rearrange some of the remaining ones in order to draw them together to create a broad unified and fairly natural-looking rocky bank thirty yards long. The site was about as unsuitable for alpines as it could have been, but over the course of time I have planted miniature rhododendrons and small azaleas and a selection of other shrubs and dwarf trees there. Some damp-loving plants – primulas and irises – form a line along its lower edge. This area links Great-Uncle Harry's pond with Uncle Albert's yew hedge, now a shapely seventy-five years old, which was planted to give that space its individual identity. It features also a leg-of-mutton shaped bed, and a screen of rhododendrons and small trees enclose its other two sides.

This screen of rhododendrons, survivors or successors of those planted by Great-Uncle Harry ninety years ago, are planted on a gentle bank which includes a wide rustic stone-stepped path. That path has now been a tunnel through the rhododendrons since they grew tall fifty or sixty years ago, and I came to realise that, with a little cunning, it could introduce this enclosed space between the yew hedge and the broad walk as a surprise, and moreover the narrow view of it which first appears half way up the steps could become wider step by step until one finally emerges and sees a panorama, with the full length of the rock garden ahead, the pond and rotunda on the right, and the keep of the Old Castle above the yew hedge on the left. I am not sure how many of those who climb the steps are conscious of this process – only a minority of those who come to visit the garden are remotely interested in what they see – but to me it is certainly the most pleasing and successful of all the small features I have tried to introduce: for the first glimpse itself is a surprise, and is followed by the gradually widening revelation of the whole scene. I hope there may be a few people who like it, even perhaps without thinking quite why. It was a stroke of luck, presented to me on a plate, and to be honest all I had to do was to plant one new rhododendron and shape a few other shrubs.

Large trees are doubly valuable to the landscape gardener: not only do they create the verticals of the frame (or, if you like, a number of changing frames as you move through the exhibition), but they are wonderful individual compositions in themselves, especially but not only beech trees, their soaring branches reflecting the arms of a stained-glass saint (or a ballet dancer) pointing the beholder to heaven. The

The Landscape Garden

trees of the early landscapers performed neither of these functions: they merely played their collective part in the shaping of clumps and spinneys. But in landscape gardens the shapes of individual or pairs or small groups of tall trees is important.

My fourth rule is that in a landscape garden one should let the kinds of trees and plants grow which want to grow, rather than coaxing those which don't. As far as plants are concerned, this applies at Hawarden mainly to three sorts of ground: open flattish sunny places, shady or semi-shady sites near or under trees, and wet sites whether in shade or sunshine. I prefer to encourage these sites to be as they want to be, rather than trying to make the rough places plain or the wet places dry. We are fortunate in several respects: our open ground tends to be made up of light soils, easy to work. The soil is acidic, so the wooded areas are peaty and the annual leaf litter provides rich nourishment. But since our land is post-glacial, areas of undrainable clay appear in bogs and on banks here and there. You can spend much toil and treasure trying to drain these wet banks, but if you succeed they have a maddening habit of reappearing not far away. Our shady sites are ideal for azaleas, which need to be shown in large swathes, though not in island beds, which tend to stick out like sore thumbs in a landscape. The more or less indigenous yellow azalea is scented, unlike so many modern hybrids, as is an exceptionally fine pink and white species of American origin, which flourishes here and either layers and thus perpetuates itself, or does so with help of a little peat-filled plastic bag.

The wild (or admittedly in some cases 'naturalised') daffodils already made a fine show a hundred years ago and they now extend right round the keep mound of the Old Castle and along the banks of the so-called 'moat' which is obviously not a moat at all but the sunken part of the ancient road; the amphitheatre, and the slope below it on both sides of the broad walk. Primroses, alas, do not do well. In dairying country where the grass grows quickly they are too intolerant of open or even semi-shaded places. There are some alongside the paths. But forget-me-nots and bluebells flourish, although the bluebells are slow to germinate and spread. Thus we now have a striking blue period to succeed the yellow period of early spring; and then the red period follows, the leading part played by campion.

People who have not attempted to encourage wild flowers tend to think that they must be easier than tame ones. Actually they are far more tricky – disregarding rarities in both cases. The main problem is

The Landscape Garden

that they need exactly the right amount of competition, and most wildflowers other than dandelions and buttercups don't like grass, which suppresses them. They like just the right amount of shade, too. Some will only flourish in shade, but others will grow in the open or in a semi-shaded spot with reduced competition to suit them. Some like chalky and some like acid soil, although many will tolerate the right kind of site in either. Few will survive on heavily grazed land, even if it has never been subjected to chemicals. Primroses and cowslips are, on the whole, only to be seen in masses where a bank is too steep for heavy grazing, and this refers not so much to the discouraging experience of being eaten by sheep or cattle but to being trodden on. We tend to forget, too, that many wildflowers are only at home on arable land: poppies in particular. Some wildflower seed, including bluebells and poppies, will lie dormant for many years, perhaps hundreds. That of course is why the Flanders poppies appeared from the subsoil as a result of artillery bombardment during the First World War, and occasionally in a British field you will see a patch of poppies where a clumsy ploughman with a huge tractor has ploughed too deep. Bluebells will wait patiently through a long rotation of beech trees until the successor generation of giant trees has grown large enough to suppress the undergrowth once more.

Gardening or farming to encourage wild flowers must be organic, and on some sites various flowers will re-emerge after some years if grazing and mowing is stopped altogether. However, just leaving Nature to do what it will is not by any means an easy answer because crops like bracken or brambles will simply take over. This is well known to those who point out that it is not the wild state of land but the state of land tamed for cultivation and enclosed with hedges since the 'agricultural revolution' of the eighteenth century that provides the most varied and abundant wildlife in Britain.

Some wild flowers will appear in odd spots for a few years and then disappear, but reappear in other spots at some future date for reasons which are difficult to fathom. Flowers of the orchid families are notably capable of this: it is one of the most pleasing phenomena of the summer season because suddenly you find a wonderful show of orchids where you have never seen them before. They may last on a particular site for a number of years, or for a single year, and then disappear as suddenly as they came.

In general, wild flowers are much more difficult subjects for the

The Landscape Garden

gardener than domesticated flowers are. The best policy is to allow or encourage the ones which do well, ensuring of course that you use no chemicals and that you mow late, preferably as late as August. With modern methods of growing and conserving hay and silage it is easy to forget that the best 'meadow hay' comes late in the season. Late mowing also avoids the massacre of millions of small mammals, mostly new-born, by modern machines which cut very low.

It is common knowledge that green is the most important colour in the garden, that there is a vast variety of greens both in colour and texture, and that these colours change as the weeks of the year move on. What I think most people with large gardens underestimate is the value of long grass in itself. Yes, people will try to grow wildflower meadows (until in most cases they discover how difficult it is) but I am thinking of just long grass, not only because I think it looks interesting and varies with the seasons, the light and the wind, but because it does contain a remarkable variety of wild flowers, not just dandelions and buttercups (and how many different sorts of buttercup) and cuckoo flowers but many more modest ones which will gradually appear over the course of years if you give them time to seed and don't cut too early. The variety of grasses adds character to swathes of long grass. Long grass, home to small mammals, helps to restore diversity.

I have used the small area of parkland south of the big house mostly as grassland, primarily to give the house space and to leave open the distant views (one in particular down the valley just east of south) both from the house and also from the park itself of the Old and New Castles. There used to be too many big trees around the Old Castle. To give it its authentic surroundings as a castle, with clear fields of view and of fire, there still are too many trees, but the number has been reduced, mainly by natural wastage, over the last half-century, and, after all, the survivors do add beauty on their own and picturesqueness to the setting. The Old Castle is a ruin, not a defended site, and as I have said a ruin should be 'come across': Nature should to some extent be allowed to take its course in this process.

I made use the open area of parkland south of the Castle primarily in order to make a connection with the lake in its enclosure rather than merely walking across a field grazed by livestock as we used to do. The prime use of this space itself is to enhance the views in all directions,

The Landscape Garden

especially the best views of the old and the new castles seen together, for which purpose I have created a wide lawn a hundred yards long leading to an eight-seater larch bench specifically or perhaps symbolically to accommodate our successor family in the Castle, Charlie and Caroline and their six children.

I like water in a garden almost wherever I can get it. I first made the big pond just beyond the low wall which marks the end of the terrace partly to try to get some interest out of an area which, rather extraordinarily, Uncle Harry had levelled as a couple of tennis courts. The pond provided partial reflections of the Old Castle from the new and vice versa; and emphasised that the wild garden had indeed begun. It might attract a few duck now and again, which has been successful mainly with mallard and occasionally teal. Sometimes a pair or two come in to rest there by night, and mallard duck will nest in uncannily concealed sites, sometimes where people pass regularly within a few feet. They give delight when they introduce their numerous clutches of tiny ducklings to the pond. Even moorhens, although they are brutes to rival species, are welcome visitors to the garden: their tiny red and black striped young are attractive. Moorhens too have made nests in some eccentric places, but if you can find a nest with only two or three eggs in it you can take all but one and go on taking one every day for some time, and she will still lay a full clutch which she can hardly cover. Lightly boiled, the eggs are delicious, ideal for a picnic or a camp. There are many house martins' nests on the Castle, and it is good to see them catching beaksful of flies over the pond and returning to the gables to fuel their young.

I enlarged the 'pond garden' from two ponds to a string of seven, alongside the south wall of the walled garden, where the red candelabra primulas in May are followed by a long mass of 'pulverulenta', the tall yellow ones sometimes nicknamed 'cowslip primulas' which produce a mass of colour with a gentle lemony scent right through to the end of August, when the last of the long succession of irises are over. Unlike most primulas, these pulverulenta must have stone for their roots to rest on at the water's edge, where they must be able to sink their tentacles.

My last 'water feature' within the garden, which I call the 'bog garden', is simply the exploitation of a field drain which had the annoying habit of moving to a new spot every time I repaired it. I thought 'If you can't beat it, join it.' It now forms a bog or a tiny stream punctuated by a couple of small ponds, forty yards long. To get the best views

The Landscape Garden

of the bog garden I have made a large larch bridge to cover the tiny stream where the field drain ran: the Bridge of Size, which leads one to the chestnut gate from the garden in to the park. The attractive grained bare chestnut boards are now ninety years old and flawless; but you must protect the end-grain.

The other ponds I made are in the park itself. For many years I had vaguely hankered after a big pond in the park beyond the terrace, knowing that it would be too expensive, if done properly, to be justified by the result. But then I came to think that my idea of scale – a big pond in a big field to set off a big house – was oversimplified, and that typical ponds in grass fields were quite small. Cheshire, a dairy county, was famous for having a pond in every field. Perhaps the best illustration of this is the view from the train from Chester to Crewe. You can see how some fields were split by the railway in the 1830s and 1840s and where ponds have been filled in or neglected since those days. But, happily, many remain. East Flintshire is dairy country too, with ponds in some of the fields. So I thought that a couple of ponds of typical size would do for the park in front of the house, although I added a deception by making long narrow ponds between these two, to suggest a former meander of the old course of a river. I think this has worked well. It has introduced some reflections of both the Castle and the Old Castle and it has added interest to a flat area visible from the terrace or the upper-floor windows, and some additional variety of wildlife too. The water supply is entirely natural, from a spring and a field drain.

The post-glacial grassland has drained itself by eroding many steep little hollows leading to a larger stream, the Broughton Brook. One of these valleys makes an attractive route to the Lake from the park.

The two branches of the Broughton Brook, one rising in Buckley and the other in Ewloe, merge above the waterfall at the old mill in Tinkersdale, and then flow through a flat boggy area at the lowest point of the park until they meet another waterfall just above the Lake. This fall is at the fault line which threw up the rock on which the Old Castle is built. Unfortunately both branches of the stream became heavily polluted by iron oxide from coal workings first at Buckley in the eighteenth century and then at Ewloe in the nineteenth, destroying its wildlife and turning the water orange – it became generally known as the Red Stream.

Above and below each waterfall (there is a third one, the Lady's Fall, just below the Lake) the stream flows through flat land where meanders

The Landscape Garden

and ponds are liable to occur, and the pond below the middle fall now forms the top end of the Lake. This pond was twice enlarged, once by my Great-Uuncle Herbert around 1890, after which it was known as Lake Superior, and then with a much larger and more costly enlargement by his brother my Great-Uncle Harry in the 1920s. In each case they laid a large pipe to take the flow of the 'red stream', so that their lake was clean, fed only by the tiny streams from the various little eroded valleys either side of it. Lake Superior had an earth dam, a short section of which was left in place and now forms the island just above the boathouse. But Great-Uncle Harry's much more ambitious enlargement involved laying a huge 30-inch pipe to take the Red Stream, and a concrete dam across the valley. He built the charming boathouse with larch-bark cladding and a thatched roof. The thatch was replaced by roofing-felt tiles after the war.

The upper part of the Lake had become seriously silted by the 1960s and I invited Blaster Bates, an explosives expert who demolished most of the great brick factory chimneys in Cheshire and Lancashire during that decade, to see whether he could blow the silt out of this area. We drained it and let it dry out until he could walk over it and put his explosive charges in place. Then we waited for a wind so that the spoil would not simply fall back into the Lake. I took a snapshot of the earth falling in the park to the north. The operation was a limited success. We did not need very deep water but the trouble is that once a bank of silt manages to get its head above water at any spot it starts to grow plants very rapidly, accelerating the process of silting.

The arms of mechanical diggers are not long enough to reach down from a bank to extract spoil. My next effort therefore was to employ a dragline, a crane-like machine which throws out a bucket on a wire from the top of its very long boom and then hauls it in. The limitation is that it then has to swing the bucket at the end of its boom to right or left so as to dump its load on dry land. This involves clearing all the trees from the swinging and dumping area. This operation was successful along quite a long part of the south bank, but it still could not deal with the whole silted area.

It wasn't until Airbus was planning to build its west factory to manufacture the wings for the Airbus A380 that I had the stroke of luck which enabled me to meet the cost of making a proper job of dredging the Lake. The Broughton Brook (or Red Stream) ran close to the site of the proposed factory in a very boggy area. The powers-that-be decreed

The Landscape Garden

that there must be a 'lagoon' higher up the stream to accept flood water for a short period so as to moderate the flow lower down and allow the water to get away rather than to flood the factory. The estate owned the land through which the stream flowed, and by reading the requirements carefully I realised that if we dredged the silted part of the Lake it might meet these criteria, for we would be creating a 'lagoon' which could hold the necessary increased volume of flood water. We could not only accommodate the additional flow, but we could control the rate at which it was released, through the pipe and valve which Uncle Harry had included in the concrete dam.

I offered to create the required lagoon provided that the planners would accept it and that the developers would pay for it. They were delighted to find a cooperative landlord who was willing to dedicate an area of his parkland in order to solve what would otherwise have been an intractable problem – which might indeed have scotched the whole project and obliged them to build the new factory on another part of their land. This would have imposed limitations in the facilities for taking off and landing at Hawarden Airport. Having rather grand ideas of their own public standing, they had been dismayed to find that they did not possess compulsory powers to purchase an adjacent site.

I had often had cause to employ a digger for various jobs, and I picked the firm which I thought would be the least cavalier in its approach. With due respect to a skilled profession, I can say that driving a digger does seem to attract a rather gung-ho attitude to environmental features. It is tempting to tidy them up by removing them, and the amount of damage which can be done in a few unsupervised minutes, even in the face of strict and plain instructions, is frightening.

We lowered the water level so as to dry out the silt and in the hope of finding a fairly firm bottom, which we did. We made a ramp to allow the two diggers and three dumper trucks to get in and out of the Lake, and we created a lagoon in the park as close as we could. This lagoon simply involved removing some soil from just inside it to create its boundaries in the form of earth banks – actually we found very sandy material through which some of the water could get away. It was on sloping ground. We started filling it at the bottom and then worked up. Soon we realised that we could simply dump the spoil at the top and let it find its level like a lava flow. We removed about 65,000 tons at just under 50p per ton. I gave the contractors the strict limit of money available from the factory builders when I gave them the specification for the dredging, and although once we had started there was a little bit of coming back for more and groaning when it was refused, they did the job well and went away happy. I had to be there every day if not all day and stern vigilance turned out to be as necessary as I had anticipated. They did some serious damage on two occasions, in each case within a matter of minutes, one of which, the reduction in size of the larger of the two islands near the top end, was irreparable.

The project was successful and whilst the upper part of the Lake was empty I saw that the remains of the old earth dam of Lake Superior and its overflow pipes were still in place only a yard below the normal water level, and realised that it acted as a silt trap. This meant that only very slow and limited silting would occur in the whole of the rest of the Lake, mainly where small streams entered it.

We did later with much difficulty remove quite a lot of silt from the south side of this main part of the Lake, hoping to make it too deep for the water lilies which had spread over a large area of the surface and were very difficult to eradicate. This was not very successful, as we could not dig deep beyond and below the bank even with Robin Wynn's digger with its boom specially lengthened for this sort of work; but the function of the old earth dam of Lake Superior as a silt trap, whether or not it had been left in place with this in mind, was a godsend, for any project to dredge the main, lower part of the Lake would have cost a fortune. As it is, the level of the bottom has hardly risen if at all in the ninety years since the concrete dam was built.

Almost all the lakes and large ponds or watercourses in the parks of British country houses are unenclosed and open features of the scenery. However, Great-Uncle Harry decided to enclose his lake and boathouse, perhaps for more privacy for boating, bathing and fishing, and he employed an expert to produce a plan for planting trees in the late 1920s. With the outbreak of war in 1939 no maintenance was possible, and when my parents and their family arrived at Hawarden in 1946 sycamores, birch and alder, which grow here like weeds, as well as oak and ash, had helped themselves to any space available. The alder, which grows at a surprising rate all round the Lake at the water's edge, had even begun to get a foothold before the war. We were faced with a jungle to clear, and Peter and I went about the task with our axes and saws during holiday visits. But the Lake itself and its enclosure have kept their wild character, forming a paradise in its own right. I vividly remember one well-travelled visitor in the early 1960s saying 'This is

The Landscape Garden

the most beautiful place I have ever seen.' We and our family have never grown tired of it. As you walk round there is a series of exquisite views of water, trees and sky, several of them enhanced by the delightful boathouse. My efforts to encourage primroses and cowslips have been only moderately successful, but there is quite a good variety of other wild flowers.

The entrance to the Lake enclosure from the park struck me as unnecessarily abrupt once we had decided not to have livestock grazing in the few acres between the Castle and the Lake. On the banks of the little valley leading to the Lake I began to create a woodland garden with azaleas, mostly seedlings and layerings from the scented yellow plants in the wilder part of the garden. It will be some years before the trees are large enough to give the azaleas all the shade they need on sunny afternoons in a dry summer, but it is now quite well established.

In the further part of the park, more or less out of sight from the Castle itself, I have replaced the Scots pine planted in clumps by Will before the First War, I suppose as a sort of tribute a predecessor who was denied the long innings which I have been fortunate enough to enjoy. I have planted an avenue of pear trees (mixed to try to ensure fertilisation) as successors of the one very ancient survivor from the time before the park was cleared in the eighteenth century. This survivor was blown down some twenty years ago but I followed the rule that the best thing to do to a severely damaged tree or shrub is nothing.

The cricket club, founded mainly by our cousins the Lytteltons in the 1860s, occupies part of the park to the south of the Castle, but we are now in the process of relocating it to Moor Lane where it will have facilities adequate for its greatly increased number of matches, now about eighty each season with presumably more to come as women's cricket becomes more popular. My successors will decide how to use the old cricket field, but will presumably keep it more or less as open grassland forming part of the Castle's breathing space. Indeed, they may decide to remove some of the trees and spinneys which I have planted on various sites, just as they may change what I have done in other ways. Whether the changes they make are large or small, a landscape garden changes every year on its own account: that is part of its charm and its challenge.

3
Watercolour Landscape

Painting landscapes in watercolours is an absorbing and challenging hobby which has given me many hours, days and late-to-bed-nights of enjoyment and satisfaction; and it is a lasting satisfaction if a picture has been a success. You can learn all the techniques as you go along, and vary them to suit what you want to achieve. To make a start does not demand any particular skill or ability – you do not even have to be able to draw well. There are however three vital requirements. The first is a love of landscape. The second is the ambition to create a satisfying picture. The third is to observe and interpret what you see in such a way as to convert an actual scene to a two-dimensional image on paper, not a copy (such as an illustrator or a common-or-garden photographer can make) but an icon conceived in your own head. With watercolours above all you interpret the way in which the light falls upon land or water.

You need to simplify the scene. This merely means putting on paper what you see when you are looking normally at a landscape rather than trying to observe a particular detail or details. Turner's sketches often show a building or a townscape in detail. He was a masterly draughtsman, and some of his early works, pictures of churches or ruined abbeys, for instance, are exquisite drawings in their own right. But their beauty depends also on his interpretation of the light, interpretation that staggers us by its beauty even in these early drawings. As his approach to watercolours developed, he gradually became more interested in the play of light than in the detail of buildings or scenery, and even if his pencil sketches were still detailed though quick drawings, he simplified them in his final image. Taking a different case altogether, Edward Lear's skill as a draughtsman is astonishing, but although his bread and butter was earned from his exhibitions of 'finished' watercolours, these images are rather wooden and lack the spontaneity and liveliness of his preliminary sketches with their bold and simple washes.

The watercolourist can eliminate the electricity wires or the cars in the car park, but essentially he must also simplify the scene by avoiding detail. We do not see detail unless we search for it, a temptation which must be avoided so that the artist can concentrate on the impression he wishes his picture to convey.

Painting in watercolour is a creative occupation in which you can have the satisfaction of getting better and better at what you are doing, not by producing a more accurate image but more often by the opposite, which enables you produce a more striking one – as long as you don't go for gimmicks or try deliberately to form a 'style'. Let your style come if and as it will. By striking I do not refer to any kind of exaggeration or by using bright colours or deliberately distorted shapes. I mean giving your picture a sense of movement – the sun and the clouds do not stand still – and by the subtlety of light and shade.

I would like to encourage others to get the same sort of satisfaction from this wonderful hobby as I have done. Relative to other activities – from yachting to shopping, although not to walking and talking, it is cheap. Relative to golf or cricket or gardening it is not time-consuming. It does not require a team. It is absorbingly therapeutic because it demands intense concentration over a short time. It is a solitary occupation, but not over long or even longish periods. There is nothing worse than being disturbed in the middle of a 'wash', when you must work quickly and at high concentration before the water dries, but that only lasts minute or two, as your family will know. Telephones don't have the right to be answered.

The fewer lessons you have, the better. You may need just one or two, and a hint now and again, but success comes only with practice, not with being taught.

My mother was a gifted artist. She gave up her training as an architect at the age of nineteen to get married, and although she squeezed some time for painting as her older children were growing up, she had three more children, bringing the total to six over a span of twenty years; then she and my father took on the challenge of reopening a large country house after the war, after the age of servants but before the age of gadgets; and the long and the short of it was that she had no more time for art until she was at the age when ladies are wont to retire; although she could knock up a pair of knitted stockings in her spare time within twenty-four hours (reading simultaneously) or create a dress for herself or a daughter or a sweater or dressing gown for one of her sons in one or two days. As she grew older and at last had some time to spare she set up a screen-printing business for a small and select band of clients, for which she did the designs as well as the printing, some of them arrestingly modern, some more in the tradition of William Morris, and the others, in my mind the finest, stylish flowing delicate yet powerful flower drawings.

I was her first child, and I had – compared with her – a very modest penchant for drawing; and she taught me two or three vital lessons which I have described in another chapter, and which were delivered in no more than three or four words. 'Fill your paper.' 'What colour is that water? Look at it.' 'Simplify.' 'It's tone that matters – not colour.' I didn't really understand these lessons at the time, but they puzzled me sufficiently for me to remember what she had said when, like her, I reached the age of sixty and thought: if I don't start now, I never shall. She had also taught me the basic principles of composition and perspective, and had told me more than once that the translucency of a watercolour depended on the whiteness of the paper showing through the washes of watercolour pigment, another lesson I remembered without understanding it.

I wanted to paint landscapes; 'landscape' in this context including skyscape and seascape, for the beauty of the British countryside depends on the light from the sky and the reflections of water. The most exquisite days are days of sunshine and cloud, light and shadow always on the move, altering from minute to minute; and of the changing seasons from the fresh colours of spring to the mists and mellow fruitfulness of autumn and the snow of winter, snow which is not white but pale gold in the sun and blue in the shade. Watercolours are suited to temperate climates, oils to the Mediterranean.

Watercolours are indeed translucent. The strength of a 'wash' does depend on the whiteness of the paper still showing through it. Obviously, therefore, you must paint the lightest parts of your picture first, with lots of water and not much pigment, and gradually work to the darker areas. This technique was invented and developed around 1800. Most of the artists who brought it to perfection were born before the year 1800 and died after it. Although they might add interesting detail to their pictures, as time went on more and more of them simplified what they saw, and then painted freely; applying the paint in washes rather than working in meticulous detail. Their colours are exquisite; but gently and economically used. They use differences in tone, not colour, to get their effects. Alas, it is difficult nowadays to find black and white illustrations in a book, or to take black and white photographs as snapshots to use instead of pen or pencil sketches: not a desirable alternative, but a very convenient one. The Stevenson screen is a home-made gadget to help with this but I found it more trouble than it was worth; or you can roll up a piece of paper and look at different parts of your picture through it; but essentially what you have to do is to be persistent in trying to see what you look at in tone not colour: that is to say, how light or dark is it in terms of white to black? It's not easy but you will improve. Tone also grows lighter with distance: that is an essential principle for the watercolourist. Variations in tone create their own perspective.

I am writing about representational painting, although by its nature it is impressionistic; and it strikes me as remarkable that the technique developed by the masters around 1800 is alive and kicking, that it has been able to continue to change and develop in style as the years have gone by, and that it is open not only to professionals but also to amateurs to gain satisfaction from it, and indeed to work out their own approach and to allow their own style to develop. And they are not 'copying' but interpreting what they see. They are interpreting the view as something personal, unique and iconic: a picture.

A large part of the pleasure I have derived from watercolours has been from admiring and studying the work of the early nineteenth century in this tradition which is still very much alive. The fact that modern work is so strongly related to a school of artists flourishing two hundred years ago enables the study of their approaches and techniques to add another dimension to the pleasure of actually painting in a way which I suggest is unmatched in other forms of visual art. Modern painters in oils can beneficially study the old masters. And if they are so inclined they can trace back the continuous history of the contemporary school through the intervening years (although this may be a contrived concept when one considers how the Impressionists burst upon the world), but there is neither the same straightforward path along the trail nor anything like the large group of watercolourists who represent this extraordinary generation – well, a bit more than a generation, but not much – of the early nineteenth century. Each of the leading artists had a distinctive style, instantly recognisable by the connoisseur, yet what they had in common was far more significant than the differences between their individual approaches.

I have already mentioned two very different artists, one (as it happens) of the early and the other of the late years of this era, whom I

Watercolour Landscape

especially admire – J. M. W. Turner and Edward Lear. One of the nice things about this large group was that a lot of them happened to have memorably distinctive names, and indeed even Turner who didn't, and requires no other label than his surname, is often referred to as Joseph Mallord William Turner, I don't know why. Richard Parkes Bonnington, Thomas Shotter Boys, John Robert Cozens, William Henry Hunt (not to mention Alfred William Hunt and William Holman Hunt), John Frederick Lewis, and a few even with an adopted third name like Michael 'Angelo' Rooker, John 'Warwick' Smith, and to crown them all Anthony Vandyke Copley Fielding. The others whose work I admire included Thomas Girtin, whom Turner considered his equal or even his superior until his early death, David Cox (senior, but junior as well), Peter de Wint, Henry Gastineau, Robert Hills, John Linnell, William James Muller, Samuel Palmer, David Roberts, Francis Towne, William Turner 'of Oxford', and John Varley; but there are more to choose from, and moreover, overlapping with these names, is the large group of the 'Illustrators' who travelled the Continent after the Napoleonic wars and produced magnificent volumes of wonderful topographical illustrations, mostly in lithograph, of Europe and beyond for gentlemen who could afford them. One is tempted to think that the camera, which gradually eliminated them (for they had no successors), was one of the worst things that ever happened in the realm of art!

So there is a broad choice of models for anyone who wants to study the schools of British watercolour landscapists from its first full triumphant emergence about two hundred years ago until today. I venture to say that there is no indigenous form of art quite like it, 'minor' art-form though it may be. (One calls them British, but nearly all of them were English. Perhaps one of England's outstanding contributions to the arts lies in 'minor' art forms, including alongside watercolours the supreme periods of walnut furniture (roughly from William and Mary until disease extinguished it in 1741); Stuart to George II silver; and domestic architecture from Inigo Jones to Queen Anne).

Yes, for the watercolourist there are plenty of models from whom to choose. But it is a mistake to have regular lessons. It is better to work things out for yourself by trial and error. That enables you to learn your own technique and create your own picture. One lesson should be followed by weeks or months of practice – until suddenly, to your surprise and relief, a certain knack comes right. I am not against small sketching groups of friends who like to work out of doors, and who can if they please criticise each other and give each other hints; but people who give lessons other than at (or perhaps in some cases even at) colleges or academies of art tend to be illustrators or instructors rather than artists, competent teachers maybe but not artists of any calibre, and at the end of the course everybody is painting the same sort of rather lifeless picture.

The ideal way to make a start, or rather to open up the possibility of success after you have spent some time practising the technique of watercolours on your own, is to persuade an artist whose work you admire to paint a picture while you watch, to comment on what he or she is doing and to allow you to ask questions. I had the good fortune to persuade Denis Pannett to do this while he was staying with us with his mother Juliet, a well-known portraitist, and painting watercolours in our part of the world. I asked him to copy a picture which I admired by Edward Wesson, a very freely painted snow scene with a frozen pond. This was a revelation to me. He did not of course create a slavish copy: that would have lacked the vitality of the original. But he painted the scene which Wesson had created in his own way. Denis taught me how to lay a wash, to add different colours to it before it dried, how to work from light towards dark, to paint with an almost dry as well as a wet brush, to give an impression of objects without painting them in detail, and also quite a lot about making all the colours one needed with just a few pigments. While we were waiting for the first wash to dry he asked me whether I had a small hair-dryer. This has been a boon to me: instead of waiting patiently after each wash one can speed up the process as long as the dryer is set to low or medium and held some little distance from the paper. Waiting can try one's patience because to start a new wash before the last one is completely dry is asking for trouble.

Denis used thick rough paper – French handmade Arches 400 gm 'Rough'. He said it was expensive but well worth it, but that one could probably get away with 300 gm which is slightly cheaper. These papers have a front and a back (you can tell which is which from the watermark) but I find they are equally good, so if you make a hash of a drawing (a common experience) you can do another on the other side. (By the way, it is correct to call all watercolours 'drawings' rather than paintings, the latter being reserved for oils.) The advantages of this paper are that it does not need stretching before use (a tedious operation); that it will not curl up or 'puddle' under a wet wash; and that its rough surface will help to create life and variety in a painting according

COBALT BLUE	PRUSSIAN BLUE	FRENCH ULTRAMARINE			
VIRIDIAN	CADMIUM SCARLET				
LIGHT RED	CADMIUM YELLOW PALE	RAW SIENNA		RAW UMBER	BURNT UMBER

This is the palette I use for landscapes – Blues in the top row and Browns in the bottom. In the middle row are a couple I use occasionally to add a tiny highlight, a bright green and a bright red. The palette is made up of three porcelain palettes each with six compartments an inch wide and three inches deep, leaving plenty of spaces for urgent mixing, which can be cleaned with a damp rag after each session. The only modern dye I use (apart from the scarlet) is the Cadmium Yellow Pale, which makes a fresh green but needs using very sparingly. My only principles are to use as limited a palette as possible and to use the old dyes, gentler than the modern ones, especially the 'earthy' yellows and browns. Apart from that, the choice is a personal one.

to the wetness of the brush or the way the brush is applied, or the speed the brush moves. Fix the paper by drawing pins or masking tape to a board sloping slightly towards you on a table.

Last but not least Arches paper will take a lot of punishment without the surface being damaged. This is nothing to be ashamed of: the supreme master, J. M. W. Turner, gave his paper a lot of punishment in the course of creating his wonderful effects, 'lifting out' which means removing pigment, either by gentle persistence with a wet brush or by using a hard little oils brush for a small area, or dabbing and rubbing with cotton wool or even scratching out pigment here and there with a sharp blade: thus he could apply a wash very freely and if necessary modify it afterwards.

Since that day I have often said that this lesson from Denis was the only lesson I ever had. All my time was then spent practising what he had taught me, and within a couple of years, although still prone (as watercolourists are) to make mistakes and consign them to the wastepaper basket, I felt, when a painting went well, that I had mastered the medium. Meanwhile I had, *faute de mieux*, begun to form my own style, to paint as I wanted to paint and not as anyone had taught me to. This ought to allow one to go on painting for years – albeit with a sabbatical now and again to restore freshness to one's efforts – and to continue to enjoy this therapeutic and creative occupation while allowing one's style to develop.

Denis and Juliet Pannett did also help me to select a palette, and this is a very useful lesson for a beginner if you can get it from an artist you admire. Then with experience you can gradually change it to your own satisfaction. The colours needed for a landscape are very different from those you need for painting flowers or birds – and indeed you need far fewer of them. To a lesser extent the same is true of still life or interiors. But the old masters achieved their superb results with fewer colours than we have, although Thomas Girtin and some other pioneers did unfortunately and unwittingly use rather 'fugitive' colours which have faded.

If you study Turner, which in one respect is difficult to do because of his many private (he kept his secrets) and complicated methods and his extraordinary skill at manipulating his pigments; but on the other hand easy because so many of his sketches – a preliminary idea or just a fleeting detail or the way of laying down an early wash – were bequeathed by him to the nation and can be consulted (many of them are published); you may be able to bring yourself to accept my assertion that to Turner there were only two colours, yellow and blue. Put less simply, colours have only two functions: light and shadow, hot and cold, aggressive and recessive. If you can believe this, you can compose all your pictures on this simple principle and you can divide all your pigments into two categories, the blues and the yellows. Then, very sparingly, you can add a third category of luxuries, which allow you, for instance, to add a little person in a scarlet hat. Turner knew, too, that to use a bright colour very sparingly – perhaps as a very thin line of bright green in the distant sunshine – is more striking than a larger area.

Turner could break the rules. For common mortals, however, it is best to confine oneself to true watercolours, avoiding opaque colours, above all Chinese white. It is also advisable to avoid modern chemical dyes, which are simply too strong, though useful for painting parrots. For instance, use good old Prussian blue rather than Winsor blue, even if people tell you that they are 'the same'.

For blues you need cobalt blue, Prussian blue and French ultramarine. Cobalt blue is ideal for 'blue' skies, and it will make shade on clouds mixed with light red. This is also useful as a coldish grey in other contexts; and with more light red will move towards mauve (to be used sparingly). Prussian blue is for dark water and, mixed with one or more of the 'yellows', for all the greens you want to create. The brightest yellow to mix with it is chrome yellow pale (a modern dye to be used very sparingly), and the darkest burnt umber. The warm and friendly greens so characteristic of the British landscape are to be got with raw sienna and raw umber – I especially value the latter.

Neither cobalt nor ultramarine work well for making greens. Ultramarine is ideal for threatening skies, especially with some burnt umber. And this is the best mixture to get a really black black, mixing in as much burnt umber as you need with not too much water. It is blacker and more lively than ivory black, which is definitely one to avoid. Another useful mixture is ultramarine and a little light red, good for distant hills and for shadows as well as stormy skies. Unlike Prussian blue and cobalt, ultramarine will not produce an even wash when it dries – try it and see.

For yellows you need light red, raw sienna (the same as yellow ochre, but I prefer it), raw umber and burnt umber. These four ought to be enough but if you want a very fresh green you can add chrome yellow pale or chrome lemon pale (both modern and rather strong – use very sparingly) according to taste. Raw umber provides some lovely midgreens, restrained and typical of the English countryside. Burnt umber is striking in foregrounds, bringing them closer. With ultramarine it will produce a great variety of browns and greys through to black; and with Prussian blue it will produce the darkest greens, whether for land or sea.

These seven or eight pigments will provide a vast variety of colours for land, sea and sky. The colours to be avoided are Chinese white, ivory black and alizarin crimson (which has a nasty habit of 'getting in everywhere' as Juliet Pannett put it) and any of the strong modern chemical dyes. Personally, I do not use burnt sienna, because it produces a rather orangey tint which I don't like, and I can get all the brown shades I need from the other pigments. However, what I emphasise is that if you start with these few, you will create pictures with a nature-driven unity or integrity which a palette with emphasis on the natural 'earthy' dyes produces, although this quality is difficult to analyse or define; and you will probably be reluctant to exclude these pigments even if you add others.

There are a few excellent books about how to paint watercolours, but they need to be read with reserve. They are best used to give hints, but the only way to understand hints is to work them out in your own time and not to copy the author's work. In the end what you are trying to achieve will come right, and after much practice you will say 'Ah, now at last I see what he or she meant!' The sort of hint that is valuable is about using lighter tones and fainter colours for your backgrounds, or in other words using colour to enhance perspective. And, incidentally, you may need to learn more about perspective than you learnt by drawing cubes at school, especially little tricks about drawing people at various distances.

Some artists who begin as amateurs and then succeed in selling a large number of pictures, and decide to become 'professionals', are tempted to overdo the acquisition of an easily recognised 'style' by exaggerating certain characteristics in their pictures, which may indeed bring increased sales. But this leads to a dead end: you see small galleries full of stylised – indeed stilted – pictures all looking much the same. Soon this ceases to be art and the artist ceases to be an artist. He or she makes a bit of money but they just become a conveyor belt.

I took up watercolours entirely for my own satisfaction, but it so happened that my brother and sister-in-law were running a gallery close by and in due course they were kind enough to say that they would like to exhibit my work. The big problem for any artist who wants to sell his work is how to exhibit it. One way is to persuade a gallery (or rather an art shop) to take a couple of his drawings on a commission basis: that is to say a 'sale or return' with a percentage payable to the gallery in the event of a sale. This would probably run at 30 to 35% plus VAT, after which your payment should be declared for income tax, unless you can persuade HMRC that you are a non-professional artist simply selling the occasional chattel, even if it is home-made; or that the tiny income can be disregarded as 'de minimis' – too small to be noticed. Before exhibiting your work you must pay for it to be mounted and framed. There is a strong temptation to do this cheaply, but in my opinion that does not pay. So it is a long campaign to get to the stage when your work is seen by more than a very few people, one or two of whom might like it enough to buy a picture, and after paying all the costs and tax on the net amount you may have about 20% of the sale price in your pocket. If you are in London you can add the extra nought or two; indeed you must do so or people will think your work not worth buying. Costs are much higher, but you have a chance of making a worthwhile sum.

Ideally what you need to find is a dedicated gallery in which, by one kind of arrangement or another, you can put a good number of works on display for, say, two or three weeks: you can then circularise your friends with a fair chance that they may come, either to a 'private view' (with refreshments) at the beginning, or at some time during the period when they are not too busy. It was my good fortune to have this facility nearby, my brother and sister-in-law inviting usually three of perhaps four artists to show their work at one of their annual or biennial exhibitions. They built up a good clientele, and I did sell quite a few pictures, the most in a single exhibition being fifty-six. That does get your work known, although maybe not many people are going to buy more than one, even if you have several exhibitions. But after a few years the time, trouble and expense of running an exhibition outran the benefits for the proprietors and, as I have explained, the actual income for the artist was minimal. After three or four of those exhibitions, the only ones I took part in were in aid of charities on their own premises. This does enable them to invite all their supporters and to motivate them to open their purses in aid of a good cause, although for practical reasons they could probably only open the exhibition for one weekend, which is not long enough for all the interested people to be able to come. Moreover, you can't fleece your supporters too often without putting them off: once a decade, maybe. And you have to be a prolific amateur to be able to hold this sort of exhibition more than occasionally. If you 'turn professional', unless you are very exceptional and have friends and colleagues around the world of art colleges and art dealers, you need your own little gallery.

I am known by my friends to be rather opinionated and I own that it is presumptuous for a mere amateur to give any advice at all about how to launch yourself into an occupation which demands a great deal of practice for all except those who possess a touch of genius and have no need for advice anyway. Furthermore, I admit to using a camera rather than always sketching, and to doing most of my work indoors, both of which are frowned on by pundits, although I sketch out of doors in pencil, or sometimes in ink, as much as I can, and jot down notes on my sketches. I am comforted by knowing that Turner did all his finishing work in his studio, and I have the advantage that a modern striplight reproduces daylight.

To those who can successfully paint in the open air, I take off my hat. I am not one of them, alas. And as for a camera, it is a dangerous ally with the strong temptation to copy it. You could say it is the friend of a lazy artist. That is a fair point, and if you allow yourself simply to copy a photograph you will never be an artist. But it is a quick fix, a short cut to a great deal of sketching, and it does what artists in bygone time could never benefit from: it fixes a sky in time – stops it – which is something you can never do without a camera while the clouds are moving and changing shape before your very eyes. Constable with extraordinary virtuosity and plenty of paint thinner – linseed oil and white spirit – used oils to adhere to his rule 'to paint a sky every day': his sketches, many of which have happily survived, are much sought after, because they show more movement (more 'life'?) than his finished oils, in spite of all his virtuosity in his large finished landscape paintings. But actually, even with the advantage of a sky fixed in time by a camera, you cannot copy it in watercolour because the medium demands so much speedy work before a wash starts to dry and you must then stop until it has done so. You simply do not have time to shape each cloud exactly as you might wish.

Constable is unusual if not unique amongst landscape artists in using oils for his preliminary sketches of skies. He spent many years before

Watercolour Landscape

he could feel to his own satisfaction that he had mastered his medium. His mastery of oils did enable him to shape every cloud as and when he saw it, as a watercolourist cannot hope to do. Unfortunately many watercolourists surrender to the difficulty of painting skies as they see them by simply abandoning the effort and developing an oversimplified, even naive and conventional, form of sky which tends to appear in all their pictures. I must admit that, looking back on some of my earlier efforts to paint a sky as I saw it, I am surprised that I did not surrender to this temptation myself: my earlier clouds look lumpy and solid, just as I say they ought not to look. True, I am referring here to days of fleeting sunshine and cloud so typical of Britain, rather than stormy skies which are much simpler to paint. (A day of cloudless blue skies is not a good one for painting, simple though the subject it presents may be.)

Clouds are not solid objects: they do not have rigid edges, they merge with each other and with their background of blue. Therefore you must paint them wet. That leads to an almost frenzied few minutes of excitement. It's like playing a salmon. If you don't respond quickly, he's gone. If you're too much in a hurry, or work too hard, he's gone. If you slacken off for a second, he's gone. And if you try too hard to steer him, you simply won't succeed.

I will finish, then, by giving you my home recipe for painting a blue sky with fairly large mainly 'white' clouds. There are all sorts of skies, an infinite variety indeed, which you can try to turn into skies-in-pictures. Did you know that the French have two plurals for *ciel*, the sky? One is *cieux*, meaning just skies, although why we need a plural at all, in any language, has always baffled me. There is only one sky. But there are infinite numbers of skies-in-pictures, *ciels*. I'll try to paint just one. Get into my head a rough idea of the size and shape of the big clouds near the top. As you go down, they get further away, smaller and easier to paint. Their bottoms will be flatter than their tops, the tones lighter. Sketch them in very roughly and faintly with a pencil if you wish, but don't expect to be able to stick to this because you must cover the paper very rapidly. Whenever you use a pencil, rub it out soon after the paint has dried. Don't leave it too long or it will be hard to get it out. Never use a pen or pencil to 'create' an outline. Let your paint do that as far as it will.

Equip yourself with two tumblers of clean water. The idea is to use one for a clean brush, the other to rinse a paint-filled one. In the

Watercolour Landscape

excitement of the moment I always forget which is which, or find I have dipped my brush into a mug of tea. But two are better than one. Have three if you wish. Also have a good roll of cotton wool and at least two or three old bits of cloth or handkerchief, the former for dabbing your pigments to create merged borders or lift out pigment where you have applied too much. You will need to dampen each bit of cotton wool as you use it – use plenty of small bits – unless you want to make a wet spot fuzzy, or prevent a puddle from forming. You can, alternatively, do most of this – but probably not all – with your brushes, if you keep wiping them with the cloths. Have your two or three biggest brushes immediately to hand, wet and ready to go.

Squeeze out plenty of paint in the little compartments on your porcelain palettes overnight so it can harden. I like to have three rows each of about eight of these little compartments on porcelain palettes, with the blues in the top row, the middle row left empty for mixing colours, and the yellows and browns in the lowest row. (Luxuries, seldom used, can go at the end of the middle row.) The more clean compartments you have for mixing, the better. At the end of every session, clean them with a damp rag.

Mix a large amount of cobalt blue and water: a big puddle. You don't want to run out half way through. I also like to mix some of the cloud-shade colour I propose to use. I prefer greyish rather than brownish. There is a lot to be said for cobalt and light red. Add more pigment to darken it as required. Ultramarine and burnt sienna is another good mixture, more savage, but on the other hand it is a good rule, even if a rule to be broken occasionally, to use only one blue (with many shades and variations, of course, by adding other pigments) for one sky. Dampen your raw sienna, as you may need it to add light to the highlights of the clouds; and perhaps some light red with it. (There are a surprising number of colours in an apparently blue and white sky.)

Take a deep breath and your biggest brush fully loaded with rather strong cobalt blue. It does need to be strong at the top, getting paler as you go down. (The lowest areas of sky – and indeed cloud – may benefit from a light second wash of raw sienna, and a touch of light red, depending on the light in the sky.)

Begin quickly with your biggest brush – the bigger the better – working the cobalt, using plenty of water, more or less horizontally across the paper but leaving the spaces for clouds blank, refilling your brush (with both water and pigment) as and when you need to. As you work down the paper each horizontal brush stroke will take up the surplus water from the bottom of the previous stroke.

Now put clean water in the spaces you've left for clouds, except where you want to leave the brightest white highlights which you must – you absolutely must – leave untouched and dry. These highlights can be quite small, or can be reduced later, but once you have dampened the paper you can never make them bigger. Use another brush as you go along to put the shadows on the clouds. (Before you start, you will of course know exactly the direction of the sun.) Darken the shadows as you get nearer their edges furthest from the sun. There will be more shadow at the sides and lower edges of the clouds than at the top. Big clouds are not just one single lump: give them shadow wherever they need it to give them shape.

Having so far worked at maximum speed so that the wash is not yet drying out, quickly go round all the edges where blue sky meets cloud, and where the white of a cloud gives way to shadow, with a barely damp brush which you will probably need to wipe frequently, so as to merge or blur the clouds with the sky and also grade your shadows from light to dark without a break. If you wish, you can use little bits of wet cotton wool instead of a brush (throw away each one before it gets dirty). During the whole of this operation you will have to judge how much wetness you need in your brush or your cotton wool.

As soon as the wash starts to dry out: stop!

It is far better to leave the job half done – to let the paper dry out completely, either with patience or with the gentle aid of a hair-drier; and then to start again by wetting it (with or without additional pigment) – than it is to go on working once it is drying out.

It is very difficult to finish a complete sky in one wash – other than a very simple and probably boring one. If you can do so, you are a master! A sky finished in one wash has more life in it, more movement and spontaneity than one which has taken several washes. But if it is not finished, don't fool yourself that it is. It may need a little darkening of the blue at the top, some refinement to the shadows on the clouds, some merging of hard lines here and there or even hardening of woolly lines at the bottom edges of the clouds, which tend to look quite solid; or some more sunlight in the far distance just above the horizon – a light wash of raw sienna or light red – or you may indeed not have had time to put in the distant clouds at all. The only important thing is not to continue as the paint begins to dry, and not to start again until it has dried completely.

Then, when you have more or less mastered one method of painting one fairly ambitious sky like this, see if you can create your own interpretations by slightly different techniques – for instance using Prussian blue which is less sugary, more restrained, rather than cobalt, and which gives you more freedom in edging cautiously towards green to bring in the light of the sun (even more important in sea than in sky). Turner relied much more on Prussian than on cobalt which only came in during his life time, and although the cobalt added a wonderful prettiness to some of his later sun-drenched mists and skies, I wonder whether he might have been better off without it?

4
Shooting

My family and I have had wonderful opportunities to enjoy shooting game on land both in North Wales and in eastern Scotland ever since I was a teenager; and to invite our friends to share our good luck. In one respect I claim to be something of an expert, namely on the driving of grouse in the Grampians, having learnt what I know from many years trudging the moor walking-up the grouse before there was any driving. My brother Peter and I walked-up the grouse at Glen Dye almost every year from 1947 until we ourselves restarted driving in 1961. We got to know every feature of this large moor, we studied where the grouse would lie in various conditions and times of year, and every time a bird or a covey rose we watched the flight line. We mostly had the head keeper with us, first Duncan Fraser and then his successor Dan Dowell from 1953. There was usually an under-keeper to fill out the line and help with the picking-up and carrying the bag. I listened to those who knew more than I did and would often be able to absorb little bits of knowledge and comments on past experiences, because an understanding of the way grouse behave is part of the pleasure of walking-up grouse. However, I do not write as an expert, pretended or otherwise, but simply to describe my enjoyment for the interest of those who share my enthusiasm.

In spite of my luck, and my opportunities on some occasions to enjoy the cream of shooting, my love of the sport depends largely on the pleasure of being out in the country in search of wild quarry, coming home in the evening with a few friends and perhaps with only a few head of game, preferably a mixed bag.

I would like to dispel two misconceptions. The first is that expensive shooting is always, or even usually, the best shooting. This is not sour grapes: I am one of the lucky few who has shot driven grouse in a good year on one of the eastern Scottish moors with its rounded hills where the butts are set to give a short skyline and the sport is second to none. And I enjoy the excitement of shooting high, fast, unpredictable and preferably curling pheasants, although I am not very good at it. But I

Shooting

am not the sort of person who gets about in a chauffeur-driven car, and during an actual day's shooting is delivered to his peg in a Range Rover.

The second misconception is that some people who are considered, not only by themselves but also by magazine editors, to be sufficiently expert to write articles for journals about shooting actually know very little about the true nature of the sport. An 'expert' recently wrote in *Country Life* that 'walked-up grouse are regarded as the world's most challenging game bird' alongside a picture of himself trying to shoot one with his footwork completely wrong. He doesn't say (as he well might) that unless you get your footwork right you will not succeed in any form of shooting, and he doesn't say that walked-up grouse are regarded by him (consequently) as the most difficult form of shooting; but he just says that they 'are regarded' without saying 'by people like me who can't hit them'. (Alongside is a picture of his chauffeur, to whom he gave the unfortunate grouse he did hit: perhaps he should have had it stuffed.) He caps the authenticity of his opinion by quoting the 'world' as his field of experience, but it is world-wide nonsense, not world-wide truth.

It would be ridiculous to argue that the pleasure of the day varies inversely with the size of the bag. But who is to say that the wildfowler who returns with one goose or even one wigeon has had less pleasure than the sportsman who shoots hundreds of reared driven pheasants, most of them flying straight, almost every day of the season? All forms of game-shooting require skill, but for a naturally gifted athlete the skill required often amounts to a knack, aided by concentration, determination and a good deal of practice.

I had learnt to shoot with an air rifle at my preparatory school, and I began shooting rabbits with a .22 rifle in Scotland in the 1930s. My 'teens passed during the war when gamekeepers were few and far between and rearing game was out of the question. Meat was rationed and anything edible we could shoot was for the pot. We had short winter holidays at Hawarden in North Wales where my father taught me the rudiments of game shooting and the rules of safety. Most of our small bag was pigeons, which had the advantage that they could be plucked and cleaned in a few minutes.

After our wartime summer holidays in Scotland we would return south by train, preferably with a haunch of venison, a couple of blue hares and a brace or two of grouse – the latter hard won by tramping for hours through long heather, for there were no gamekeepers to burn

Shooting

it. We had to do all the cleaning and plucking, which added to the satisfaction of consuming this luxurious addition to our rations.

During our postwar holidays, by which time we lived at Hawarden, Peter and I often walked out to get a few pigeons and occasionally a duck or a partridge or a pheasant. Peter had a clever sheepdog which he had rescued as a puppy from a reed bed on the Severn and appropriately named Moses, who found our birds but had to be pursued rapidly before he could himself eat them (as we wished to do); but one January day when I was out on my own I shot a duck over water, stripped my clothes off and swam out to retrieve it. It didn't occur to me at the time that this might be a stupid thing to do. Both Peter and I became teachers, and the school summer holidays in those days still ended at the end of September (Michaelmas Day under the ancient calendar, when the harvest was gathered in and the young men could be spared to return to their studies) so we were able to shoot the partridges on the farm land.

Fields were much smaller than they are now and every farm had at least two or three small fields – mostly about three to five acres – of root crops: turnips and potatoes, although these crops were also grown in larger fields. We would walk around the surrounding grass fields and stubbles, getting a few long shots at partridges if we were lucky, and driving most of the coveys into the roots, where they would sit tight. A covey might get up from a root field in a flurry or they might get up one by one, or a few at a time, but it was here, walking back and forth, that we could make our bag, which was usually around four or five brace; our record was ten brace. There were quite a few brown hares on the 'low ground', delicious if jugged. One day I shot a partridge which almost fell on a brown hare, putting it up, so it too was despatched When we retrieved the hare, we found a second dead partridge close by. A hare and a partridge in one shot, or a hare and a brace of partridges as a right-and-left, was a rare achievement which I mentioned occasionally when two or three sportsmen were gathered together to 'shoot a line'; but some years later Peter was taking part in one of these conversations, and he claimed that it was he, not I, who had got this right-and-left. He may have been right; or he may not; we shall never know.

The fields are much larger now on this land, sloping down from the road between Broughton and Hawarden to the flat fields below, which had been saltings, covered at high tides, until the Dee was canalised in the 1730s. In some of these meadows the old meandering ditches can

Shooting

still be seen, while others were of such excellent alluvial quality as to be worth levelling and draining for arable farming. Most of these reclaimed fields were large, even in those days, and a few hedges have since then been ripped out. Lapwings bred there and flocks of them wheeled around in winter. A curlew appeared from time to time. In wintry weather redshanks and golden plover appeared in large flocks, and snipe and jack snipe settled in the few small fields which had defied drainage and were full of rushes.

My uncle gave me his Scottish property in 1960, and throughout the Sixties while I was working in Sussex we went to Fasque near Fettercairn every year over the New Year with a few friends. The pheasants were all wild birds. Not a bird had been reared there since 1914, which marked the end of the era of record bags. My uncle's predecessor, another bachelor, Sir John Gladstone, had succeeded his father in the big house with a full team of servants in the 1880s, devoting much of his life from then onwards to shooting and fishing. He inaugurated grouse driving at Glen Dye in the 1880s, and resited many of his original lines of butts in 1912; but around the turn of the century there had been a full decade of lean grouse years, and he turned his mind and his money to rearing pheasants at Fasque, achieving a record bag of 3,000 pheasants in one day in 1905. By my day the only people who remembered those years at Fasque were the Queen Mother, the old Earl of Southesk, the late estate joiner's daughter Jemima Towns who had worked as a youngster in the kitchen, and the daughter of a gamekeeper, Lilian Menzies; but there were also full records in the game books.

John Gladstone admired the work of Scottish keepers on the high ground, but he did not think they knew much about pheasants and partridges. He therefore imported two keepers from Suffolk on the recommendation of his Fellowes uncle: Bert Dingle as the head keeper and Mrs Menzies's father as his assistant. Lilian had attended the estate school (which had closed in 1914) and had suffered cultural pressure to obviate her East Anglian accent in favour of the proper Inglis spoken by the Scots. She herself married one of the gardeners – he was the glasshouse man – who however had lost a leg in the First World War and never fully recovered.

Eastern Scotland, like East Anglia, is good ground for wild pheasants and partridges. In the era of traditional farming, good keepering and fair weather were enough to assure good sport – but not record bags in

Shooting

the competitive climate of Edwardian affluence. Dingle was a master of his trade, for not only could he organise the rearing of pheasants in big numbers, which apart from his regular staff of keepers involved taking on eleven casuals for the rearing season, but he could also devise and mastermind the strategy and tactics of a day's shooting to provide both famously high birds and record-breaking bags.

One man working full-time in those days could be in charge of just 250 pheasant chicks and poults, hatched and reared by broody hens and then fed egg mixed with breadcrumbs, laboriously prepared by the keepers.

Having reared the pheasants and put them out to cover, the problem must have been how to kill 3,000 on one Scottish November day before the advent of motor cars. The time available amounted to about six hours, from just after 9 a.m. to just after 3 p.m. There were three drives at Fasque, as I believe was the case on most other large shoots. And it was vital to get at least half the bag in the first and biggest drive. There were eight guns, each in those days still with three guns and two loaders. The hammerless ejector had in theory made it possible to achieve the same result with two guns and one loader, but the habits of old and experienced guns die hard, and anyway it was easier to keep three guns going round than to keep passing two guns between a gun and one loader.

The pheasants had to be sent over more or less the whole line in a steady stream but without flushes. This could best be achieved with the main lines of flight not at a right-angle to the line of guns, but at a slant so that birds not killed by one gun could mostly be floored by the next. For the first drive at Fasque, named after a folly called the Octagon at the top of the wood, most of the birds must have been flushed from a fairly small area, and although they were high and fast most of them were flying straight.

For this first drive from the Octagon, the birds were walked into the wood by beaters from a wide area. Under-keepers would then assist Dingle to control them, and he would put them up from a number of short v-shaped or w-shaped fences, a few at a time.

To make the arithmetic easy let us consider a bag of 1,600 at the first drive, and perhaps 800 at the second and 600 at the third. The average kill for each gun at the first drive would be 200, but the hottest spots must in practice have needed to kill nearer 300. I am sure that all the guns achieved five kills for six cartridges, if not better. They must have needed a rest – and lunch – before the later drives.

Shooting

All this came abruptly to an end in 1914 and no birds were reared at Fasque until my brother Peter with his family arrived there in the 1970s with a brief to diversify the activities of the estate. All the birds we shot during the Sixties were wild. I let the shoot to a syndicate of retired business and professional men from Glasgow, sporting people who were not out for large bags, on condition that I could have two shoots over the New Year. One of these shoots was in the better coverts where we usually got close to 100 birds, mostly pheasants, and the other was essentially a day of rough shooting when we would get a mixed bag of perhaps thirty or forty head. On the third day we went over to Glen Dye.

The covert shooting was rather different from a shoot at reared game nowadays, more improvised and haphazard, and the wild birds were more unpredictable than reared ones. You would be shown roughly where to stand but could move if necessary: 'Adjust yourself, doctor' as the keeper, who could not get his tongue round Chenevix-Trench, said to Tony. Most of the birds were high, but they were all fast and seldom flying straight. We were usually five or perhaps six guns: myself and Rosamund, my brother Peter and sometimes my sister Penelope (Francis was mostly in the United States), usually Tony Chenevix-Trench who was then head master of Bradfield and Michael Ricketts whom (like Tony) I had known at Oxford and who was one of the housemasters there; Nicholas Headlam (the only non-schoolmaster) and in the later years Alastair Graham who was teaching at Eton.

We slept in the east end of Fasque, where the rooms although large were smaller than in the rest of the house, and heated with coal fires in the evenings. We had our meals at that end of the house also, in the former senior servants' dining room, a charming room with a barrel-vaulted ceiling, where the butler, the housekeeper and the cook had been served by junior maids, next to the pantry, now the kitchen. Miss Towns and Mrs Menzies came in and looked after us.

Our sitting room was at the opposite end of the house, quite a walk away through an arctic temperature. This was the 'business room', the late Sir John's sitting room, never much given over to business. Smaller than the drawing room and the billiards room, it was nevertheless the size of a two-storey three-bedroom council house, except that the ceiling would have had to be about a foot higher. We heated one end of it by a big log fire and an old-fashioned electric fire facing each other, with our armchairs on either side facing inwards, and amused ourselves in the evenings by playing Battleships.

Shooting

These shoots at Fasque were some of the most enjoyable I remember. The wild pheasants on day one were fast and unpredictable. Driving them over the farm cottages at the top of the hill, Tony bet Peter that he could not drop one through the pyjamas drying on the washing-line: Peter got quite close, but needless to say exactly how close was never resolved, the distance tending to diminish with the passing years. The second day covered a large area of farm and woodland with many spinneys, ponds here and there, and little valleys with tinkling burns. You never knew what would come out next, perhaps a pheasant or a duck or a woodcock. You mostly had to shoot on sight, but part of the fun of these small drives was that you could often see your neighbours' targets before they could. We would shout 'blackbird' or 'moorhen' to Tony and he usually had a shot at it, for there was no time to pause and consider.

Each little spinney required a brief tactical plan depending on the wind and other considerations, and most of them rewarded us with a couple of wild, cunning, fast pheasants, or perhaps three or four. There were a few wheeling partridges on the remaining stubbles which could be driven over us by the two or three keepers and beaters, and the occasional high pigeon.

These rough days provided the most enjoyable sport I ever remember from a day's shooting, with many memorable incidents to cover fully in the evening's conversation. Yet I suppose that the cream of these holidays was on the third day when we would shoot the wild pheasants at Glen Dye, over the Cairn O'Mount to the north of Fasque and thus truly in the Highlands. The snow often used to come between Christmas and the New Year. If there was a sprinkling at Fasque, the Cairn road might be impassable, although in those good old days it was ploughed by the Kincardineshire County Council immediately, and often kept viable even with several feet of drifted snow either side of the road near the top. The economy of this little county between Aberdeen and Angus depended on the agriculture of the The Howe of the Mearns, famous for its potatoes and raspberries, its malting barley and its Aberdeen-Angus beef. It was a top priority to keep every farm lane as well as the main roads clear of snow. Land Rovers were few and far between (and draughty) but if we could not get over the Cairn in a two-wheel-drive car we could usually go round by the Slug road via Stonehaven.

January, so foul in England and Wales, is often the best month of the

Shooting

winter in eastern Scotland. There may be snow, but that can be coped with. It is cold, but the cold is a dry, bracing cold and there are many days with cloudless skies. The sun is low, making the whole landscape look like a film-set; and in this exquisite glen with its steep terraces, tumbling river, clear brown pools and foamy waterfalls, what a film-set.

The head keeper Dan Dowell used to feed the wild pheasants at a few spots in the hope of drawing them in to an area where they could be driven over us. Even if they rose quite close to the guns they could fly like bullets, climbing at about 60 degrees and looking the size of tennis balls. The day's shooting consisted of working down the Dye from the point near the Lodge where the moorland ceased and the woods began. The rough land near the river in the valley lower down is covered by scrub birch, its undergrowth reduced to grass and rushes by the sheep and cattle for which it provided ideal shelter with grazing in hard winter weather.

Higher up the sides of the glen are the big woods of pine, larch and spruce of all sizes, every tree self-sown since the 1953 gale and the simultaneous onslaught of myxomatosis which had eliminated the rabbits and made planting unnecessary.

Sometimes the guns would stand at fixed spots, but in two little drives, one at Tillyfumerie and the other just below the Bridge of Dye, the line of guns along the river bank would walk upstream parallel to the beaters who were up on the steep river terraces covered in scrub and bracken and Scots pine. Here and there they put up a pheasant or two, which would rise and curl stupendously, aiming for the other side of the river. Everybody could see more or less every bird and admire the occasional triumphant shot. Year after year our bag for the day was likely to be between twenty and thirty pheasants with perhaps the odd duck, pigeon or woodcock: not a vast bag, but an unforgettable day's sport.

Peter and his family went to live at Fasque, and one of his enterprises was to develop a shoot, including many drives on the upper ground which had not been feasible before the advent of Land Rovers. The estate has a small grouse moor and below it a strip of forestry. Below the trees is a belt of rough grazing with a few arable fields, and below that again some good agricultural land. Modern transport and modern methods of rearing made it possible to exploit the higher ground, ideal for showing high fast pheasants in exquisite surroundings, notably along the several burns which rose on the moor and flowed through the

Shooting

forest in steep little glens. Our New Year holidays, which had been predominantly rough shooting, now became covert shoots as challenging as anyone could wish, sometimes more so. Very few of the pheasants were out of shot, as they are for instance on some of the best-known shoots in North Wales, and very few were flying straight: those which were were crossing the valleys, requiring extreme quickness if they were to be felled. In a commercial shoot most of the income has to come from the biggest shoots in November and December: after that one is more or less mopping up, but the quality has become even more challenging.

The Fasque pattern was applied at Glen Dye on a much smaller scale, still working down the Glen from the edge of the moor to the lower parts of the forest.

A few years previously we also started to build up the Hawarden pheasant shoot in north-east Wales for the first time since the 1930s, but here the object was much more modest – to create a family shoot in which a few friends might play a part in order to defray the cost. In 1968 Peter, who was then still a master at Shrewsbury and thus within fairly easy reach, found for the first time since Dingle had retired soon after the war a wonderful keeper in Ellis Davies, the kind of person who inspires the thought that keepers are born, not made. Vermin was soon under control and he started to rear a few pheasants under broody hens. Peter was convinced that there was no reason for Hawarden's old reputation for low birds to continue, since there were some spinneys and high banks, although most of the estate's woodlands in terms of acreage consisted of one big block of about 400 acres, unsuitable for a shoot. I planted three small spinneys, each of about half an acre, in suitable spots because I thought that covert shooting proper with a full team of guns would never be affordable on a family shoot and I wanted to create a good rough shoot for the next generation. But modern methods of rearing pheasants were just beginning to come in: first with turkey 'starter crumbs', ideal for pheasant poults, and then with improved incubators and warm electric lamps in rearing sheds which allowed one to dispense with broody chickens.

Ellis started to catch some hens in the spring and collect their eggs, and to prevent in-breeding we used to exchange some cocks with neighbouring estates. Eventually Ellis was rearing about 3,000 birds each season.

Shooting

I had no knowledge or experience of creating a covert shoot from an area of farmland and woods, and I sought advice from what was to become the British Association for Shooting and Conservation. The advice was well thought out and could be reduced to a number of basic aims and methods. One lesson walking round the potential coverts taught me what to aim at. The essence was to feed birds away from the areas where they had been reared, to woods where they could effectively be flushed to provide high shots on their way home; to remove or split up ground cover where it was too dense, and to plant more undergrowth where it was too sparse. On this basis I devised seven drives around one large release pen on the south side of the Lake: three from the west – the Dogs' Graves, Will's Plantation and the Old Castle; two from the east – the Triangle and the Broughton Belt; and two in the Beech Wood to the south. These drives, developed over the years in the light of experience and adjusted in response to the growth and removal of trees, have remained the core of our shoot ever since. We also had a drive near Ellis's house (the 'Elysian Fields') and we made two more pens. One was in the wood called Poverty, former farmland of such poor quality that it had been fenced off and allowed to go wild for partridges before the First War: this served the Old Cathedral, named for its lofty vault of beech, now all fallen; the (tree) Nursery, the Elders and The Square, the two latter long since defunct. The other pen served the Dingle and the Firs Wood, providing two valuable afternoon drives. There are not many coverts where the birds will come to feed in the morning and then happily stay around all day until disturbed in the afternoon.

A few other drives were used for some years, and almost all the drives have changed, especially the Firs Wood and Will's Plantation where by natural causes (gales) and selective felling we have been able to draw the guns back to the water's edge and provide a challenge second to none with the birds flying over high trees at the top of the banks. What a stroke of luck it has been for me to develop and adjust this shoot on our home ground over the course of forty years. We do not aim for big bags but we do aim to spread the sport out over the season.

The whole of our shoot occupies certainly not more than 250 acres. Much of the pleasure derives from the fact that all the beaters and stops and pickers-up come because they enjoy the day, and they all become friends. The team has changed gradually over the years as old members retire and young ones are recruited, often their sons and daughters. Ellis in his eighties continued to come out, although he puffed a bit and liked a lift up the hills in the Land Rover. This is the long wheel-based Land Rover I proudly bought in 1969, just about when Ellis came, although in its mature years it needs sympathetic coaxing across difficult ground. Ellis in his eighties was an invaluable stop in the trickiest positions, because he possessed the rare virtue of knowing how to stand still in exactly the right place.

When Ellis retired a successor recommended by him was appointed but turned out to be unsatisfactory. He was removed at quite an early stage of his first season and the situation was gallantly rescued by two of our most skilled supporters, Gerry Evans and Dave Pope. Gerry, an early-retired telephone engineer, then took over and acted as our part-time volunteer keeper with entire success for many years. Our team of beaters, stops and pickers-up was kept together and, like our member guns, has continued ever since, refreshed after the retirement of veterans with younger recruits. Over the years Gerry's keepership in partnership with my own management has enabled us to continue to evolve the various drives with the objective of showing an improved proportion of fast, high and unpredictable pheasants. Several drives have been improved by the establishment of small game crops, none more than half an acre in extent, and all now able to provide nine guns with a prospect of a good shoot.

When eventually Gerry retired, Dean Eagles took over from him, a professional tree surgeon but a sportsman up to the eyeballs. I retired as Shoot Captain and fortunately Chris Maddock, who farms near Buckley, agreed to take over. This has turned out to be a very fortunate succession, bringing a fresh look and further development, of which so far the most notable characteristic has been an improvement in the proportion of birds which fly high and fast, and also in the quality of the earlier shoots.

Three years later I retired as a gun. I had always insisted that this should be a walk-round shoot in order to retain the atmosphere of a family shoot, replaced by a group of friends who were interested in what went on and not merely delivered to their pegs in total ignorance of the countryside and wildlife around them, or why the pheasants might behave as they did. Fortunately for me the next two generations of our family enjoy shooting and the countryside: our sons Charlie and Rob continue to come every year. Our grandsons Jack, Tom, and Will are already fully-fledged participants, with Felix and Piers following on. One or two of the girls have had a go occasionally but so far only the boys have wanted to continue.

After the war my uncle continued to invite the family to the shooting lodge at Glen Dye for the summer holidays. As in wartime, there was no manpower to burn the moor in the postwar years, although vermin was still effectively controlled, and it would take a long time to get a burning cycle going again. With taxation at penal rates there was a general view that 'big' shooting, including all grouse-driving and pheasant-rearing, would never return. However, during the early 1950s it was clear that the grouse were coming back. Our daily bags rose from just a few brace to perhaps occasionally twenty or thirty brace on our best days in the late 1940s and early Fifties. By 1953 we might be getting fifty brace on the best day or two of the season. As the Fifties wore on, came the stupendous days when we reached a hundred brace on two or three of the best days of walking-up, with just four or five guns. This itself posed a logistical problem since our entire transport column on the moor consisted of one pony.

My uncle never liked to have more than four guns – occasionally five. He thought that to have a long line would present too many problems and too much work for the keepers to cope with. Shooting with this fairly small line was, however, what made it possible to obtain big bags. A long line of eight or nine guns takes much longer to change direction, and is liable to greater delays in picking up any bird which is difficult to find. The best areas as August wears on are often on the shoulders of hills, with good drainage and sheltered sunny spots and good crops of blaeberries. Adjustments in the direction of the line and minor movements up or down hill, or to get the top end or the bottom end forward in response to the wind as one works round a hill or a ridge, are much easier with a short line. These tactics are vital if one is to get the best sport, and it helps too if the guns are experienced and know each other: a hand signal or a word passed down the line will do the trick. If a bird falls a long way off it is sometimes possible for a keeper with his dog to go after it while the line is still moving.

In a strong wind the top gun may put up birds which produce exciting driven shots for those at the bottom. Grouse like to stick to their own 'hill', although precisely what is meant by that word is not straightforward. They like too to follow a contour rather than flying up

GROUSE DRIVES ON LOCHNAWEEN

One Mile

The upper and lower lines of butts are almost in a straight line and each provides 'return' drives facing in opposite directions, marked 1,2,3,4. A variation is the little drive A along a ridge lower down. The 'balloons' show approximately the ground taken in by each drive, and the lines with arrows show the tracks of the beaters and the flight lines of the grouse. They show how the birds tend to follow the contours and will not cross from their own hill or ridge.

Shooting

hill or down (it is this which makes driving possible) and they will tend to fly back to their home ground if and when they can. This again, like the concept of 'their own hill', needs qualification: their movements will also depend on the weather (they like ground sheltered from wind) and the supply of water and of food – at first insects but then primarily the shoots of young heather; and a week or two later berries if they are to be had. The ideal line is one in which the guns understand these points and know why the head keeper or the gun who is master-minding the line wants to make adjustments. Apart from anything else this greatly increases the interest of the day's sport. Nothing is more infuriating than a gun (or an enthusiastic young keeper) who gets in front of the line. You almost always see your neighbour's birds when they rise before he does, and a person in front of the line is liable to put them up just out of range, and at the same time to reduce the already narrow angle for safe shooting. Getting in front is even worse than getting behind, which is dangerous if birds rise or fly behind the line. This is another reason why a short line (if one can afford such a luxury) of people who understand these matters is an advantage.

Our younger brother Francis came on stream during the Fifties: Peter, he and I were all extremely fit, which is essential with a short line if one is to get the best of a day's sport, although it is counter-productive to walk fast. Each step needs to be careful and deliberate, ensuring a firm base if a bird should rise. Our father and uncles had by now retired. The numbers were made up by two or three cousins or friends – Ernle Gilbert, Andrew Burnaby-Atkins, Michael Merriam and Nicholas Headlam were amongst those who were often with us. Our cousin John once shot seven grouse with a right and left on the flat ground of the Leggie, and received a stern ticking off from Duncan Fraser.

Duncan, the mastermind from the time of the resiting of the butts in 1912 until the end of the great decade of the 1930s, eventually retired in 1953 and was succeeded by Dan Dowell. We did not know it at the time, but Dan was to develop as another master of the driven grouse – a rare bird if one may use that metaphor.

We used to shoot four times a week, on Mondays and Tuesdays and on Thursdays and Fridays, leaving the weekends and Wednesdays free for family activities: visits to the beach at St Cyrus on fine days and to Dunnottar Castle on wet days, for example; or fishing for sea-trout and grilse – and the occasional salmon – on the Feugh if the water was right,

Shooting

and for little brown trout, plentiful in those days, 'breakfast fish' as they were known, on the Dye with the children.

Occasionally there was a chance of some other shooting. Once when walking up on Heatheryhaugh we rose more than a hundred mallard from the floe ground, which consists of groups of small narrow ponds all about a foot deep characteristic of little plateaus at the tops of hills where the rock has been consolidated and flattened by a massive weight of permanent ice; and we walked out the next morning to flight them at 4 a.m, having started soon after three.

In September we might be able to walk-up the partridges on the farm land during one or two mornings or afternoons, provided that there had been an early harvest. There were still stooks of corn in the small fields in those days, where birds might take cover, creating excellent sport. On the lake at Fasque there would probably be some duck, mostly mallard, wigeon and teal. There were four butts on the narrow part of the kidney-shaped lake where they might be in range as they took flight, each butt shared by two guns for a short but frenzied shooting as the duck flew off. One day I was sharing a butt with Adele Smyth-Osbourne, and four duck flew rapidly past us from left to right. Being the right-hand gun I took the two leading birds, and down they came. Adele had the presence of mind to take the other two, and down they came too. We congratulated each other – I felt strongly that she had done (even) better than I had; but she would not have it. 'No,' she said, 'it was you who did well.' It took me some time to realise that she had not fired at all: I had killed all four with my two barrels. Whether that was clever or not is a moot point.

Walking up grouse can provide easy sport on a hot day early in the season, and very difficult sport on a windy day in early September. After that, the grouse are too wild for walking up: they nearly all rise out of range unless shot over dogs.

If the weather is fine during the first week or two after 12 August the birds sit tight and the excitement arises when a covey explodes quite close at hand. If the whole covey gets up together the old birds will be the first to rise and (by general if not universal agreement) the best to kill because the average grouse only lives for about three years. (Peter argued that it was best to leave the old ones as they had proved that they could rear a brood.) The experienced gun will polish them off, before quickly reloading and having a go at the young birds. Quickness is essential, but a hurried shot will often fail. Even more important than

Shooting

quickness is good footwork: that is to say to get your feet firmly planted, left in front of right, even if this takes up a few precious seconds on rough ground. If you are experienced in this respect and a covey gets up quite close to the line you may be able to reload two cartridges and get a right and left at the young birds, or even wait until two are in line and kill three with two more shots. Even a fortnight or more after 12 August on a very hot day the birds may sit close and get up all round you in twos and threes – calling for a calm as well as a quick method.

In a very dry year many of the coveys may lie along the banks of burns. But after about three weeks they have grown in strength and they get canny. On a wet and windy day they will rise steeply at extreme range and you almost have to throw your gun at them to kill them: it is remarkable how far out you can kill a steeply rising or crossing bird with a very quick swing. Especially difficult are strong birds which have settled on the banks between peat-hags, steep-sided natural ditches running directly down hillsides where much of the peat has been eroded and what survives consists of narrow banks or ridges. The grouse always get up at the most awkward moment, just as you are struggling to get up a bank or have unloaded to jump down one.

Walking up grouse in a good season is a wonderful sport: hard work in magnificent countryside shooting wild birds which give an unpredictable variety of shots. On a hot day early in the season with plenty of strong coveys it can be almost too easy for a 'natural' and experienced shot: my friends the Leslie-Melville twins, Sandy and Geordie, found it so easy that by the age of about fourteen they would only shoot from the hip. Yet I have seen brilliant shots at driven grouse completely flummoxed by walked-up birds, getting more and more angry (and thus more likely to fail) as one miss follows another. They are accustomed to standing in a butt with a firm level floor, where correct footwork comes naturally and easily. In tufty heather the technique is different.

I have also seen people who are good shots at walked-up grouse sadly humbled by their first experience of driving. Instead of shooting on sight they think 'Shall I or shan't I?', and by the time they have decided 'No' and turned round the grouse are almost out of sight. Eventually they decide to give these birds a shot in the tail, with no effect except to leave themselves unloaded for the next covey.

Driving grouse is a very different matter from walking-up. If you know the moor well and are willing to work your own dog and carry

Shooting

your own game, a couple or more of you can walk-up without any professional help, although it would be unusual not to have a gamekeeper with you. But for driving you need a full team of beaters, a few pickers-up, five or six experienced flankers and a couple of keepers who know the moor well enough and have the personality to take charge of the two lines of beaters; although as the season progresses and the grouse get wilder and their flights get longer you can manage with fewer beaters. This therefore is a sport only available to the very fortunate.

My uncle gave me the moor in 1960 and the subsequent year I told him that I intended to try a couple of days' driving. He did not think that we would know how to get the birds over the butts and, if we succeeded in that, he did not think that we would know how to shoot them. However, we came back with a hundred brace the first day and he was delighted.

I felt that since I had the rare good fortune to own a grouse moor, I must enjoy it; also that I must enable my family, and preferably some friends, to share my luck. Many owners let their moors for most of the season, perhaps reserving just a day or two to themselves. But that was not good enough for me, neither was I prepared to blow the capital of the family estate in order to have a good time for a few years. We had three gamekeepers and a boy (a 'loon'), and neighbouring keepers who would help. We also had a team of foresters, some of whom could be volunteered as beaters for a few days for a year or two while we were getting going. And there were some older people around who remembered the 1930s, and had a good idea of what was needed to do the vital job of flanking. But we still needed a large team of beaters for these earliest ventures. It just so happened that I had lent the big house – Fasque – for a holiday to a large 'family' of war orphans, now teenagers, who had been taken on by a remarkable friend of one of my first cousins. They were only too delighted to have a go. Thus we managed two successful days' driving in our first year. We then established a programme for bringing all the lines of butts gradually back in to use. At much the same time I started a ten-year plan to build tracks for the use of Land Rovers to serve all the drives, although in some cases there was still a long walk to the butts. I did so not because our family party required them (we were willing to walk long distances) but because in this era of high taxation I thought that within ten years we would not be able to keep the moor unless we were able to let it for some weeks each season to foreigners, probably Americans. This

Shooting

programme cost almost nothing because the government wanted to encourage hill-farming and considered motorable tracks for the shepherd's use to be necessary, and therefore provided generous grants. We realised that the drainage of these tracks was of paramount importance and we learnt the best techniques of construction from our mistakes as we went along.

There was an Approved School – the euphemistic nomenclature for something one step milder than a Borstal – in Aberdeen, with an enlightened head master who wanted not merely to confine and punish his mischievous clients but also to give them some training in the hope of making them better citizens. He wanted them to learn to look after themselves and to be presented with some challenges. One or two enlightened landowners had offered them an outbuilding but, although they were well supervised a minority of them had always contrived to commit the odd misdemeanour such as stealing the neighbours' chickens or using their furniture for firewood. I, however, much admiring the efforts of the head and his staff, was able to offer them a cottage and some small buildings at the Charr, right in the middle of the moor far away from any dwelling, and to accept the risk that one or two of them still might get up to mischief. It was not difficult to find volunteers to take part in this training – almost anything was preferable to being confined in that school. Equally, to cut a long story short, they were happy to volunteer for 'the grouse' as beaters, for which they got paid a small statutory wage.

There was not much scope for mischievous activity on the moor itself, and no point in absconding. A small group of them did on one occasion manage to remove one of our guests' cars from the track, but fortunately not where there was a steep bank, and it was easily recovered. One day one of these 'loons' came up to Dan during the lunch-break and proudly showed him the contents of his lunch-box – an adder. But happily no harm resulted. We needed more or less twice as many of these boys as with 'normal' beaters, but the logistics were simple because they all travelled by minibus with a teacher as driver – the teachers enjoyed the day on the hill just as the boys did. For about fifteen years this scheme solved our problem of beaters in a very economical way, and a beneficial way too to those involved.

We told one of our guests, a major in the Grenadier Guards, that they were Lancing boys (whose head master I was) and at the end of the day he said to Rosamund 'I'm surprised that Willie doesn't seem to chat more to the boys.' She told him that his leg was being pulled and they were Borstal boys. That evening we told him that actually they were Lancing boys. He believed what he was told all three times. Actually Lancing boys were not unfamiliar with Glen Dye because they used it in winter for the Duke of Edinburgh's award scheme: so I was in the happy position of enabling my grouse moor to play two parts in the education of the young. I also persuaded the Royal Navy engineer officers under training (with the ethos of 'go anywhere, do anything') to convert the old stables as a Cub Scout pack holiday centre. The midges were rather too much for the Cubs, but in later years when the moor was let for part of the season this accommodation came in handy for 'normal' beaters, many of them students. By these methods I made the driving of grouse affordable to an owner for the first three weeks of driving, letting it later in the season for two weeks to genial parties led by Rob Robel, an American professor of biology, and by a group of Italians who had migrated to London as waiters and then made a fortune by launching Sphagetti Houses. I was able with the encouragement of the Inspector of Taxes to pay the wages of one keeper from the farm and one from the schedule D woodlands, thus avoiding a monstrous tax bill if they had been employed for sport, and simultaneously reducing farm and woodland profits, taxable in those days at up to 83p in the £. The three keepers worked as a team – and what does it matter if you cull the red deer or the foxes on farmland or on the heather or in the young plantations? You are still benefiting both the farm and the woods.

Thus we were able to enjoy three weeks of driving and to entertain our family and friends. There was little opportunity for us when I was head master of a boarding school to entertain any but official guests – governors, lecturers, preachers and members of the staff and their families. This summer holiday made up for that, although it was hard work for Rosamund. But we used to advertise every year in *The Lady* for two young ladies to come and do the cooking. Letting the moor for the two later weeks repaid most of the costs of the shooting, and fortunately Dan Dowell was as good with our tenants as he was with the loons from the Approved School. He had the natural authority of a regimental sergeant major, never having to raise his voice. But above all he was a brilliant driver of grouse.

Even after an early and successful hatch it is preferable not to start driving until the second week of the season, when all the young birds will fly strongly, especially on high ground where the chicks and the heather growth come late. The season is, however, a short one: every week must be taken advantage of, and many moors do start driving on or soon after the Twelfth. Until 1751/2 it was 1 August, but the calendar had to be switched forward by eleven days to correct eleven centuries of error.

The flights of the grouse gradually get longer as the season progresses, until they will sometimes fly the full length of a drive, depending on the character of the moor. Glen Dye is a very big moor, but not mineral-rich, so the average size of each territory of a pair of grouse is extensive and the drives are long, though shortened in the early days. It is essential to have an area of 'settling ground' about 100 to 200 yards in front of the butts, in long heather where the early coveys will be happy to alight before being risen again to fly over the butts.

Grouse tend to follow a contour, not precisely but in general terms, and on the round-topped hills of the Grampians they prefer to fly right round their own hill to get back to their home ground, although late in the season and especially when the coveys have left their territories and joined together in 'packs', and especially in a high wind, they may take off and fly away a long distance, along a ridge or over a valley. But when they are following a contour and sticking to their home ground, their chosen flight may even be almost 'S' shaped, perhaps over a small depression and then right round a hill. Quite recently I showed a new keeper and his boss how to take one such drive. Before the season the boss said to me, 'He's nervous about the Lochnaween drive.' 'Tell him not to worry,' I said, 'the grouse will do it for him.' The boss duly reported: 'You were right: they did.' This makes grouse driving sound easy, but it isn't: this anecdote is on the contrary an example of the fact that the grouse will fly where they want to.

A full understanding of every feature of the terrain, its shape and orientation and character is an essential starting point. At the same time you must understand the wind, for the same wind will not blow in the same direction all round a hill or a valley, and it will be at its fiercest on the top of a ridge. You must know the sort of places where coveys are likely to settle, especially where one alighted covey will have the effect of 'calling in' others, and you must be able to stop the line every time a covey rises. Then towards the end of the drive you must nurse the remaining grouse off the settling ground over the butts covey by covey, and still prevent any beater from getting within dangerous range of the butts until, at the very last minute, this is unavoidable and the guns must be told to stop shooting in front.

The other essential is to have efficient flankers who will keep fully concealed to allow all the birds on the right line to fly over the butts, yet at the same time will be alert enough to give misaligned coveys a quick flick of their flag while they are still far enough away to change direction. In a strong wind the downwind flankers may need to be stretched out at right angles to the butts, but in some cases where the top butt is at the top of a hill they may need to be almost parallel, or even in a few unusual cases actually sloping backwards from the line so that coveys creeping above the butts will calmly turn more than 90 degrees downhill before resuming their chosen direction. There is one particularly fascinating line of butts on the Cairn O'Mount where in an ideal wind the majority of the grouse will approach the line of butts after a long almost circular flight; and although some will come straight through the line others will work their way up the butts, often not flying fast but changing height bewilderingly – almost hovering as they struggle into the wind, apparently easy targets but in fact the very devils to hit; and then turn through the line at or beyond the top butt. If they see a flanker in exactly the right spot here, some way beyond the top butt and just behind the line, they will turn down the back of the line, now picking up speed in the following wind, and provide a further chance of shooting, this time getting faster and higher as they curl away. This is the champagne of grouse-driving.

On moors where the butts are on flat or flattish land these refinements do not occur to anything like the same extent. The beaters have a more straightforward task and the flankers merely add V-shaped wings to the line of butts. Often the birds can be seen a long way off, and some of the coveys don't want to fly through the line but fly about in front of it giving crossing shots. This tends or tended to be the case on some of the Denbigh moors in North Wales when the higher land had been afforested and only the flatter land (over-grazed by sheep whose owners had common rights) was left for the grouse, and also on some (not all!) Yorkshire moors which involve a steep climb to get up to them but are more or less on a plateau. It also occurs on some drives on some of the Grampian moors where the butt lines were created in the early days of driving and have never been changed. The resulting drives do not provide the special quality of sport achievable where the butts run directly up and down hill and are well concealed.

Shooting

Where the hills are rounded or steep the butts were often originally placed, mostly in or around the 1880s, on or near the tops of ridges on flattish ground which had been identified as sites over which large numbers of grouse were known to fly. Eventually it was realised that they could be funnelled much more effectively over a line only three or four hundred yards wide on the side of a hill rather than at the top, and that the butts could be sited to give the guns an ideal average horizon of about thirty yards; so that birds flying straight through the line would be seen at about forty yards distant and would not have time to take avoiding action before they came under fire. If you kill a bird about twenty or thirty yards in front it will probably land just in front of your butt, but many of the birds you shoot in front will land behind.

In a moderate breeze – ideal conditions – many coveys will not come over at right angles but will work their way up the line at an angle, and if they are low you will have to be extremely quick to get a shot at them while they are visible between the peat banks, so there is plenty of variety in the shots. On other days they will curl and swoop down the line very fast indeed.

In a strong wind, or late in the season, or even early in the season with birds coming fast straight through the line, it is seldom effective to turn round and try to shoot them in the tail: they are already out of range, and although there are sometimes a great variety of crossing shots to be had behind, some of them may be easy but others are extremely difficult when birds are curling away from you as the rate of swing required reduces rapidly as you prepare to shoot.

The best advice for a beginner is always to shoot your birds in front, and if you do turn round turn back and reload at once, and try again. Sometimes there are a couple of butts at the top of the hill where the land is almost flat and many of the grouse will be flying on a flat trajectory. These are much the best places for beginners and give them a measure of confidence, provided that the nearest flanker has the sense to keep out of range: there are very few places where a flanker at the top of the line cannot sensibly be out of shot, certainly where the land is flat and a gale is not blowing.

Grouse driving requires meticulous attention to safety, especially in avoiding shooting down the line, which is a temptation to be avoided at all costs when the grouse are flying rapidly and there is only a split second in which to shoot them safely: the most humiliating shot is the one which kills the grouse behind the one which you are aiming at.

Shooting

Perhaps one ought to be equally humiliated by killing more than one bird with one shot, but this is more likely to be savoured as a notable feat: I did once kill five with a right and left, but my neighbour Willie Mitchell had a short-sighted personal picker-up with thick round glasses called Cowie, and at the end of the drive he had all five on his master's butt before I could get to them: it served me right, no doubt.

As soon as one reaches a butt, the safe angles can be identified and if necessary marked by a stick, either on the butt itself to prevent a dangerous swing, or on the horizon just a few yards away if a neighbouring butt is not visible. Sometimes one can identify a small feature – a heather bank or a boulder perhaps – which helps to mark the ideal place at optimum range to make a kill, as if one were shooting a grouse coming through an imaginary gate.

We were essentially a family party. Peter and I were there for the full three weeks, Francis for most of them, and Andrew the youngest of the four brothers for a week. Our sister Penelope shot effectively during the earlier years. Rosamund achieved excellent bags and never wounded a grouse. Our sons Charlie and Robert came on stream as the years passed. Our cousin John came from time to time: he was very tall, sticking up from his butt like a lighthouse, and once complained that the grouse flew too low! But a low grouse is as good a target as any, swooping down the line and taking its speed off the heather, skimming it with his lower wing almost touching it in the same way as one sees a fulmar flying with extraordinary virtuosity over the sea.

From my mother's side of the family my uncle Vernon Erskine Crum, with his cheerful wife Rosemary (and later their son Douglas), came quite often. He was much my youngest uncle, closer in age to me than to my uncles on my father's side: a brigadier and soon a major-general after a distinguished career in the Scots Guards and then as Mountbatten's aide; tall, spare and broad-shouldered, he strolled across the moor, his gun looking almost a toy in his hands, his observations on human nature encapsulated in a word or two. Sadly he was to die at the age of fifty-two of the heart failure which had done for his father at forty-six.

Fortunately I liked all the close friends Rosamund made before we were married. Before you propose marriage check out your future spouse's friends – it's a good indicator whether the match is likely to last. She liked my old friends, so we made a good start in that respect before we got to know more people in our Lancing and Hawarden years. Some of these friends we invited to Glen Dye year after year, others more occasionally. But pride of place has to go to Ernle Gilbert, who had taught me and my cousins to tickle trout in the burn at Fasque in the prewar years. He was a few years older than us, buccaneer son of a buccaneer father who was a close friend of my uncles and father: a gifted sportsman who had played cricket for England (though 'only' against the West Indies), who never bothered to clean his gun except after shooting rock doves: which meant shooting birds from the cliffs from a boat, when the gun would be suffering from salt water. He kept the accounts for their small rough shoot in Herefordshire and I remember seeing my father's copy for one pre-1914 season after which the surplus had been 6/- (six shillings or 30 new pence) to share between the members. His mantle had fallen on his son, an inventive sportsman who would modify the orthodox methods of catching fish where circumstances required. Ernle was godfather to our elder son Charlie, and then when Rob's godfather died he was roped in in an honorary capacity to be his godfather too. He was a good shot. 'Actually,' he said, 'I don't swing: I know about how much lead to give them.'

Two friends of Rosamund's were Gina Hill-Wood who married Richard Holt and Sally Isdell-Carpenenter who married Teddy Elliott. Agewise their families fitted with ours and their children used to come with them to Glen Dye. The Holts were one of those clever but totally 'unacademic' families for whom the linguistic-based education which had dominated our schools for centuries (and hung on grimly until the 1990s) suited neither Richard nor their son Nicholas; but give them (or Gina) a pack of cards or the odds at a race meeting or (more importantly?) an insurance risk, and they were at home. Richard, blessed also with charm and the power of persuasion, was successful in Lloyd's and they migrated gracefully to a beautiful house in Suffolk. Nick runs Holts, a leading firm in the sporting gun trade. Gina was one of those stalwarts who radiates a gentle confidence while quietly holding everything together in any difficulty.

Teddy Elliott is a Harrovian Cambridge engineering graduate who claimed (rather less convincingly than the Holts) not to have shone even dimly at school but who, together with the (now) Lord Vinson, pioneered plastic coatings. He and Sally live in his family's Sussex farmhouse near Pulborough, in that still unspoilt part of west Sussex which we so much loved when we were at Lancing. We have enjoyed countless happy times in their company (one of our refuges from boarding school pressures) and Sally never lets her friendships get 'out of repair'.

Shooting

Also among our regular guests at Glen Dye were two school friends of mine, already mentioned in other contexts, Michael Merriam and Nicholas Headlam. Anne Merriam had a wonderful way with children, never talking down to them, and she was a gifted artist, especially an illustrator with a gift for the quick caricature. Nicholas became my solicitor after I had parted from Freshfields (Mr Freshfield had been John Gladstone'e solicitor in the 1830s, so it was a wrench) when they became so grand that private clients were passed down to the more junior partners. Nicholas masterminded all our family trusts. He left London and joined a firm in Monmouth so that he and Jane could be near her ageing parents, the Scarletts, but he shrewdly kept in touch with the leading London QCs. Jane came out on the hill with Nicholas whatever the weather, and put at least one of the shivering menfolk to shame. My respective godsons Andrew Merriam and Anthony Headlam joined walking-up the grouse, four men and a boy.

Andrew and Caroline Burnaby-Atkins often came, the perfect couple, handsome and entertaining, and loyal friends. I had known him at school but we became close friends when we lived at Baldwin's End at Eton when I was master there and he the adjutant of the Corps. A Rifleman, he had won two MCs in the 1944–45 campaign and had then become one of General Montgomery's team of nice young men – Johnnie Henderson was another such.

Dickie Birch-Reynardson of the Grenadier Guards had also become a close friend of mine when he also was adjutant of the Eton Corps when I was commanding officer, and I was later able to rope him in as a governor of Lancing because he had the knack of identifying what mattered and what didn't. He was a brilliant shot at grouse. He was the classic lazy man who von Moltke said should be the commander-in-chief, so I could rely on him to do the work of the commanding officer while I did the much more difficult and demanding donkey-work and detail which was properly his as adjutant, and thus got my way, for in education the devil is often in the detail. His delightful wife Mary, a gifted watercolourist who (like me) learnt a lot from my mother's gentle criticism, fulfilled a similar role on their domestic front. She introduced Mary's Game to our regular evening recreations at Glen Dye. Two other couples who came from time to time were Mark and Tubby Evans, whose family also overlapped with ours and became good friends; and Peter and Barbara Hextall who were particular friends, farming near Lancing.

Shooting

The core of our line of guns was thus made up from the family and filled out by several of these guests staying for a week. Our three weeks at Glen Dye became a gathering of old friends in familiar surroundings, the ideal recipe for a holiday. There were not many spaces in the line to invite local people, but there were a few special friends, all of whom were good shots to boot. Indeed my old school friends Geordie Leslie-Melville, and occasionally also Jamie Bruce, who had been my contemporaries both at prep school and at Eton, were both outstanding shots. Our other two regulars were Bill Bradford of Kincardine and Willie Mitchell. Bill had escaped as a prisoner of war by walking and sailing from the north of France in 1940 to North Africa, and had then played a distinguished part in the Normandy campaign, being awarded the DSO and the MC. He qualified for my award of the description as a Typical Black Watch Brigadier (in the orthodox sense there is no such thing: no two are alike). He had had his sons down for my house at Eton before I departed to Lancing. Willie Mitchell had inherited some money from his family's Glasgow tobacco firm, bought a beat on the Dee and spent every day of his life thereafter fishing, except Sundays or when shooting. ('Willie, do you ever get tired of fishing?' 'I haven't yet.') He had taken the shoot at Fasque from me for some years, and had been an excellent tenant.

I cannot believe that there is any more glorious form of sport than shooting driven grouse on the rounded or steep heather hills of eastern Scotland where the butts are placed to give a short skyline and the coveys cannot see the line far enough away to take evasive action. The shooting gets more and more difficult as the season progresses: the 'October' grouse is a notoriously difficult target. A five-star drive is a rare experience, never forgotten. It depends on a combination of circumstances of which the wind and the weather are important, and it brings perhaps twenty minutes of continuous excitement as one challenge follows another: early on perhaps an unwary pair killed flip-flip well in front; then a covey flying straight at the butt but stretched out with just enough time for two shots in front and two behind. (The very best shots – not including myself – might take three in front and two behind early in the season, but not later.) Then the birds begin to sweep down from the top and if the top gun has the experience to shoot early at long range he will turn the coveys and they will offer shots to two or three butts lower down as they try to cross again. I remember two such drives in different terrain. In the former the grouse would try to cross three times – this was in a modest landscape, at the end of the day, where they had gathered perfectly from the earlier drives and came over with a light wind in their faces. Every butt got wonderful shooting and the day ended with that warm collective exhilaration which helps to make the occasion a long-remembered one. The other drive was on high ground, in a high wind, late in the season, when the coveys had just started to join together in packs; and it was the only drive I ever took part in which yielded a hundred brace. The birds wanted to make for the top of the hill, the quickest way home; but they could be turned by excellent flanking and quick shooting in the top butt or two, and as they crossed again several packs gave four butts a chance, four right-and-lefts. But there were masses of lower coveys as well, trying to cross more or less at right angles. The dogs were so tired after picking up a hundred and seventy-five birds at this last drive of the day that we called a halt and returned the next morning. Our beloved Leggie picked up seventeen of the remaining twenty-five, an amateur Labrador putting the professionals in the shade.

Critics might say that enough is enough: why does one have to kill so many? Well, as far as reared birds are concerned I agree. If reared birds are encouraged to 'go wild' my preferred aim would be that they should hardly ever see a human being. Hand-feeding in selected places should not be allowed. And I would not allow anyone to shoot with two guns and a loader. Unfortunately there are still a few 'commercial shoots' where the aim is not challenging sport but big bags to boast of: and that can only be eliminated by peer-pressure. But if the people responsible work hard at a shoot they can ensure that at least most of the shots are really challenging. Grouse, however, are entirely wild birds, and if too large a stock is left at the end of a season disease will set in during the winter and at least nine out of ten birds will die. This argument may be countered by saying that big numbers are only achieved by good keeping, which in itself is 'artificial'; but good keeping also benefits both farming and the diversity of wild life. Personally, although I never did allow two guns and a loader (and I would never dream of allowing a magazine-loaded gun), these are subjective rules which can only be perceived as reasonable by consensus. I think they reward skill, and I think that shooting driven grouse is quite difficult enough without needing artificial limitations. It can be enjoyed by any keen sporting person once they have got the knack: they may be indifferent shots or

Shooting

good shots or brilliant shots or outstanding shots. This last category are rare: they contrive to kill birds which a good or even a brilliant shot would not even consider as 'possibles' especially low birds at long ranges often beyond their neighbours' butts. The few people I have ever met in this category always perform without a flourish: economy is of the essence of their art.

Index

And please consult family trees pp. vi–viii

Adams, Mr, head gardener at Hawarden, 107
Adie, C.J.M., Eton housemaster, 184
Alexander, Mr, manager of Lloyd's Bank, Hawarden, 121
Alington, Cyril, head master of Eton, 100
Alllman, Mr, head forester at Hawarden, 106; retires 1958, 113
Alston, John, Lancing musical director, 151
Armstrong, Robert (Lord Armstrong of Ilminster) 20
Arnold, Dr Thomas, 91
Astridge, Pembrokeshire, family holidays at, 46–9, 59

Babington Smith, Harry, comes to stay at Astridge, 47
Baden-Powell, Norman, rector of Hawarden, 122–3, 124; and son Ralph, 123
Barber, Hilary, 87
Barker, Harold, 30
Barlow, Peter, transfers to Hawarden building maintenance team, 108; 110, befriends Alec Lamb, 172
Barlow, Terry, son of preceding, plasterer in building maintenance team, 113

Basnett, Chris, forester, succeeds Robert Charmley, 113
Bates, Blaster, 228
Beaton, Barbara ('Baba'), Rosamund's mother, see Hambro
Beaton, (Sir) Cecil, 167–8, 179, 180
Beaton, Ernest Walter Hardy, Rosamund's grandfather, 179–80; m. Esther Sisson, two sons, two daughters (see family tree), 180
Beaton, Nancy, see Smiley
Beaton family, history of, 179
Beeching, Dr, life peer 1963, author invites to speak to Lancing sixth form, 147
Bell Jones, William, Hawarden postmaster and local historian, 121–2
Bennett, Mrs, Baba Beaton's cleaner, accompanies them to Exmoor, 171
Benson, Jeremy, 54
Betjeman, Sir John, 151
Bickersteth, John, later Bishop of Bath and Wells, 87
Bickerton, Bruce, chartered surveyor, 126
Birch-Reynardson, Dickie, and wife Mary, 272
birds (Fervour 1), numerous species mentioned, 183–200; decline in

Index

population, 183; habitats familiar to author: Eton and surrounds, 184–90, 192, Wales, 191–2, Hickling Broad, Norfolk, 192–3, Hawarden, 193–5, Glen Dye, 195–8,
Bird Sense, by Tim Birkhead, 199–200
Birkenhead, John and Denis, partnership in dairy business with author, 116–17
Birley, Robert (later Sir), head master of Eton, offers author job teaching history, 100
Blake, Robert (later Baron Blake, life peer), 79
Bland, Michael, author's godfather, 1, 19; and sailing, 19–20, 21; *Birds in an Eton Garden*, 184
Blomfield, Arthur, architect, 89
Bodnant, Lord Aberconway, 207
Bonsor, Sir Brian, MP, m. Libby, second daughter of Angus and Vanda Hambro; author remembers their elder son Nicholas as oarsman at Eton, 169
Bowood, Marquess of Lansdowne, 107
Bradford, Bill, 273
Briggs, Asa, life peer 1976, 152
Brighton, 159
Britten, Benjamin (later life peer), 151
Broadlane Hall, Hawarden, Sir John Glynne, 206
Brock, Professor David le M., designs author's mother's new house at Hawarden, 137
Brown, David, Shrewsbury master, 94, 95
Brown, Lancelot, 'Capability', 204

Bruce, Hon. James, author's contemporary at school, shooting at Glen Dye, 273
Buggy, Valerie, family help, 164–5
Burge, Mr, Birkenhead photographer, commissioned by author's parents in 1953 to create album portraying Hawarden estate employees, 110
Burnaby-Atkins, Andrew and Caroline, 272
Butler, David, chair of Hawarden High School Governors, 128

Caban, Alice, housekeeper at The Old Farm House, 141, 143
Callaghan, James (life peer 1987), and Selective Employment Tax, 156
Callender, David, 52
Campbell, Colen, 212
Castle Howard, 213
Cator, John, 58
Cawkwell, George, 81
Chadwyck-Healey, Cherry and Viola, 153
Charlesworth, Michael, Shrewsbury master, 94, 96
Charmley, Robert, forester at Hawarden, 113; recruits Chris Basnett (q.v.), dies in his mid-fifties, 113; 114
Chatsworth, Derbyshire, 212–13
Chattock, Cada, sister of Zandra and Rosamund's paternal grandmother, two daughters – Tess (Ellert), and Tecia (Fearnley-Whittingstall), 180; her sister Jessie Suarez described in Cecil Beaton's *My Bolivian Aunt*, 180
Chenevix-Trench, Tony, later head master of Bradfield, Eton and

[278]

Index

Fettes, at Christ Church with author, 83–4, 84–5; and wife Elizabeth, 85; 91–2; shooting, 253
Chetwynd, Richard, m. Peggy Jephson, 168
Chichester Festival, 159;
Christ Church, Oxford, author attends 1946–49, 79–88
Churchill, Sir Winston, 146, 147
Clinton, Lord (21st Baron) and Lady, and family, 44
Cole, Mike, bricklayer at Hawarden, 113
Collins, Commissioned Gunner (T) 'Jumper', torpedo officer HMS *Wrangler*, 77
Colman, Stacy, Shrewsbury master, 91, 92
Connah, David and Peter (cousins), 119
Constable, John, 243–4
Cooper, Mr, gardener at Hawarden, 101
Cooper of Stockton Heath, Lord (life peer), speaks at Lancing, 148
Cork, Nathaniel, Hawarden rector, 122–3
Corlett, John, 3
Cowell, Ned, author appoints to help administer estate, 111–12
Cowes Regatta, 21
Crace, Mrs, Sunday school for infants, and son Christopher, 10
Crathes Castle, and National Trust, 218–19
Croft House School, 161, 170
Crofts, Billy, forester at Hawarden, 106
Cross, Canon Dr, Christ Church, 85

Crow, Graham, farmer, 117
Crum, Sir Walter Erskine, author's maternal grandfather, and wife Violet Forbes (q.v.), 1; dies young, 24

Dancy, John (later Professor), precedes author as head master of Lancing, 142; notes on masters for author, 144
Daniel, Lieutenant, HMS *Wrangler*, 77
Dashwood, Francis (later Sir, 11th Bt) 54–5, 58
Davidge, Christopher, 52
Davidson, Clair, see Gladstone, Deiney
Davies, Ellis, gamekeeper, and wife Doris, 114–15; succeeded by Gerry Evans, 115; 256, 257, 258
Davies, Joe, forester at Hawarden, and wife, 106
Davies, John, tenant of land in the park during the war, grandfather of David Edge (q.v.), 117
Davies, Revd Philip, rector of Hawarden, 124
Dawson, Harry, Shrewsbury master, 91
Deacon, Tom, Lancing PT instructor, 140, 155, 156
de Trafford, Dermot (later Sir, 5th Bt), 87
Dickin, Revd W., 124
Dingle, Bert, gamekeeper at Hawarden, 106–8; and (second) wife and children, 108; 114, 118; 251, 252, 256
Douglas-Home, Charles, lecture at Lancing, 148–9
Dowell, Dan, head keeper Glen Dye, 248, 255, 265, 266

Index

Drake, Miss, author's junior school, 11

Eagles, Dean, gamekeeper at Hawarden, 115, 258
Eames, John, 206
Edge, David, farming partnership with author, 117
Edward VII, HM King, shoots at Milton Abbey, 178
Elizabeth, HM The Queen Mother, 251
Ellert, John and Tess (see Chattock), 180
Elliott, Teddy and Sally, 151; and family, 271
Ellis, Armon, solicitor in Mold, with clerk Haydn Rees, 109–10
Ellis, Ossian, performs on harp at Hawarden, 151
Elphick, John, 126
Elphick, Mr, worker on Hobbses' Sussex farm, 153–4
Elphinstone, Revd Hon. Andrew, m. Jean Hambro, 3rd daughter of Angus and Vanda Hambro, a lady-in-waiting to the Queen; marries author and Rosamund in Chelsea Old Church, 169
Erskine Crum, Donald, author's uncle, in Malaya, and has son, Simon, 67; joins RAF in war, on Mountbatten's South-East Asia staff, 67; 153
Erskine Crum, Elizabeth, author's aunt, marries John Garton, 67
Erskine Crum, Vernon, author's uncle, captain in Guards Armoured Division, wins MC; serves as aide-de-camp to Mountbatten at end of war with Germany and later when Mountbatten was Viceroy of India, 67, 68; shooting at Glen Dye, with wife Rosemary and son Douglas, 270
Eton College, author at, 52–9; author teaches at, 139
Eton shopkeepers, 3–7, 8
Evans, Dan, in forestry department at Hawarden, rears geese for Christmas estate party, 106; and wife, 106
Evans, Gerry, succeeds Ellis Davies as gamekeeper, 115, 258
Evans, Mark and Tubby, 272
Exmoor, family visits to, 162

farming neighbours at Hawarden, Edges and Bellises, Arden and Wrench families, 117–18
Fasque, Kincardineshire, 41–6, 66, 211, 251, 253, 254; duck on lake, 262
Fergusson, Brigadier Bernard (later Baron Ballantrae, life peer), speaks at Lancing, 147
Fisher, Dr Kenneth, biologist, head master of Oundle, arranges trip to Hickling Broad, 192; son James a noted ornithologist, 192
Fleming, Mr, architect, advises author on new building work at Lancing; author meets again many years later, 158
Forbes, Arthur, author's godfather, 23
Forbes, Violet, wife of Sir Walter Erskine Crum (q.v.), 1; at Henley, 24, 30, 67, 68; golf and articles for press, 68
Foster, Michael, Christ Church, 87–8

[280]

Index

Forster, Michael, Warden of St Deiniol's Library, 125–6
Francis, Revd Peter, 127
Fraser, Duncan, head keeper at Glen Dye, 63–5; 191, 248
Fraser, Lieutenant (E), engineer officer HMS *Wrangler*, 77
Friedlander, Elizabeth, cartographer, 98
Fulton, John (life peer, 1966) vice-chancellor of University of Sussex, 151–2

Garton, John, author's uncle (see Erskine-Crum, Elizabeth), 67; three sons, Ian, Clive and Robin, 67
Gibson-Watt, Andrew, 51, m. Pammie Hambro, 178
Gibson-Watt, David, MP, brother of preceding, m. Diana Hambro, 178
Gilbert, Colonel, 30; and red kites, 191
Gilbert, Ernle, 271
Gladstone, (Sir) Albert, 5th Bt, author's uncle, 1; takes over Manley Hall, 26; 27, awarded MBE,, 28; 30, 31, moves with author's Aunt Kith to Hawarden Castle, 40 ; and Fasque (q.v.), 41–6 , inherited from bachelor cousin, Sir John Gladstone; and Glen Dye, 62; and shooting, 66; he and sister leave Hawarden Castle at beginning of war to live at Broadlane nearby, 68; 101; chairman of Representative Body of the Church in Wales, 120; supports William Bell Jones (q.v.), 122; organic gardening, 203; grounds at Hawarden, 211, 215, 221

Gladstone, Andrew, author's youngest brother, 52, 60, 133; career and family, 134–5; dies, 135
Gladstone, Annie Crosthwaite, née Wilson, author's grandmother, 25, 26
Gladstone, Catherine, author's Aunt Kith, 26, 27, 33–4, finances, 36–7; reads to children, 38; car, 38;moves to Hawarden, 40; 101, organic gardening, 203
Gladstone, (Sir) Charles Andrew, 6th Bt, author's father, housemaster at Eton, 1; ornithologist, 15 (and see birds, Fervour 1); introduces author to carpentry, 15 ; and motor cars, 16–17; and crossword puzzles, 18–19 ; 27, oarsman, 28; war service, 28–9; 35, 49, choice of Scaitcliffe, 50; announcement of forthcoming birth of author's brother Francis , 59; difficult to get away from Eton in wartime school holidays 61; at Glen Dye, 61, 63, 64; chairman of Hawarden bench and chairman of Representative Body of the Church in Wales, 120–1; hands over running of estate to author in late 1960s, 136; death of, 136, 165; author's family visits in Lancing school holidays, 162; 183, 184, 185, telescope, 188; bird-watching excursions with author, 190–1; teaches author about gardening, 15, 202, 203–4; 221–2
Gladstone, Charles Angus, author's son, 60, 112; birth of, 143; 144, 153, 160, 161

[281]

Index

Gladstone, Deiney, author's uncle, awarded MC, 28; 30; and wife Clair Davidson, 30–3; four children, see family tree; 37, 40, buys house, Lewins, at Crockham Hill, Kent, 40; holidays at Glen Dye with son Stephen and daughters Felicity and Anne, 61, 63, 64; author visits at Lewins, 69; 101

Gladstone, Edie, author's aunt, 32; (Mrs Tom Stamper) and see family tree

Gladstone, Francis, author's brother, 52, birth of, 59–60; friend of Ralph Baden-Powell, 123; career and family, 133–4; and tribute to brother Andrew, 135; curator with wife Jo of mother's artistic work, 137–8; garden at Hawarden, 215

Gladstone, Helen, author's sister, 60, career and family, 134; and mother's artistic work, 137

Gladstone, 1st Baron, Henry Neville, author's great-uncle, and wife Maud, née Rendel, 36, 37; he dies 1935, Maud moves to Plas Warren, 40; 101, 210–11, 215, 221, 222, 228

Gladstone, Herbert, 1st Viscount, author's great-uncle, Act for the Protection of Birds, 183

Gladstone, Isla Margaret, née Crum, author's mother, 1; artistically gifted, 1–2, 14, 202–3, 204, 233–4; and 'good taste', 13–14; shopping trips to London with author, 17–18; 30, new house at Hawarden, 137; artistic work, 137; and Isla Gladstone Conservatory in Liverpool, 137–8

Gladstone, John, author's cousin, 33; and see family tree

Gladstone, Sir John, 3rd Bt, at Fasque, 251

Gladstone, Melissa (author's niece), m. Nick Beare, 133

Gladstone, Penelope, author's sister, 2, 11, 33, 59, 65; career and publications, 135; 163, shooting, 253

Gladstone, Peter, author's brother, 2, 5–6, 12, 16, school, 51; oarsman, rowing blue, 51–2, 105; 59, 65, 84; works with author on garden and old castle grounds at Hawarden, 104, 230; National Service in Palestine Police, 105; teaches at Shrewsbury, 105; finds new gamekeeper, 114; 116, and Saunders Rees, 122; 133, career, 135–6; wife Jeannie and son Xenny, 166; interest in birds, 188; shooting, 248, 250, 253; he and family live at Fasque, 255

Gladstone, Robert, author's son, born 1968, 169

Gladstone, Rosamund, née Hambro, author's wife, 48–9, 58, 60, 96; before marriage, 141–2; marries author September 1962, 142; birth of Charlie, 143; her Mini, 143–4; culinary skills, 156; mother Baba and upbringing wiith sister Zandra on Exmoor, 161; Croft House school, 161; and ponies, 161–2

Gladstone, Revd Stephen, author's grandfather, rector of Hawarden, married to Annie Wilson

('Muzzie'), 25; buys Manley Hall, 25; death of, 25
Gladstone, Vicky, author's daughter, born 1967, 160, 161
Gladstone, W.E., 4–5, 25, 38, 91, 120; founds St Deiniol's Library, 125; political papers, 127; 130, 209, 210
Gladstone, William, nephew of author's grandfather Stephen, lives at Hawarden, 25
Gladstone Diaries, The (Michael Foot and Colin Matthew edd.), 127
Gladstone Playing Fields, 129–30; and Harry and Herbert, W. E.Gladstone's youngest sons, 129–30
Gladstone v. Bower, author's successful suit to recover land at Manor Farm, Hawarden (see also Seymour), 170
Glen Dye, three summer holidays at, 61–2; 162–3; author's three brothers with families, and sister Penelope, join in shooting, 163, 270; cook Debbie, 163; life at Glen Dye, 163–4; red kite, 191; shooting, 248, 252, 253, 256, 259–75; Leggie retrieving, 274
Glyndebourne opera, author and Rosamund attend, 159–60; and Christie family, 160
Glynne family, 205–6ff
Goodhart-Rendel, Hal, designs stone-built pavilion at Hawarden, 210
Goodwood Races, 159, 160
Gould, Dick, and wife Erica, 85–6
Graham, Alastair, 84; shooting, 253
Great Dixter, 219

Grey of Falloden, Viscount, takes Teddy Roosevelt to Burnham Beeches, 189; 190
Griffiths, Revd Tudor, rector of Hawarden, 125

Hadley, Peter and Valerie, entertain author and Rosamund at Goodwood; and son John, 159
Hall, William, establishes firm of chartered surveyors, working from Hawarden estate office, 112; and son Anthony, 112; way of thinking chimes with author's, 112
Hambro, Alec, Rosamund's father, 166; 174, memorial in Milton Abbey Church, 177
Hambro, Angus, father of preceding, MP, married (1) Rosamund Kearsley, two children, (2) Vanda St John Charlton, four daughters, 168; Zandra and Rosamund fond of, 170; 174
Hambro, Barbara ('Baba'), née Beaton, author's mother-in-law, 142; 161–2, 166; Exmoor, 170–1; moves to Chelsea, acquires cottage near Exford, 171; pancreatic cancer, dies aged sixty, 171; buried at Hawarden, 172
Hambro, Calmer, moves from Hamburg to Copenhagen in 1770s, son Joseph sent to Hamburg where he establishes firm of C. J. Hambro & Son in 1800, 175
Hambro, Carl Joachim, Danish baron, founds family Bank in London; acquires Milton Abbey

[283]

Index

in Dorset, 177; model landowner, when wife dies passes on estate to son Charles Joseph (q.v.), 177

Hambro, Sir Charles, eldest brother of Angus (q.v.), chairman of Bank, 178; daughters Diana and Pammie marry David and Andrew Gibson-Watt (q.v.), 178

Hambro, Charles, Rosamund's uncle, gives her away at wedding to author, 142; and diamond brooch, 142; 174

Hambro, Charles Joseph, inherits Milton Abbey in 1877; MP for Weymouth, then Dorset South, 177; leaves estate to nephew Henry Charles ('Harry'), 178

Hambro, Everard, youngest son of Carl Joachim (q.v.), buys Milton Abbey estate, 178; senior partner of Bank, leases Gannochy, philanthropist, 178

Hambro, Henry Charles, and maintenance of Milton Abbey; sells property to his uncle Everard Hambro (q.v.), 178

Hambro, Percival, brother of Everard (q.v.), 178

Hambro, Zandra, see Lamb

Hambro family, origins of (see Hambro, Calmer above), 175; Denmark history during Napoleonic era, 175–6; Joseph Hambro moves to London 1815, raises loans for Danish government, 176–7; and son Carl Joachim (q.v.), 177

Hampton Court, 205

Handbook of British Birds, The, 193, 198–200

Harden, Peter, 120

Hardy, H.H., headmaster of Shrewsbury preceding Wolfenden, 91

Harper, Mr, part-time gardener at Hawarden, 107

Harris, C., manager of Lloyd's Bank in Hawarden, a member of the Representative Body of the Church in Wales's finance committee, 121

Harvey, Chris, headmaster of Hawarden High School, 128, 129

Hawarden, some village features, 130–1; aircraft connections, 131–2, 229

Hawarden Castle, 25, 36, 40, 44, 68; author visits, 68; 101–38; home to Stamper cousins during school holiday before the wars, 102; RAF officers' mess in the war, 102–3; Uncle Albert offers opportunity of living there to author's parents, 102; dilapidation attended to, 103; daily helpers at, 103; programme of replanting woodland starts in 1958, 105; farm shop and garden centre, 114; farming problems, 115–18; creation and development of estate, see 'The Landscape Garden', Fervour 2, 201–31; map of garden, 216; pheasant shoot, 256–9, authors sons and grandsons participate, 258–9

Hawarden Electric, 103

Hawarden Embankment Trust, 132–3

Hawarden Golf Club, 118–19

Hawarden schools, 128–9

Headlam, Nicholas, 54, 57–8, 66; shooting, 253, 272; author's solicitor, 272; wife Jane and son Anthony, 272
Hedley, Prescott, 141
Henderson, Johnnie, 272
Heron Walker, Sir James, 5th Bt, Baba Hambro works for, 171
Heseltine, Michael, life peer 2001, 155
Hextall, Peter and Barbara, 151; come shooting, 272
Heywood-Lonsdale, Colonel Arthur, on Shrewsbury Governing Body, 97–8
Hibbert, Ken, headmaster of Hawarden secondary modern school, 128
Hickmott, Mr, building maintenance at Lancing, 157–8
High Glanau Manor, Monmouth, 219
Hill-Wood, Gina, later Holt, 142, 271
Hilton, Captain A. R., MC, helpful to author in research on *The Shropshire Yeomanry*, 98
Hobhouse, Richard, 87
Hodgkinson, Hugh, headmaster of Milton Abbey school, 168
Hogg, Quintin, 2nd Viscount Hailsham, and inquiry over proposed aircraft runway, 154–5
Holt, Richard, 142; and family, 271
Homan, Dick, 87
Hope-Simpson, 'Juggins', Shrewsbury master, 93
Horton-Fawkes, Nicholas, 54, 56–7, 66
Houghton, Norfolk, 212

How, Mr and Mrs, farm at Wiston, 154
Hubbard, Jasper, 87
Hudson, Martin, 54
Hughes (later Pownall), Dorothy, in Hawarden estate office, 110; succeeded by Jane Lloyd (q.v), 112
Hyland, Philip, 174, see Lamb, Zandra

Isdell-Carpenenter, Sally, m. Teddy Elliott (q.v.), 151, 271

Jagger, Revd Peter, and St Deiniol's Library, 126, 127
James, Eric (life peer 1959, Baron James of Rusholme), vice-chancellor of University of York, 152
Jekyll, Gertrude, 219
Jephson, Selwyn, m. Peggy Hambro, sister of Alec, 168; daughter Judith m. Richard Chetwynd, 168
John, Hywel, 124, 129
Johnson, John, and family, 'Greenacres Farm Park', 120
Jones, C., decorator in Hawarden, 103
Jones, Don, manager of Hawarden garden centre, 215
Jones, Elizabeth, member of Hawarden council, chair of High School governors, 128
Jones, Hector, plumber in Hawarden, 103
Jones, Ian, 119
Jones, Idris, Hawarden postmaster, and wife, 122
Jones, Norman, forester at Hawarden, 106

Index

Kaunda, President Kenneth, author invites to lecture at Lancing, 146
Kay, David, 131
Keay, Miss, author's junior school, 11
Kentell, Bill, and wife, Lancing Chapel verger, 156
Kenyon, Lord (5th Baron), host at Lloyd's Bank lunches in Liverpool, 121
Knole House, 213

Lamb, Alec, son of Micky and Zandra, qualifies as stone mason, works in team at Hawarden; tree surgeon in Australia; Cambodian wife Heng and son Angeko, 172
Lamb, Roger, son of Micky and Zandra, degree in engineering, works on major irrigation scheme in New Zealand; he and wife die in accidents in Morocco; four sons looked after by mother's sister Charlotte and her husband Rupert Sebag-Montefiore (q.v.), 173
Lamb, Micky, comes to Glen Dye, 163; moves from Zimbabwe back to Gloucestershire; intensive pig-farming venture destroyed by fire; Cotswold house at Frith; doing up and selling houses, 172; an adventurer, 173; hang-gliding accident, then dies after motor accident, 174
Lamb, Zandra, Rosamund's sister, wife of preceding, living in Zimbabwe, 142; 161–2, 166; children Alec, Zara and Roger born in Africa, 172; leaves Frith after husband's death for smaller house near Cirencester, 174; marries Philip Hyland, who dies after twenty-five years, 174; moves into Cirencester, 174; 177; 179
Lamb, Zara, daughter of Micky and Zandra, at school; marries; administrative and secretarial work, 172–3; son Jasper at Cambridge, 173
Lancing beach, author acquires hut from the Ellerts; Leggie lifts a leg, 154
Lancing College, 139–65; author appointed head master, 139; accommodation, The Old Farm House, 139–40, ideal family home, 160; improvements to house and garden, 142–3; visiting lecturers, 144–9; Archbishop of Canterbury preaches at centenary of laying foundation stone of Chapel, 150; swimming pool, 155; lawns and paths, 157; maintenance of school buildings, Mr Duke and Mr Hickmott, 157; school holidays, 161
'Landscape Garden, The', Fervour 2, see Hawarden
Law, Hubert, Hawarden estate joiner, 110
Lawton, Warden Revd Dr Stuart, 125
Lear, Edward, 232, 235
Leeding, Grant, foreman of Hawarden building maintenance team, 113
Leggie, author's dog, 144, 154, 274
Leslie-Melville. Hon. G. D., 51; shooting at Glen Dye (and twin Sandy, later Earl of Leven and Melville), 263, 273

Index

Lewis, Revd David, rector of Hawarden, 125
Lintott, Mr and Mrs, housekeepers, 140–1
Littler, Mr, fencer and ditcher at Hawarden, 108
Llandulas, holidays at, 38–41
Lloyd, Jane, succeeds Dorothy Pownall as office manager, 112
Lorimer, Sub-Lieutenant Ken, 78
Lowe, Very Revd John, Dean of Christ Church, 87

MacCallum, James, Hawarden estate manager, from Fasque, 108–9; appointed Lieutenant-Colonel, Home Guard, 1940, 109; retires, 111; 116
McCann, Mr, manager of Lloyd's Bank, Hawarden, 121
McKenzie-Hill, Victoria, marries Xenny Gladstone, elder son of author's brother Peter, 166
Macmillan, Harold, 1st Earl of Stockton, 102, 148, 149–50
Macpherson, Colin, 54, 58
Maddock, Chris, and Hawarden shoot, 258
Manley Hall, Cheshire, author's paternal grandmother's home, 17, 24, 25; 26, 32–4; staff, 33; visits to Chester and Liverpool, 33–4; 35–8; left to author's father, 40; lies empty, 44
March, Laurie, and wife Pip, 116
Marley, Fred, helps Rosamund and Zandra with pony, 161; 162
Mary, HM Queen, 50–1
Mascall, Revd Eric, Christ Church chaplain, 87
Masser, Ken, Captain of Boats at Shrewsbury, 97; meets author twenty years later at Eton, 97
Masterman, J. C., later Sir John, 90
Matthew, Colin, 79, 127
May, Phyllis, 'Nanny May', 2–12; foundling, brought up by nuns, 2; with author's mother's siblings before coming to author's family, 2; walks with author up Eton High Street, 3–6; influences on author, 8, 13; funeral, 12; at Manley, 35
Mayall, Eric, wizard at finding birds' nests, 183, 185–6
Mayes, Charles, Eton housemaster, 7
Mellor, C. I. ('Cim'), 81–2, 83, 85
Menuhin, Hepzibah, 150
Menuhin, Sir Yehudi, opens new music school at Lancing, 150–1
Menzies, Lilian, 251, 253
Merriam, Michael, 54, 55–6, 57, 58, 66, and wife Anne, 272
Middlemas, Keith, lecturer University of Sussex (Professor 1986), 152
Mills, Frank, succeeds Allman and Shaw as head forester at Hawarden, 106
Mills, Walter, clerk in Hawarden estate office, adjutant (Captain) in Home Guard, 109; claimed to have been youngest soldier – drummer boy – to have joined the Army in First World War, 109
Miss Scott's School, author attends, 10–11
Mitchell, Willie, 270, 273
Mitford, Hon. Nancy, 36
Montgomery of Alamein, Field-Marshal 1st Viscount, speaks at

Index

Lancing on 'Leadership', 146–7; 272
Moody, Vera, nurserymaid, 11
Morgans, Rob, joins Hawarden outdoor maintenance department, 114
Morris, William, 219, 234
Morshead, Dr, Lancing presented with his watercolour collection 147
Morton, Anthony, 1st lieutenant in HMS *Wrangler* (later Admiral Sir Anthony), 75–6
Mountbatten of Burma, Rear-Admiral (later Admiral of the Fleet) Earl, 67–8, 270

Newport, John, 114; and brother Geoffrey, 118–19
Nicholls, Bernard, publisher of *The Shropshire Yeomanry*, 99
Nickson, Geoffrey, 100, 167
Noel, Robin, 85

Oldham, Basil, 93, 94
Owen, Arthur, joins Hubert Law (q,v.), takes over from him in early 1950s, 110; widow Vera still living on estate 2015, 110; befriends Alec Lamb, 172
Owen, Dennis, Scaitcliffe, 5, 52, 133

Palgrave-Brown, Alan, 82–3
Palgrave-Brown, Alastair, 82–3
Pannett, Denis, 237
Pannett, Juliet, mother of preceding, 237, 241
Parish, Christopher, 39
Parry, Gordon, Hawarden primary school, 129
Parry, Mr, handyman-chauffeur at Hawarden, 103

Passey, Mr, Lancing gardener, 157
Pawson, Tony, 86
Pears, (Sir) Peter, at Lancing, 151; later performs at Hawarden, 151
Pemberton, Christopher, 51
Pemberton, Roger, 51, 87
Percy, Hugh, 58
Peterson, Jack, succeeds Wolfenden as headmaster of Shrewsbury, ex-housemaster at Eton, 100
Phillips. Alan, Shrewsbury housemaster, author his house tutor, 96
Piccozzi, Nick, and hen harriers, 197–8
Pickthorn, Charles, 66
Pope, Dave, 258
Powell, Eric, 28, death in Alpine accident, 30; keen ornithologist, 184
Powell, Michael, Shrewsbury master, 94; commanding officer of the Corps, 96; rowing coach, 96; persuades author to start a Naval Section, 96
Pownall, Mr, fencer and ditcher at Hawarden, 108; nephew Arthur marries Dorothy Hughes (q.v.), 110
Pownall, Ron, 110
Pridding, Mr, no 2 in garden at Hawarden, 107

Quarterman, Mr, gardener at Eton, 15

Rees, Revd Saunders, rector of Hawarden, 122
Reeve, Brianne, starts playgroup for Lancing masters' children, 161

[288]

Reeve, Jamie, 153, friendship with author's son Charlie, 161
Repton, Humphry, 204
Ricketts, Michael, 84; breeder of Leggie the Labrador, 144; shooting, 253
Riddle, Dr, Lancing G.P., 160
Robel, Professor Robert, 266
Roberts, Dr Emlyn, Hawarden organist and choirmaster, 123-4
Rolfe, Neville, 30
Rowlatt, Charles, author's Eton housemaster, 53

sailing, 19-23
St Deiniol's Library, Hawarden, 125
Savill Garden, Windsor Great Park, 207
Scaitcliffe preparatory school, 11, 13, 50-2, 133; and Mr Pike ('Pikey') master, and 'KP' (Revd Kirkpatrick), 133
Schmoller, Hans, head of design at Penguin Books, 99
Scouting for Boys (Baden-Powell), 15
Scott, Sir George Gilbert, advises Carl Joachim Hambro (q.v.) on restoration of Milton Abbey Church, 177
Scott, Sir Peter, 198
Sebag-Montefiore, Rupert, and wife Charlotte, rescue four orphaned Lamb nephews and give them home in Hampshire, 173
Seymour, William ('Bill'), author and chartered surveyor, agent for Crichel Down estate, Dorset; m. Mary, youngest daughter of Angus and Vanda Hambro; and right to buy back requisitioned (Crichel) land, 169-70
Sharpley, Major John, park keeper at Hawarden from 1954, 104-5; journalist daughter Anne, 105
Shaw, Mr, ex-Forestry Commission, in charge of tree replanting programme at Hawarden, 113
Shrewsbury School, author teaches there 1949-50, 89-100; geographical location between town and school 'ideal', 94
shooting, Fervour 4, 248-75
Shropshire Yeomanry, The (1953), researched and written by author, 97-9
Sissinghurst, 213
Sladden, Mrs C. E., wife of Eton housemaster, and son Duncan, 10
Smiley, Sir Hugh, Bt, marries Nancy Beaton, 166-7; son John and daughter-in-law Davina, three grandchildren, Melinda, Christopher, William, 167; 168
Smyth-Osbourne, Adele, 262
Smyth-Osbourne, Douglas, 30
Snow, Philip, 100
Sopwith, T. O. M., 22
South Downs, walks on, 158-9
Southesk, 10th Earl of, 251
Spedding, Commander H. R., author appoints to administer estate (with Ned Cowell, q.v.), 111; leaves, 112
Squelch, Mrs, 102
Stamper, Tom, author's uncle by marriage (see Gladstone, Edie), 32; MC and two bars, 32; Indian Civil Service, 32; 35; retires, 40; visited by author, 69; 101

[289]

Index

Stanley, Hon. Hugh, 58
Stern, Sir Fred, introduced to author and wife by Dossie Parish (author's cousin) and advises on Old Farm House garden, 143
Still, W. C., Rosamund's nanny, 171
Street, J. M., Shrewsbury master, 91, 92
Stuart, Charles, 79
Suarez, Jessica, see Chattock
Sussex neighbours and friends. Gorings, Donald Scotts, Howards, Nathans, Hobbses 152–3,
Swire, John, 58

Taylor, Tom, Shrewsbury housemaster, 92, 94–5
Temple, Paul, 131
Thatcher, Lillian, nanny, 61, 102
Thorold, Revd Henry, 151, 220
Toller family, Hawarden, 129–30
Treherne, Sir Cennydd, author succeeds as chairman of the Reoresentative Body of the Church in Wales, 120
Towns, Jemima, 251, 253
Trevor-Roper, Hugh (later Baron Dacre of Glanton, life peer), 79, 87
Trinder, Peter, Hawarden church organist, 124
Tschihold, Jan, Swiss typographer, 99
Turner, J.M.W., 232, 235–6, 239, 240, 243, 247
Tydd, Bill, Lancing bursar, helps author in public inquiry over aircraft runway at Shoreham, 155; and woodwork instructors, 155–6; 157

University of Sussex, 151–2

Veysey, Geoffrey, county archivist, 127
Vickers, Hugo, 168
Vickers, Richard, Scaitcliffe, 51, 52, 133
Vickers, Ronald, Scaitcliffe, 50, 133
Vidler, Revd Dr Alec, warden of St Deiniol's, 125
Vincent, Jim, warden of Hickling Broad, 192–3

Waddesdon, 205
Wainwright, Ralph, ex-Forestry Commission, consultant at Hawarden, advises Robert Charmley (q.v.), 113
Wakeman, Sir Offley, Bt, on Shrewsbury Governing Body, 97
Warren, Lt Cdr Edgar, captain of HMS *Wrangler*, 71–2, 73, 75
watercolour landscape (Fervour 3), 232–47; artists admired by author, 235–6; illustration of palette, 238
Watson, Camilla, commissioned by author to compile photographic album of Hawarden past and present employees and local independent business proprietors who had worked regularly for the estate, 111
Watson, Steven, 79
Wesson, Edward, 237
Whitcombe, Philip, 86–7
White, Jeremy, 11
Wilkinson, Denys, Eton Ornithological Society; retires to Gower Peninsula, visited there by author, 184

Index

Williams, Jack, bricklayer at Hawarden, 110

Wilson, Bertie, brother of author's paternal grandfather, 34–5

Wilson, Maud, unmarried sister of author's paternal grandmother, 34–5

Wolfenden, J. W. (life peer 1974), headmaster of Shrewsbury, 89–91, 96, 97; leaves to become vice-chancellor of Reading University, 100

Wood, Frank, 140

Woodruffe, Jack, director of Hambro's Bank, m. Tish, eldest of four daughters of Angus and Vanda Hambro, 168; they retire to Phesdo, Kincardineshire, derelict property owned by author which they restore, 168–9

Woodruffe, Simon, son of preceding, at Eton, joins Hambro's Bank, 169

Worthing, 159

Wrangler, HMS, author's service with, 70–8

Wrench, John, inventor of modern method of harvesting silage, 118; and son John, 118

Wyndham, Hon. John (1st Baron Egremont, 1963, 6th Baron Leconfield, 1967), visit to Lancing, 148–9